NORTH AFRICA

Tunisian Adventure On A 150CC BSA Motorcycle

TED & EMMA SELIG JONES

iUniverse, Inc.
Bloomington

North Africa
Tunisian Adventure On A 150CC BSA Motorcycle

iUniverse books may be ordered through booksellers or by contacting:

iUniverse
1663 Liberty Drive
Bloomington, IN 47403
www.iuniverse.com
1-800-Authors (1-800-288-4677)

Because of the dynamic nature of the Internet, any web addresses or links contained in this book may have changed since publication and may no longer be valid. The views expressed in this work are solely those of the author and do not necessarily reflect the views of the publisher, and the publisher hereby disclaims any responsibility for them.

Any people depicted in stock imagery provided by Thinkstock are models, and such images are being used for illustrative purposes only.
Certain stock imagery © Thinkstock.

ISBN: 978-1-4697-9563-8 (sc)
ISBN: 978-1-4697-9564-5 (ebk)

Printed in the United States of America

iUniverse rev. date: 03/08/2012

Dedicated to
T. R. Malthus *(1766-1834)*
whose insight gave us the key
to a better quality of life for mankind.

INTRODUCTION

In the spring of 1954 the authors were working in the Ann Arbor School system, Ted was teaching Biology and Emma was a School Nurse. After three years it was decided that they were not suited to remain in one location for thirty years. The possibility of a ten month European—North Africa tour on a very limited savings account was discussed. Financial constraints dictated that such a venture might be done by camping on a motorcycle.

Tickets were purchased, furniture sold, required shots taken and farewells said to friends made over the previous three years. The announcement to our families in Pennsylvania brought the reply, "They are crazy!" Despite that opinion, and the warning, "If you get into trouble don't wire us for money," our goal had been determined and embarkation from Pier 6 in Brooklyn on the Dutch passenger liner to South Hampton, England September 23, 1954 took place as scheduled.

Hotel prices in London quickly determined that a bed and breakfast location would be our only way of survival. Mrs. Burk and her husband, refugees from Austria, provided a "home away from home". For three dollars a day Mrs. Burk provided a delicious breakfast, large bedroom and a most pleasant atmosphere. A month was spent in London seeing "the sights" and searching for an economical means of transport. Mr. Ernie, Marble Arch Motors, came to our rescue. For $350.00 he sold us a new BSA 150cc bike with windscreen and heavy-duty rear luggage carrier. Our first adventure was learning to control that bike while circling Piccadilly Circus driving on the "wrong side" in heavy traffic. The London drivers were very tolerant.

Leaving the security and excellent accommodation provided by the Berks was very difficult. We left them with the hope that they would soon be repatriated to their former home and printing business confiscated when the Russians occupied Austria. On a cloudy, rainy morning we rode out of London, headed for Wales, Europe and Tunisia, North Africa.

TUNISIAN ADVENTURE ON A 150CC BSA MOTORCYCLE

In 1954-55 we purchased a motorcycle in London and traveled for ten months through Europe and Tunisia N. Africa. This is an account of the four months we spent in Tunisia, N. Africa during that trip.

As we cleared the docks in Palermo, Sicily, and started across the Mediterranean to the port of Tunis, Tunisia in North Africa, it was dark. The sea was very calm, there was no moon light, and the stars were bright. It would take all night to cross and the crossing would have been relaxing except for the fact that we were aboard illegally—without any official papers. It was difficult to deal with the confusion in Palermo. The language barrier made communication impossible. Customs either could not, or would not, stamp our papers for the bike or for us. Just before the ship was ready to leave the dock we jumped on the bike and rode up the narrow plank and into the hold.

All members of the crew with whom we made contact were courteous and friendly. One officer arranged for us to occupy a pleasant stateroom. The procedure was interrupted when the Captain sent another officer who informed us that the Captain requested our presence—immediately.

1

The Captain was an average-sized, middle-aged man. He appeared stiff and uncomfortable. He wore a tiny mustache and a starched white uniform topped off with what appeared to me to be cardboard on each shoulder. His hat had a lot of gold braid and the usual black eye-shield. He was the Captain! He wanted everyone to know, and to understand that he was the Captain. We had no problem with the fact that he was the Captain; we were just pleased that we were not one of the crew. I know that I was!

As we entered the office he stood, as if at attention, behind his large, very neatly arranged, desk. The officer stood at attention. To us the Captain spoke only one sentence, "We are at sea and you two are aboard my ship illegally, without the proper official papers". I agreed. He then turned to the officer who had brought us in and spoke in French. They talked for some time—that is, the Captain talked and the officer listened. When the Captain was finished the officer returned with us to our stateroom.

After the officer left, Emma and I discussed our situation, the officer, and the Captain. I told her that I thought that we were aboard a ferry that ran between Palermo and Tunis. After our visit with the Captain I thought that we might be aboard a French Battleship. During my four years in the US Air Force I had to deal with several men like the Captain. I made a habit of trying to stay away from them.

We know nothing about ships, how they are operated or commanded. The Captain may have had very good reasons for acting the way that he did. It seemed that the officers were French; the crew was made up of Italians and Arabs. After our visit with the Captain everything went smoothly.

Actually, before we were able to fall into our bunks there was a knock on the cabin door. When Emma opened it she was served a tray of sandwiches and hot tea! In the morning a waiter appeared with hot coffee and biscuits! We do not think that could have happened without the permission of the Captain.

As our ship slowly made its way into the Bay of Tunis, the sun came into view as a glowing red ball of fire in the East. It was a brilliant show of color as we entered a completely new, old land. To our right, port, we were able to make out the famous ancient cities of Carthage and Sidi Bou-Said. They both face the open waters of the Bay. Ever so slowly the iron cranes of La Goulette, a water-side port, appeared and faded from view behind us. Next we crossed a wide, shallow lake. We were in the port of Tunis!

During our approach to the harbor our conversation turned to two history courses that we completed while in college. One was, "The History of Civilization", the other, "European History". Dr. Guterman was our professor and he brought the events of history to life. Between the two of us we were able to recall some of his comments on, The Barbary Coast of North Africa, the pirates, and their notorious activities.

Dr. Guterman described the pirate coastal hideouts from Morocco to Libya. He vividly described their inhumane activities at sea and along the coasts of Europe, and as far away as Iceland. Thousands were killed and thousands were sold into slavery. Barbary pirates, also called Ottoman corsairs, controlled the Mediterranean, and much of the Atlantic from the time of the Crusades until the 19th century. He explained that the frequent wars in Europe played into the hands of the corsairs. European countries, at times, hired the pirates to prey upon their enemies.

Residents along the coasts in the Mediterranean, and as far away as England, Holland, and Iceland were not safe. Some coastal areas were abandoned. In other areas watchtowers and fortified churches were constructed. When Dr. Guterman described "Redbeard", one of the most "famous" corsairs, one of two brothers, he was on his feet in front of the class; I thought that I could see "Redbeard" swinging his sword!

In the late 15th century Spain expelled the Moors. Most of those Muslims migrated to coastal cities along the North African coast. There, with the help of local Arabs who resented the Crusades, organized expeditions called "razzias" designed to disrupt Christian sovereigns and, at the same time, capture slaves and white women who were much in demand for the brothels of the East. If a captured person could raise enough money, he might secure his freedom. Some escaped slavery by professing the Moslem Faith. In some areas of the Barberry Coast the area was under complete control of the pirates and the financial support was derived from piracy on the high seas and raids of coastal villages. Hundreds of European ships were taken or sunk and thousands either killed or sold into slavery.

In 1784 the first American ship was seized by Moroccan pirates. The US paid $60,000 in order to reach a settlement. In 1785 Algerian pirates seized two American ships, everything was sold and the crews put to hard labor. Thomas Jefferson and John Adams met with the ambassador from Tripoli in London. When they requested an explanation for the hostile action the following was the ambassador's answer—

It was written in the Koran, that all nations which had not acknowledged the Prophet were sinners,

Whom it was the right and duty of the faithful to plunder and enslave; and that every Moslem

Who was slain in this warfare was sure to go to paradise. He said, also, that the man who was the

First to board a vessel had one slave over and above his share, and that when they sprang to the

Deck of an enemy's ship, every sailor held a dagger in each hand and a third in his mouth; which

Usually struck such terror into the foe that they cried out for quarter at once.

By 1793 about a dozen American ships had been captured, goods stripped and everyone enslaved. The Early 1800s saw the formation of the US Navy and the Marines. With the cooperation of several European powers, it was agreed that action had to be taken against the Barbary pirates. The Barbary Wars followed during which several pirate strongholds along the coast of North Africa were attacked and bombarded. England and Holland assisted. Some of the bombardments were very intense. The US Marines landed in Tripoli and that action led to the line "to the shores of Tripoli", the opening of the Marine Hymn.

A combined fleet of British and Dutch war ships bombarded Algiers. That action terrified the pirates of Algiers and of Tunis, so much so that Tunis gave up 3,000 prisoners. Tunis and Algiers agreed to keep the peace—In short order Algiers renewed its piracies and slave-taking. In 1824 the British again bombarded the city of Algiers. The city remained a haven for and a source of pirates until, in 1830, France completed its conquest of Algeria.

Piracy on the high seas was brought under control. It was not eliminated in North Africa or the East. The scene from the deck overlooked a veritable beehive of activity. The Arabs on the dock and boarding the ship reminded us of the pirates of about 100 years ago. There can be no doubt that those dock-workers are carrying many of those pirate genes. Emma squeezed my arm firmly and said," At last, we are in Africa!"

Several of the pirates attacked our luggage and the bike. They were very determined to unload the ship and put everything on the dock. Maybe they thought that we were Crusaders! It required an unusual amount of gesturing, and shouting, before we could get them to leave everything in place. Finally, an officer appeared, he probably heard the shouting. He spoke Arabic and they melted into the mob.

The officer arranged for us to get to the tourist office. There we were introduced to an Arab who spoke perfect English. His first question—"What do you intend to do in Tunisia?" Our answer, "Camp, and travel around the country". "You will not be able to camp out in Tunisia as we are having a war just now". Emma and I looked at each other—We were thinking the same thing. That is why the Italians acted the way that they did when we boarded the ship in Palermo.

The English-speaking Arab must have been an official. He was very cordial, and he stamped our passport. He also gave us explicit directions as to where the bank was located and the Youth Hostel. The maps and travel information proved to be most useful. His last advice, "You must stay in the Youth Hostel, especially at night. You will be quite safe during the day. If you are stopped, speak English at once, not French." There was no danger of our speaking anything except English.

The cab ride through parts of the city of Tunis in an elderly Renault that sounded very much as though it should either be repaired or replaced was an adventure in itself. The cabbie wore a red fez and western clothing. The vehicle was maneuvered through impossible congestion made up of other vehicles, trucks, street cars, wagons and carts with four and two wheels, and a mob of pedestrians dressed in combinations of eastern and western clothing beyond verbal description. The driver swore at everyone and everything in at least three languages. He had an extensive vocabulary of English profanity.

The cab was required for two reasons—The bike and our baggage could not be released until we cashed some American Express traveler's checks and paid for our passage. And—It would have been impossible for us to find our way through the narrow, twisting streets and onto the spacious, tree-lined European section where the banks and American Express offices are located. The contrast was startling! The European section was pleasant—The Arab section had far more character, history, and variety. We looked forward to returning to the Arab section or Medina as soon as possible and with our own mode of transportation.

The cabbie stopped in front of the bank and indicated that he would wait for us. It sounded as though everyone employed by the bank spoke at least three languages. Several people became involved in our transaction. We were cashing American dollars, but the currencies being used at present are Tunisian francs and French francs. The shipping office had to be contacted in order to determine the currency that they would prefer. Italian lira became involved at that juncture.

An English-speaking bank employee emphasized that we should pay 14,000 French francs when we returned to the ship. Back at the ship we learned his reason. They requested that we pay 23,000! When we refused to pay the 23,000 they settled for 14.500. We later learned it was a fair price. I have the feeling that the shipping line never received any of those francs.

The Arab Pirates unloaded the bike and our suitcases onto the dock and departed. The entire dock area that had been bustling with activity was deserted. It required some time for us to get everything back in order and back on the bike racks. Then it was off to find the Youth Hostel Office. The directions were accurate and we were back in the European section. "Yes" the cute little Arab girl said, "You are welcome to stay at the Youth Hostels anywhere in Tunisia". (She was not wearing a veil.) It would cost two dollars a day for a bed, use of cooking facilities, and a prepared dinner. Emma commented, "Sounds too good to be true." My thought was, "I will be eating less stew!"

The Arab girl at the hostel office invited us to have coffee with her at the little coffee shop near-by. She indicated that she would give us an introduction to Tunisia—it must have been obvious to her that we needed it! She began by suggesting that we refer to the people in Tunisia as Tunisians.

They are mainly a blend of original Berber stock and Arabs from the East. However, she said, the spirit of nationalism is very widespread and the people like to think of themselves as Tunisians.

We learned from her the paramount importance of religion to the Tunisians. Their religion, even more than that of say, Catholicism governs every phase of their lives. There are about 920,000,000 Christians throughout the world. (I never wondered about that!) People know a great deal about Christianity and Judaism, she thinks. (I wonder.) Anyway, she told us that there are about 13,000,000 Jews in the world. There are approximately 450,000,000 Muslims! We know that there are a lot of them but, again, how many people are aware that every fourth or fifth person on the planet is a Moslem? The fact is that we learned everything that we know about the Arabs—I mean the Tunisians, from our history courses with Dr. Guterman.

Our cute little Tunisian informant continued—The Muslim religion was founded by Mohammed, a merchant who lived in Mecca, now a city in Saudi Arabia. The word Islam means "submission to the divine will". People who are Moslems are offended when referred to as Mohammedans, Mohammed was not their God, he was a prophet—the last and revered Prophet. What he said was recorded in the Koran, the equivalent of the Christian Bible. Another collection of Mohammed's sayings is called the Sannah—neither of us had ever heard of that book. Well, the truth is that almost everything that she said was new to us.

The Moslem God is Allah, and Allah is the one and only God, and Mohammed was his prophet just as Jesus Christ was a prophet so far as the Moslems are concerned. No priest stands between God and a Moslem, their contact is direct and personal. There is no mediator, no middle-man. Moslems do not believe that death ends life, they think that there will be a Judgment Day or Resurrection and that, on that day, everyone will be judged according to their religious fervor during their lives. The wicked will fall into hell, the good will enter Al Jannat, a garden with trees and meadows and cool flowing streams. (That would seem like Heaven to someone who had spent his life in the desert, in the Arabian Peninsula, where Islam had its beginnings.)

"Our religion is clear cut—we are all equal" the hostel girl told us. "In the Koran women have the same rights as men, women have the right to end a marriage in the courts and they can own and dispose of property. There are no mysteries in the Moslem religion, no rituals. The Imam, an honorable person who is not a priest, leads the prayers and calls the faithful to prayers five times each day. Formal services are conducted on Fridays in the Mosque, or church. The Mosque is a holy place, a place of prayer, a place of peace and quiet, a place where one can rest, meditate, or read the sacred word. Attendance at the Mosque is never compulsory. A Moslem, when he prays does not ask for aid, he does not request that his sins be forgiven; his one purpose is to praise Allah. Five times a day the Muzzin calls people to prayer from the minaret at the top of the Mosque

Everyone is asked to remove his shoes before entering a Mosque. Some Mosques are open to people of other faiths and some are not, in many cases it depends upon the history of the Mosque. For example, French soldiers invaded the Mosque in Kairouan, a very holy place to all Moslems, they desecrated it, and now, at certain times it is open to people of other faiths.

In the Moslem religion there are five main commandments:

1. to pray five times each day—no matter where one might be—at sunrise, noon, afternoon sunset, and misdeeming.
2. To recite the creed of Islam. "There is no God, but God and Mohammed is His Prophet".
3. To give a tenth of ones income on alms, known as zakat.
4. To make a pilgrimage (hajj) to the Holy City of Mecca, or send a deputy.
5. To fast during the month of Ramadan between sunrise and sunset. This means not eating, drinking, smoking, having intercourse, or transacting business.

No alcohol is permitted by the Moslem religion and the use of any animal form in art work is also forbidden. Music may be a small part of worship but it is not important. Polygamy is permitted. (I wanted to ask Emma about that one but did not have any opportunity.)

She said that there are several sects in the Moslem religion just as there are in other religions. (I think that there are so many in the Christian religion that it is confusing, at least to me.)

Was I surprised? Confused? Indeed! I did not expect her to be so "modern" if that is the correct word. Where had she been educated? We never found out. I did not really know what to expect in Tunisia but I did not expect that! We tried to remember everything that she said but it was all very new and different information, I can only hope that we have been able to recall it correctly. I have to ask, "Why did she do that? Was she trying to make an impression? Was it just part of her job? Was it because most visitors are so poorly informed? Had she lived in Paris?" Yes, I was confused and surprised as we said good-bye and headed out toward the hostel.

The Hostels are great places to stay. We preferred camping but, in the hostels the necessities are provided. They are affordable—And very often you meet and talk with interesting people from all over the world. There were times in Europe when it would have been more pleasant and more economical to have used the Hostels

When you hitch-hike, or ride a bike through a country you experience a "feeling" a familiarity with the people and the environment. Maybe it is an emotion or a "sense". It is something that you do not experience when you are in a vehicle. To my way of thinking, the only thing better then riding a bike through an area would be to ride a horse. A horse is much better than a bike! But, I doubt that I could have gotten Emma and the suitcases on a horse!

Tunis created a "feeling", an uneasy "sense" that we could not explain. In order to reach the Hostel it was necessary to ride through the Arab section and out into the country. No one said or did anything unfriendly. They just seemed to go about their work in a methodical fashion. The best description that I might offer would be to say that there was a "tension in the people and in the air". We were in a foreign part of the world—The Arab World. The appearance, dress, manners, and attitude of the people gave us the feeling that all was not well. We found out what it was after we reached, and got "settled" in the hostel.

When you arrive in a foreign country it is difficult not to compare it with your country of origin. Different people have different experiences, environments, problems, and they deal with conditions in their own way. It is not easy to change our way of thinking, our way of seeing conditions. Every country that we have visited so far has been different. That is what makes traveling worth the time and effort. If travel fails to make one think, to see things in a different light, to appreciate the problems of other people—Then it would be better for them to stay home. The way in which we have been reared is not necessarily the only way—In fact there is a very good chance that it might have been the wrong way! I tend to be very critical. I know that I have to make a greater effort to accept foreign people and the conditions under which they have and are living. Americans seem to think that their way is not only the only way; it is the best way!

Our background, our inheritance, is European. Emma is German. I am German and Welsh. The Arab World is very different from the European—Every fifth person is an Arab. We need to learn much more about them. If we do not understand anything about the Arabs how are we going to be able to deal with them? Deal with them? Understand their problems? We can not even talk with them! Many years ago a group of people tried to get a common language organized and accepted world-wide. The idea failed.

That probably was a very serious mistake! We certainly wish it had caught on.

The truth is that I am not able, that I do not have the vocabulary to describe what we see here. Travel, I feel, should stimulate and excite. It should educate the traveler. Travel does create problems and frustration but, over-all; it should be a pleasant and an educational experience. Travel through a country, seeing the creations of nature and man—Those things should stimulate and cause feelings of exhilaration. A person should be glad that he is there, happy to be alive and a living part of the environment.

Man is a fortunate animal. He has evolved on a spectacular planet. Everything necessary is available. It is a crime against nature that we have not taken better care of our planetary home. But much is still left to appreciate and stimulate. Travel should increase our appreciation of what we have. Of course we do have to have the inborn ability, the intelligence, to appreciate what we see and experience. John Anthony wrote an interesting book, <u>Tunisia</u>, in it he stated—"If we return from a voyage without a feeling that our own ways are a little peculiar, we might as well stay home."

Back on the bike we headed for our first Youth Hostel stop in Tunisia. Some of the streets were paved, some of rough cobble stone, and many with trolley tracks that created problems when they had to be crossed. The variety of people and types of conveyances boggled the brain! I tried to keep my attention on the congestion in front of us. Taxies, private cars, carts, mules and donkeys with gigantic loads on their backs and in baskets on each side, and human beings, loaded like the donkeys with huge loads on their backs. Some of the women wear veils, some do not. Most are covered from head to toe with black or white robes. Women were carrying everything on their heads! Pots and pans, huge earthen jars, baskets loaded with fruit, vegetables, or almost anything! The noise was terrible—People shouting, horns blowing, traffic officers blowing whistles and waving their arms in unbelievable distortions, shop-keepers barking in order to attract attention. But, it was not a mob. Everyone was headed somewhere. Is it possible to have an organized mob?

That was a brief glimpse of the Medina or Arab Souk—the market. The European, French, quarter was very organized, neater and cleaner, paved streets, sidewalks, rows of beautiful palm trees, etc., etc. In short, the European section had nothing of interest to offer. (Not to us.)

Along the paved highway out to the hostel, a distance of several miles, we passed several nomad bands with camels and donkeys loaded with all their earthly possessions. Most of the men rode donkeys; the women walked behind them, most carrying children. There were many, many children. Some of the children were carrying children. The women do not wear veils; various designs are tattooed on their faces. One is given the impression that beasts of burden include camels, donkeys, women and children. Almost all the caravans included herds of sheep and, or, goats—As well as some very unfriendly-looking dogs.

The nomads follow the rains. They move into areas where the pasture is likely to be the best available. They carry their black goat-skin tents and all necessary cooking materials with them. Some build semi-permanent huts of sticks and brush plastered over with mud. A potential disaster during infrequent heavy rains. Sanitation is not a problem.

The name of the hostel is "Bir el Bey. The Bey of Tunisia is said to have had a summer palace in the area. The Bey is a figure-head "king" appointed by the French. As we rode along the highway the French Foreign Legion was very much in evidence. Legion troops were not frequently seen in the Souks or market but they were very much in evidence in the European area and along the highway. In fact, not far out of Tunis, we saw the headquarters of the Legion, apparently for that area. They seem to have a good supply of WWII American trucks in which the Legion troops are transported.

Our short ride through, and out of the capitol, Tunis, and out into the country has impressed upon us that we are in an occupied country. That is why we had that "feeling" shortly after we left the ship. That is why we got the uneasy sense that "something is wrong here". Americans have never had to live in an "occupied or "protected" country. We have been fortunate—so far. What we have been is "lucky". To date two oceans and Canada have protected us—not intelligent diplomatic work. Our southern border is not protected—Our visits to Mexico seem to indicate that some action should be taken along that border. Even though we are just visiting Tunisia, just tourists and do not really have much background relative to the problems involved, we sense that these people do not want to be "protected".

TUNIS NORTH AFRICA
JANUARY 15 1955

A blue and white sign, "Bir el Bey" came into view. What a view! The whole area is beautiful! A sandy road leads back some distance to the white hostel buildings through a very large grove of Eucalyptus trees. The trees are just getting ready to produce clusters of yellow flowers. The area is sandy because it is part of the beach along the Mediterranean Sea. The hostel area is located in a somewhat protected cove along the bay. The location could hardly be improved, it is ideal. The ocean waves can be heard crashing softly upon the beach. To the right along the entryway several white buildings are located. At this time we do not know their function.

The hostel area is made up of three very white one-story buildings. The central structure houses the French couple who operate the facility. To the right of that a dormitory for men is located. To the left of the central building the women's quarters are located. I think the arrangement is a futile attempt to keep the boys and girls separated. The dorms are furnished with double-decker cots and a large central table with a couple chairs—that is it. The central building, as I mentioned, has an apartment for the custodians, a long serving counter, and wooden picnic tables. The furnishings are Spartan—but the location more than compensates. For those who might find the furnishings too primitive—I suggest that there are a variety of hotels just a few miles away in Tunis.

The custodians are French, very French! Of course they speak only French. She seems to be a very pleasant woman, quite attractive, with a calm manner and a ready smile, perhaps a little too heavy, but neat and clean. Everything is kept neat and clean.

Her husband is a rather large man, heavy-set but muscular. He is clean-shaven and exhibit's a definite military bearing. Having retired from military service he has been given this position probably in addition to a small pension. His wife's attitude and smile more than makes up for his lack of sociability. He seems to exhibit the attitude and mannerisms of a former officer. In the Air Force I once had to deal with a second lieutenant with such an attitude—neither of us enjoyed our time together.

Since we arrived in Tunisia it has been necessary to deal with French people only. Everyone in any position of responsibility has been French. It makes you wonder where all the Tunisians are. Of course the fact is that Tunisia is an occupied country. Since the Treaty of Bardot in 1881 the French have been "protecting" Tunisia. Tunisia, like most of the African continent, has been carved up by Europeans and placed under the "protection" of the "more advanced" white race. Tunisia, because of its geographic location, is a unique and strategic piece of property. That location has caused many invasions over the last thousands of years.

The present crisis in Tunisia is the result of greed and the self-centered arrogant attitude of several European powers. England, Italy, and France have been involved. Cape Bon in Tunisia projects to the north. It divides the Mediterranean into the more European west and the Arab east. The north coast of Tunisia faces Europe' the east coast faces the Arab World. Would it not be great if Tunisia could bring the two cultures together! England wanted the Rock of Gibraltar and both France and Italy wanted Tunisia. The English wanted Corsica. So, Britain cut a deal with France and they left Italy out in the cold. Britain got to "protect" Corsica and the French generously agreed to "protect" the Tunisians. How fortunate for the natives of those countries!

For us the hostel has proven to be an ideal location. After camping out in the cold, snow, and rain, we find the accommodations quite comfortable. But, so far, the hostel has proven to be an invaluable source of information. All kinds and types of travelers frequent the hostels. In just a few days we have met young people from several European countries and some from Australian and New Zealand. A young couple from Denmark proved to be very well informed. As we sit and talk with them every evening after dinner we are impressed with their background in history and current affairs and our ignorance. The US educational system is in dire need of repair. We could learn so much from the Europeans—and certainly from the Arabs if we would just go to the trouble of setting up a communication system with them. We would have to overcome the unjustified attitude that we already "know it All".

Generalization is always dangerous and usually inaccurate. But, we all seem to do it. As we camped through France we were able to talk to a variety of young and older people. It was something of a surprise to learn that, for a country with so many colonies, most of the people seem to be unaware of the current situation. The young people seem to be more informed and more concerned. Most of the people using the hostel are young, they speak English and understand the situation-that the Tunisians are on the verge of gaining their freedom, and the days of colonial empires are limited. The French will have to give up their coveted naval base at Bizerte

At the moment the French appear to be firmly in control. Foreign Legion troops are everywhere. Their presence gives one (me) an uneasy feeling. It is obvious that everyone is being watched. This is our first experience in an Arab country. We are profoundly ignorant with respect to the culture of these people. It will be necessary that we look and listen to what they have to offer. That is, of course, if they feel free enough to exchange ideas with us. History has taught the Arabs not to trust people with a European background and culture. They have not forgotten the Crusades carried out with the assistance and the blessings of the Pope in Rome. Protestant missionaries have added to the problem. If only we could learn to mind our own business! We have more than enough to do if we would concentrate on our own problems.

TUNIS NORTH AFRICA—BIR EL BEY—THE HOSTEL
JANUARY 15, 1955

Somewhat like the geography of Tunisia, Tunis, the capitol, presents two faces. The Old Quarter, the market, the Medina, and the new section built by the French with Arab labor. The Medina has changed very little over the last thousand years. The streets are narrow and winding. Specialized shops line each street. Most of the shop-keepers arrange as much of their wares outside as space permits. The merchant stands outside hawking his wares. "Please to come in, have tea, just look". Jewelry is sold along one street, another offers leather goods, another iron work. All kinds and types of pots and pans occupy one entire area. Most of the men ware the burnoose, the long heavy robe that covers them from head to foot. It also has a hood for protection during foul weather. Some of the men wear western clothing and some a mixture of both Arab and western. Women also seem to be in a period of transition. Some wear traditional long robes and expose only one eye. Others wear a very loose veil that might be dropped if they think that you are going to photograph them. We have seen young girls wearing shorts. In some areas the streets are covered, you have the feeling that you are walking through a long hallway. One day we were wandering around—the street became more and more narrow. We found ourselves in a cul-de-sac and had to retrace our steps. Over the past several days only two Europeans have been seen. If there is any danger we have not been aware of it. People either ignore you and go about their business or they nod and smile in a friendly manner.

The history of the area now known as Tunisia, and the present capitol, as well as the background of the founding of the present Tunisian Capitol, Tunis, is long, complicated, and interesting. The United States, compared to Tunisia, is nothing more than the blink of an eye when it comes to survival over a period of time. The present people of Tunisia can trace their origin back more than three thousand years. At the beginning of recorded history the Berbers had lived along the coast of Africa for an unknown period of time. History indicates that the Phoenicians first visited the area of Tunisia during the 10th century BC. They sailed from Tyre, now located in Lebanon. The Phoenicians were excellent sailors, and tradesmen. They established trading ports all along the North African Coast, past the Pillars of Hercules at the western end of the Mediterranean, and down along the coast of west Africa at least as far as present-day Senegal.

From that primitive trading post the city of Carthage grew. Carthage, over time, dominated the western Mediterranean Sea. Carthage fought, and won, a series of wars with the Greek city-states. The settlers brought with them their religion and culture. They worshipped a pantheon of gods.

Carthage became an independent political power. As history goes, the Carthaginians had no more than established their power along the coast of North Africa and Spain when they come into conflict with Rome. Three wars were fought. During the second, Hannibal, the most famous Carthaginian General, led an expeditionary force, including his famous trained elephants, across the Straits of Gibraltar, and down into Italy to the very gates of Rome. If Hannibal had been successful, our history, the heritage of the Western

World would have been quite different. He returned to North Africa and the area of present day Tunisia.

In the second century BC Rome attacked Carthage. They were finally successful and showed no mercy. The city was completely destroyed, the people killed or sold into slavery and all traces of the culture obliterated. Tunisia then became one of the granaries of Rome. It was Latinized and Christianized. During the 5th century AD, when the power of Rome began to weaken, the area was conquered by the Vandals only to be taken by the Byzantines emperor during the 6th century AD.

In the 7th century the Arab conquest began. Starting in the south of Tunisia, the village of Kairouan was founded and a huge Mosque constructed. Kairouan then served as a base from which the Arab forces and religion spread out to encompass all of North Africa. The native Berber tribes, in general, accepted the Arab religion. A few did not and there were rebellions from time to time. During the 12th century the coast was held briefly by the Normans from Sicily. The Arab recon quest successfully wiped out the last of the Christians in North Africa. As I have mentioned, the Christians, with the assistance and blessings of the Pope in Rome, made several attempts to re-establish a Christian footing in the Arab east. The Crusades were a complete failure. They established, in the Arab World, a lasting hatred for all Christians.

During the late 16th century the coast of Tunisia became a pirate stronghold. (The Barbary States) Next, Spain seized much real estate along the coast only to be ousted by the Turks. Under the Turks Tunisia finally achieved virtual independence in 1705 the Hussein dynasty was established which lasted until 1957 by which time Tunisia had achieved freedom from the French and the Bey was deposed. The Beys were actually the equivalent of kings.

From what we have heard and seen we would not consider having tea in a French restaurant. The hostel is guarded after dark by an armed guard with a police dog. It is mandatory that we be there before dark. Several French restaurants and social centers have been bombed. French military outposts are frequently bombed or attacked by well-armed ten-man teams of partisans. When possible it seems that the Partisans prefer to cut the throats of the French Military. Being stopped by French Military Police patrolling on motor cycles is not unusual. Still, we move about at random, we go where we wish and take many pictures. Our explanation—being young and very naïve, and being curious. (And probably having an almost complete lack of common sense.)

The hostel organization provides a great way to travel. It would have been a great idea to have joined in the US at the start of our journey. The cost of joining here in Tunisia is 40 francs. Rented sheets are 50 francs per night. Lunch 145 francs, dinner 145, and breakfast 40. Breakfast consists of coffee and bread, not quite what Emma makes when we are tenting. But lunch and dinner are very substantial. The food is very good, tasty, and served in a pleasant fashion. This is a very good deal! Last evening, for 145 francs, we had two bowls of soup each, more mashed potatoes than we could eat, plenty of bread, meat, fruit, and cheese—and a lettuce salad. And, as I said, it was dam good food!

One morning after breakfast we rode down to Sousse. Sousse is located on the Gulf of Hammamet. It has been a busy port since the days of Carthage. Carthage was the Punic settlement founded about 2000 BC. The Tunisians hope to make a resort out of the area. Beneath the ancient Kasbah (citadel) there are several miles of Christian catacombs. They date from the 2nd and 3rd centuries A.D. At that time Rome ruled the region. Every Sunday a camel market is held in a field behind the city. We missed the camel market but the ride was interesting—especially the protective walls and the souk, the market place.

The souk in Sousse is similar to the one in Tunis—but, it is not the same. Many of the "streets" are very narrow, not wide enough to allow passage of any size wagon or cart. Conditions in the Medina are very bad. There is a large Jewish section and the sanitation is about non-existent. Some sections do not have electric power. The Jews have migrated into the area from the east and the west. Many were forced to leave Spain during the Spanish Inquisition. At other periods they were expelled from various eastern countries. Actually, we were told that Sousse was a busy Phoenician port before the founding of Carthage. Small ships in the harbor were loading olive oil and various agricultural products, probably for transport along the coast. The soil is richer and more productive farther north but the area surrounding Sousse can be irrigated from shallow wells by means of pumps. The Arabs refer to the area surrounding Sousse as the Sahel.

The population density around Sousse varies from about 130-190 per square mile. Since the French military occupation, the problem of the exploding population has become more serious. Sanitation and medical facilities have been much improved. Infant mortality reduced and the life span lengthened. That has been both desirable and undesirable. Nothing has been done to reduce fertility—and nothing can be done about fertility. There are now more people than the natural resources can support.

In addition, the French have confiscated large areas of the most productive land and introduced mechanized farming. They have also done much to destroy the local tribal structure. The result has been massive unemployment. Landless people, formerly self-sufficient, have drifted into the cities seeking employment. The situation has resulted in the creation of bidomvilles, (shanty towns).

The French, in an effort to rectify the mess, instituted a scheme under which selected areas would be parceled out to certain Arabs provided that they would plant olive tree shoots. Providing that they grow, it takes about ten years to reach the first fruiting season. That is providing that the rains do not fail or that they are tended and watered. The poor soil between the trees was to be plowed and planted. Loans were promised to get the project started but the money was never made available! A crisis developed during which some of the more successful farmers took advantage of the less prosperous. Most of the people wandered away seeking a way to feed themselves and their families.

The French meant well. What did the man say?—"Please save me from well-meaning people". It is unwise and dangerous for people who do not really understand what they are doing to tinker with a system or culture that has developed over thousands of years. What the French really wanted was control of the most productive land along the Sahel, or coast, of Tunisia. By changing the land laws they managed to accomplish that. Their underhanded methods were questioned by, the British—some of the officials, and by the Italians who had been left out in the cold.

During the evenings at the hostel we were able to meet, and have long conversations with, travelers whom, we found were very well informed on the history of North Africa and the French "protectorate" in Tunisia. Two young Tunisian Arabs spoke English very well. They stayed at the hostel for several days because they had government business in Tunis. They did not provide us with details relating to their mission but, it was obvious that they were waiting for the termination of French Imperialism in Tunisia.

It was very interesting to note the attitude of the warden and his wife with respect to the people visiting the hostel. On week-ends young French groups from Tunis would arrive. They were well-dressed and full of energy and life. Everyone had an enjoyable week-end including the warden and his wife. They all laughed a lot, visited, and spent time along the sandy beach.

The young Arabs did not arrive on the week-end. It would have been very interesting if they had. The atmosphere changed abruptly upon the arrival of the Arabs. The custodians were civil, but very formal. There was no laughing and no smiling. For us it was an awkward situation. Our food was served with a smile. The Arabs were served. We looked forward to visiting with the Arabs-It is their country! But, we do not want to antagonize the custodians or hurt their feelings. The Arabs left early this AM, we plan to visit with them this evening and get some information on the country and the people.

It is possible for us to make much better time and travel farther in a day when the bike is not loaded. It is also a lot easier to balance it. Every once in a while it falls over—When loaded it takes the two of us to get it back on it's "feet".

Bir El Bey makes a fine base from which we are able to survey the country of Tunisia. The over—night ferry from Palermo, Sicily did take the entire night to get us here. Now we learn that the most northern tip of Tunisia in only 85 miles from the most southern point in Sicily. The actual distance that the ferry had to travel was much farther than that. But. Tunisia is a relatively small country. It is wedged between two giants—Libya to the east, and /Algeria to the west. Tunisia is actually about 500 miles long and 150 miles wide. The width varies on either side of 150 as we move south. The Atlas Mountains of Algeria extend into northern Tunisia. The Mediterranean borders the north and east coasts. To the south the Sahara Desert takes over and runs on into Libya.

Our brief one-day expeditions into the north, west and south of the country have proven to be very informative. Tunisia, very much a part of the Arab World, has much to offer. The Atlas Mountains in the north extend over into the Cape Bon peninsula, the finger of land that point toward Sicily and Europe. As we travel south the country dries out and finally becomes part of the Sahara. Along the entire east coast lies the beautiful Mediterranean Sea. The coastal areas of the north and east extend for about 800 miles. The land area is about 60,000 square miles. Tunisia seems to be a relatively dry country. Only one river flows all year long. A man in Tunis thought that there might be about 5 million people in the country. The population could become a problem in the future. The population is / Arab by far, about 98%. There are a few Jews and foreign nationals. We do not know yet how many French colons are here and there are several thousands of Italians.

The climate, so far as we have been able to determine is temperate in the north. Typical of Mediterranean countries. It is cool and damp now in January. As we travel south the country gets dryer and hotter. The north seems to be the best area for farming. There is a great deal more mechanization of the farms in the north. Along the Sahel, the coast toward the south there are huge areas of olive trees.

As of this date we have made it as far south as the port of Sfax. It seemed to be a long ride and it has not been possible to spend much time there. It will be necessary for us to return to Bir El Bey and pick up some things, then ride down to Gabes and the island of Djerba for a few days. From there it will be possible to visit places out in the desert—Or close to it. Right now we have to return to the hostel and visit with the young Arabs while they are there. Not many people in the country speak English.

Our dinner was served in the usual manner. The hostility between the Arabs and the French is obvious. When they appear the atmosphere turns suddenly cold. The Arabs know that the custodian and his wife do not speak or understand English. They make the most of it. The conversation turned to the French protectorate at once. "We resent the presence of the French Foreign Legion troop on Tunisian soil," one of them said with genuine hatred in his voice and manner. The other joined in, "They have taken over all the best farm land and given it to French settlers." Then, "How would you

29

like it if a foreign power took over your country, confiscated your best land and gave almost all positions of control and authority to their nationals?"

Emma and I were tentative listeners. We did not know enough about the situation to even ask intelligent questions. As tourists it is best not to get involved in the affairs of any foreign country—But, it is most interesting to know about what has, and is, happening. One comment explained the tension that we sensed as soon as we left the port "Ten-man resistance fighters have been formed. They attack /French outposts at night and try to slit the throats of as many troops as possible. Such an attack had taken place not far from Bir El Bey.

These evening sessions took place every night after dinner for three nights. Not all their comments were critical of the French. One was, "The French have done many good things. They have built, with /Arab labor, roads, schools and hospitals, and they have done much to improve sanitation." It was a surprise to hear them say anything complimentary about the French.

Later, when we discussed what was said, there were questions—best not asked. What was the nature of their "business" in Paris? They said they were on their way from Paris to Sfax in the south, on the coast. It was best for us not to know about their relationship with the "ten-man-teams". One evening one said, "We want all the French to leave as soon and as quickly as possible. We know that such a thing is not possible. The French have made sure that we do not have the trained personnel needed to run the country. They have the huge naval base at Bizerte on the north coast. It will take years to get them out of there—if it is ever possible."

These were two very dissatisfied young, educated Tunisians. Obviously they came from well-to-do Tunisian families. They had been educated, no doubt, in Paris. They had been educated but not indoctrinated. Certainly they realized our complete ignorance with respect to what has, and is, taking place in Tunisia. They did not want Tunisia to return to the "old days", they wanted progress, progress as they saw it—Not as the French wanted it. They made us think about what we were seeing.

There was considerable discussion relating to a man named Habib Bourguiba. Emma and I had heard of him but we really knew nothing about his importance with respect to Tunisia and the effort to get the French occupation forces out of the country. He, along with several other educated Tunisians have organized, and directed, the long struggle for freedom in Tunisia. Bourguiba was born in Tunisia in 1903. He has had to live through the usual jail terms inflicted upon most reformers. In Paris he studied law and political science. That did not surprise me. Most reform leaders get their education in the country that is occupying their homeland.

Bourguiba organized what our informants called the Neo-Dustor party. He was prosecuted by the French for that. He then founded a militant newspaper which he used in order to unite opposition among the people to the French occupation. Bourguiba was in and out of jail in various places around the Mediterranean. While in jail he organized the resistance movement.

Bourguiba could have worked with the Nazis during their occupation of Tunisia but he refused. He did not think that

31

Germany could win the war. He felt that the best way for Tunisia to obtain its freedom was to wait out the war and try to negotiate with the French. One of our new-found Arab informants was very passionate when he declared, "It is impossible to negotiate with the French. They have taken over our country and given the best land and the best jobs to Frenchmen. They will not train enough Tunisians in administration so that we will never be able to run the country ourselves. Our only option is military resistance. That is the reason for trains being blown up, and the bombing of French cafes and business places as well as the organized ten-man teams of partisans who attack French outposts and French soldiers"

When the name "Bourguiba" was mentioned I was watching the Hostel warden. His ears really perked up. It was obvious that he was quite familiar with that name. It is a real loss to us that we are not able to talk with him in French. We are quite sure that Bourguiba is not a popular hero to the French. Emma and I were talking about the attitude of the French towards the native Tunisians. From what we have been able to observe, the French dislike the natives, have no respect for them, and, in fact, resent them. Emma expressed our feelings at this time when she remarked, "This is a very strange situation. The country belongs to the Tunisians; they should have a right to run it as they wish." Right now I agree with that 100%. We feel that, if we do not like the conditions here, the sanitation for example, then we should go home.

As I think I mentioned above, an isolated French garrison, not far from the hostel, was attacked the other night. All the soldiers had their throats cut. Obviously there is very deep-seated hatred for the French occupation forces. The

French troops are just about everywhere. They are all along the roads, always several together. They are constantly being moved around the country in truck convoys. They are holding parades, with great fanfare in the streets of Tunis, the capitol. The only place that we have not seen them is in the souks, the Arab market place. We think that we can figure that one out. In such a crowded place they would surely be killed. Many of the "streets" are so narrow that you have to flatten yourself against one wall when a loaded burrow passes.

The old market place of Tunis is one of our favorite destinations. The activity never ceases, that is until the markets close at sundown and all the shopkeepers go home. Then it does become rather "spooky". Imagination has much to do with it. It gets dark very fast. Then the people in their long robes and the women in their veils do seem to cast a spell. The shopkeepers remove everything from the side of the "streets" and the "sidewalks". The frenetic activity and the noise that is heard all day suddenly subsides. The constant tapping of the tinsmiths ceases, the children working with their hands and feet disappear. Where do they go? Where and how do they live? Many of the children operate a lathe with their feet while they fashion something with their hands.

Schools seem to be few and far between. Education is a real problem. Along the roads we frequently pass families of nomads with all their earthly belongings loaded on the backs of donkeys and camels—and women if there are not enough pack animals. Almost in every instance there are many children. How could they go to school every day? How could the children that we have seen working in the souks ever have time enough to attend school? The children not working are employed, and directed by, professional beggars. One adult will supervise several children. They are very good at what they do.

Education of young Tunisians is a problem for the Tunisians and for the French occupation forces. What would the young Tunisians do with their education? Education for what? The French do not want them to be educated. If the French give the native Tunisians too much education they will become a serious problem. The French claim that the Tunisians are not able to run the country. They will never be able to run the country if they are not educated. But, if they are educated, then what excuse would the French have for occupying the country?

The old Arab city, the souk, the market place, has to be one of the most interesting places in the country. The many ruins of Phoenician and Roman origin are, of course, an insight into the past. But, when you slowly stroll along the narrow passageways and observe Arab life as it is being played out at this moment, as it has been for many hundreds of years, you are living in the present and in the past. That has to be a very rare, and unique, experience. As Emma said, many times, "We are so fortunate to be here and be able to see and experience all this." I never get tired of hearing that.

On one of our many forays into, and through, the souks, we thought it might be interesting to look for a book shop. Well, we found several but Arabic script is very difficult for us to read! Arab script is written from the "back" of the book to the front. But the Arabs say that we write from the "back" to the front. Anyway, we did find a bookshop that not only carried Arab, French, and English books—The shopkeeper also spoke as many languages-and he spoke English like an Englishman!

The bookshop keeper is a true Arab. He talked very freely after he found out that we were not in sympathy with the French. He emphasized that if we are ever stopped for any reason start to speak English at once. He had several books in stock and recommended three of them. One was a relatively late edition of Gunther, Inside Africa. It is a recent edition but the section on Tunisia is well-worn. Another good one that we bought is entitled Tunisia A personal view of a timeless land third, and one that is of great value to us is, Tunisia Today by Leon Laitman. It was just published last year, 1954 and, to us, it is a very objective view of the situation in Tunisia at the present time. We are going to have to do a lot of reading and thinking during the evenings at the hostel.

The bookshop keeper seems to be very well informed with respect to the present situation in Tunisia. As Gunther states in the opening of his section on Tunisia, "Tunisia is a country in crisis".

BIR EL BEY—THE HOSTEL TUNISIA NORTH AFRICA
JANUARY 16 1955

It is now quite late in the evening. We have been on the bike riding through the Medina (old Arab quarter where the market or Souk is located), and along the Grand Avenue with its wide pavement and palm trees and fancy French business offices. The day included visits to the Kasbah (formerly a fortress overlooking the city and the palace of a Barbary State ruler) now a great place for tea and/or coffee.

The French village or quarter (called the Villa nouvelle) could be called the Paris of Tunisia. It is not Paris and it certainly is not Tunisia. So, we go to the French Quarter when we have to, otherwise we are to be found in the Medina, where the Arabs are.

First, this morning was the Kasbah and a glass of strong, hot, very sweet tea. Maybe there would be an Arab present who just happened to speak English? No luck! Emma was the only woman present. We did not know what to expect. To our relief everyone was very pleasant. To date we have not encountered an unfriendly Arab. They all seem to realize that we are ignorant foreigners. That we are not familiar with their customs. We have no reason to be apprehensive in the Medina—and we have been there early in the morning and rather late in the evening. All Arabs have the reputation of treating guests with respect. We are certain that they expect to be treated in like manner. It probably would be very unwise to try to visit or live here if you do not have the ability to accept the people as they are.

From what we have seen and heard, the French Colons are learning that the hard way.

Well, having struck out at the Kasbah we took the short ride through the massive Sea Gate (the French call it the "Porte de France" into the French Quarter. We thought that we might get lucky there and find a Frenchman or an Italian who would be able to speak to us in English—No luck! What were we thinking? We had great difficulty in France finding anyone who would speak English—Even if they could! I do not think that we would have been able to recognize an Italian if we had fallen over one.

Back to the Medina and the book shop. We have been trying to read the information in the books that the book shop owner had sold us. It is not possible to spend much time in Tunis, or Tunisia, and not realize that the French and the Arabs do not like each other. When he started talking about the Italian situation that was news to us!

In situations like that a tape recorder is a must. It is not possible to remember everything that is said and remember it correctly. Italy is very close to Tunisia. It is only about 85 miles from the northern tip of Tunisia to the most southern point of Sicily. During the 18 hundreds many Italian colonists moved into Tunisia. There did not seem to be any undue friction. The government of Italy was known to be interested in the welfare of its people in Tunisia.

Of course, at the same time, the French were interested in grabbing up as much real estate as possible. All the European countries were dividing up African territory just as if they had a right to do so. Remember, it was the white mans duty to "civilize" all the natives of Africa—Whether they needed it or not!

The Italians must have done something wrong. Maybe they did not do anything at all! At any rate the French and the British got their greedy heads together and hatched up what they considered to be a "fair" scheme. This was happening during the early 18 hundreds. The French would not interfere with the British takeover of Cyprus. The British would turn a blind eye to the shenanigans of the French in North Africa. That clever, underhanded maneuver left the Italians out in the cold.

Imagine the attitude, the lack of character, the superior attitude of those so-called diplomats. They were nothing more than short-sighted, greedy politicians! The French were already well established in Algeria. On the concocted excuse that some Tunisian Berbers had invaded "their" territory, the French marched an army of about 30,000 men into Tunisia. The French invaded Tunisia by way of Algeria.

At that time the head of the Tunisian government was a ruler called the Bey. He was a dictator but a very weak one. The Beys of Tunisia had been set up by the Ottoman Turks when they took over much of the Mediterranean coast during the 14 hundreds. (If I have the dates right) At any rate the Bey was weak and in financial difficulty. Too much foreign debt, especially to the French, which is just what they wanted.

By 1880 the French had complete control of Tunisia. The French dictated the Treaty of Bardot under which they took complete control and left the Bey without power as a figurehead. The average Tunisian peasant, the "fellah" had not been doing very well under the /Beys, from what we have been able to see in the area of Tunis, they have not done any better under the French.

As the day passed people were constantly entering, and leaving, the book shop. He does far more business that we ever would have expected. Many of the customers were Arabs in western dress. Almost all the Arab men wear the round, red hat or cap called the Fez. In the Souk just about any combination of Eastern and Western dress is encountered. From what I have been able to see, many of the women cover their dresses and blouses with the ever-present long, black shawl. Some wear the veil, many do not. As I might have mentioned, some women drop the veil if they are aware that I am trying to get a picture. Those that do are quite attractive. (I have not mentioned that to Emma.) Many of the women wear European style shoes. And, it is possible to buy, in the Souk, any style clothing that you might desire. It was late when we left the book shop. That man has been a fountain of information to us. In spite of that, we would like to get the French and Italian points of view. He did give us an English translation of an Italian paper. I am going to go over that, it might be what I am looking for. I can not see that the Italians would be pleased about the French-English deal.

It was late when we reached the Hostel. The woman is very pleasant; she kept our dinner warm and served it with a smile. When I write up my notes she works in the kitchen. She has never tried to rush us out. The French Colons are not in a very desirable situation here in Tunisia. It does not help their situation even if someone is found to be at fault. The only thing that can be done is to go on from here. But, what will the /Colons do? Return to France? Stay and accept Tunisian rule?

BIR EL BEY TUNISIA
JANUARY 17 1955

Tunis, the capitol of Tunisia, is located "behind" Lake Tunis. It does not face the open water the way Carthage did. Carthage was bold; it was located on a promontory facing the open sea. Maybe the founders of Tunis, after learning the final fate of Carthage at the hands of the Romans, consciously decided to secure as much protection as was available. About 2,000 BC the Berbers founded a village where Tunis is now located. It never developed and was taken over by the Carthaginian Empire in the 9th century BC.

What I wanted to mention are the "houses" scattered all along the road leading into Tunis. They seem quite temporary. They are constructed of mud-covered frameworks of a mixture of available, local, vegetation. Some of them have apparently been here for some time because grass is growing on the mud-covered roofs. A few roofs are constructed of corrugated, rusted metal. During the summer it must be very hot inside. Windows, if there are any, are very small and placed as high as possible just under the very narrow eve. The door is narrow, low, and without any door other than a flimsy curtain

Emma and I have stopped and tried to visit with some of the people. It is impossible to communicate with them without an interpreter—and they are not available. Usually only women and small children are in or near the mud-hut. It has not been possible for us to get into one of them. Everyone has been friendly but, when you do not speak their language you have hit a stone wall. We smile a lot, pat the children on the head and give them hard candy. The adults often get into the line for the candy.

They are very poor people. They seem to have little more than the ragged clothes on their backs. The women seem to spend the day taking care of the numerous small children. We see those collecting sticks for the fire, and any edible vegetation that they can find. The women maintain the house, tend the ever-present garden, and carry water in heavy earthen pottery containers. The water jugs are very heavy and they have to carry those long distances. The base of the jug is pointed, not flat. That makes it easier to stand the container upright in the soft soil and sand.

Many of the men spend the day standing in front of the employment office in Tunis. They will accept any kind of work offered. That must make the employers very happy. A constant supply of cheap labor is always available. The French "Protectorate" has created this crisis. Before the "Protectorate", these Bedouins, of mixed Arab and local Berber heritage, were spread about the country. They were small farmers and herdsmen of cattle, sheep and goats. They farmed the fertile plain surrounding Tunis and the fertile area extending along the east coast of Tunisia. Extensive olive orchards were created and an industry was built up based upon olives and olive oil.

Originally farming was labor intensive. It would take days to plow a field using a camel and a donkey. The "Protectorate" changed much of that. The huge farms created by dispossessing the locals, are farmed by tractors. A tractor can do in a day what it would take a local Arab farmer

41

a week or more. Those former farmers, now landless and homeless, have moved toward the cities in hopes of earning some money. They do not understand a cash economy and the French do not want them to understand or take part in it.

At the same time, the French have improved medical care and sanitation. That has greatly reduced the mortality rate. More children survive—to do what? There are too many people now for the country to support. If the children are educated, where will they find employment if the French Colons have all the technical positions. ?

The word is that Tunisia will be given its freedom within the next year. The French, if I am correct, are leaving the Tunisians with a real mess. It will take years to undo the injustice. It is not possible to be objective when you see these poor, uneducated, people suffering. We have to be careful, we do not understand what has happened, we do not have the required background necessary to pass judgment. We do have to attempt to describe the situation as we see it.

Emma and I wonder how those people are able to exist in those tiny huts. We know that they do whatever they have to in order to stay alive. But, what kind of a life is it? Certainly they go to bed many nights' hungry, not knowing where the next food will come from. The huts remind us of those on the waterfront in Naples where, on Christmas Eve the poor Italians had fires in front of their tiny huts. While those poor Italians were trying to keep from starving on Christmas Eve, we had just left Rome where the Pope was celebrating with lavish pomp, ceremony, and unlimited expense.

Here the natives do not have the Pope to deal with—They have the Moslem Religion. There are elaborate Mosques all over the place and they are the most elaborate buildings in every town and village. Too bad that effort, money, time, energy, and resources could not be expended in an effort to help the natives. The same situation exists throughout Europe.

One family really got our attention. The woman was cleaning up around the mud-hut. There were several children running about. The husband was probably in Tunis looking for work. The woman just looked so thin and weak and the children were thin and dressed in tattered rags. Still, she tried to be friendly and smile. There is a small village a few miles away. Emma said, "We have to go shopping". We rode over to the village and stopped in front of an open-air meat market. The meat hung on hooks around the front of the market. It was not possible to see the meat. It was black, covered with flies. Emma tried to find out what it was—I never did. She purchased a large chunk of it.

Next, she walked along the street where a great variety of fresh vegetables were on sale. She filled the Halfa Grass basket that she carries with a variety of vegetables and she picked up a bag of cous-cous. Cous-cous is the national food in Tunisia. Apparently it is made from wheat grain. It tastes very good when cooked with meat and vegetables over an open fire.

Emma got on the bike, holding onto her shopping bag which was full, and heavy. "Take me back to that woman, those children and that mud-hut". I followed that order. When she went up to the hut with that bag of food it was not necessary for the woman to speak English or any language. Her expression told us more than we wanted to know. We had to leave.

After that visit it was late afternoon. We decided to ride on into Tunis and walk through the Medina. (Souk) the market is never the same. The leather shops produce the most beautiful leather work that we have ever seen. The cloth souk is a riot of color with samples hung out across the narrow passages. Emma spent a lot of time looking at the carpets. The geometric designs each have a special history and significance. Each pattern indicates where the carpet was created. By the time Emma finished checking the jewelry stalls it was dusk and the shopkeepers wanted to close and go home. So did I!

We reached the Hostel the French lady had kept our food warm and we were very hungry. There we found an Englishman eating his dinner. He was in Tunisia in order to see and study the ruins of Carthage and that is what he wanted to talk about. We have not yet visited Carthage, just a few miles from Tunis and we were very interested in what he had to say. He gave every indication of being very well informed with respect to Carthage and its history. We needed all the information that he had to offer so he had two very attentive listeners. It was late when the conversation was concluded. It was not really a conversation—it was a lecture on Carthage. And it could not have happened at a more opportune time for us. Of course we had heard of Carthage and the Punic Wars. Dr. Guterman, our European History Professor did the best that he could with us. After listening to him we wanted to go over to Carthage the next day. However, that was not possible.

Tomorrow, January 18 we have an appointment in Tunis with the US Consulate. I think it is the Vice-Consulate that we have to see. (I wonder if he is in charge of American advice in Tunisia.) Anyway, we will take care of that tomorrow and then ride over to Carthage the following day.

BIR EL BEY TUNIS TUNISIA
JANUARY 18 1955

We have just returned to the Hostel from Tunis and a visit to the US Consulate. Talking to the Vice-Consulate reassured Emma and swapping stories with him was interesting. However, about a half-hour later we talked with a local store-keeper. He said, "He knows more than we do? Nobody knows. It is too quiet. I do not like it." He is right, it is quiet. Maybe the store-keeper does know. He lives here. He added, "It is better when they make speeches, now they do not say anything. They make bombs!"

Yesterday there was a rally or meeting here of Youth Hostel leaders. We could not take part in the program, it was all in French. Some of the participants spoke English and we were able to talk with them. They have mixed ideas. They all seem to agree that, at the moment, the situation is stable. They thought that the north is safer than the south. One man said, "Best not to go off the main roads." That was their advice.

Well, if we do not go off the main roads we will not really see the country. Of course it is wise to be careful, but not too careful. It is necessary to take some calculated risks—and that is what we plan to do. If we are so worried about taking chances we should have stayed home, maybe in bed! But then I would have to worry that one of us might fall out and suffer a fatal injury! That is what I told the Principal of the high school in Ann Arbor. We had taken my biology class on a week-end nature trip into the Upper

Peninsula of Michigan. It was necessary to take the ferry across the peninsula and we had to camp out. There was an incident with a bear, but no one was in any danger. Living an over-cautious life must be terrible. Is living in constant fear really worth the effort?—Maybe living like that does not require any effort?

After talking to the Youth Hostel Leaders we rode down to Nabeul where they make pottery, pipes, tiles, etc. Nabeul is a "typical" Arab village with all the usual open-air shops along the market street. A great variety of fresh food is available—to those people who have jobs and can afford to buy it. Of course, if all the best positions are held by French colons, the locals might not have much cash to spend. These people are so very fortunate to be under the "protection" and the "enlightened guidance" of the "super-civilized "French. The native people seem to pay very little attention to us. All the store-keepers are friendly. When we photographed several shops, people shopping and some camels being offered for sale everyone either smiled or simply ignored us. No one has been unfriendly; we have no reason to be afraid of the natives.

On the road to Nabuel we stopped to photograph a farmer plowing a field with a very primitive plow and a camel. Nabuel is located along the coast and, we are told, the land there is more fertile than it is farther south toward the northern edge of the Sahara. The "plow" appeared to be a wooden stick. It did not seem to have a metal tip and no moldboard. It required a great deal of effort and was barely scratching the surface of the ground. The "harness" attached to the camel consisted of an arrangement of old ropes tied together. He was trying to work the soil among the trees in an olive plantation. He may own the plot of land or he may be working for another Arab or a Frenchman. Whatever the conditions, he was expending a lot of energy in order to obtain what would have to be considered a meager return. Again I have to mention the stark contrast between that Arab farmer and the huge mechanized French farms. We doubt that the Arab farmer will ever be able to purchase and operate a tractor.

When we stopped we" asked" an Arab walking along the road if we could take the picture. We showed him the camera and pointed to the farmer plowing. He smiled and shook his head "yes". When the Arab plowing saw the camera, he and his family helping him, became very excited. They appeared to be afraid and angry. When they started running toward us we jumped on the bike and headed down the road! I doubt that they would have actually attempted to harm us.

Later we learned that the very religious Arabs feel that it is against their religion to take pictures of people. They seem to accept pictures of popular individuals but, when we checked out Arab newspapers we found no pictures. We should have realized that we have seen no pictures of any animals in any Arab art work. No "graven images". In the souk, all the tapestry and carpet designs are geometric. Someone said that taking a picture "robs them of their soul". We prefer not to have another incident like that one.

From Nabuel we rode to Korbos located on the Cape Bon Peninsula that extends into the Mediterranean from the northeast tip of Tunisia. The tip of the peninsula is only about 85 miles from the most southern point of Sicily. It is easy to imagine that primitive man could have made his way back and fourth across such a narrow stretch of open water. Some anthropologists and archeologists think that evidence has been found that establishes that belief as a fact . . .

The Cap Bon Peninsula has been very important throughout the known history of the Mediterranean Basin. The narrow neck of water between Sicily and North Africa has facilitated cultural exchange throughout history, and far earlier. The same thing is true with respect to the Straits of Gibraltar which is only 12 miles wide. These two narrow stretches of water have served as connections between Europe and Africa for many thousands of years. It is thought that very early in the history of man migrations took place across these two points. Carthage, located across the Gulf of Tunisia, on the African mainland, was able to control all shipping passing through the waters between Europe and North Africa. That is between the eastern and western Mediterranean. We look forward to visiting Carthage.

Cap Bon (Cape Bon) is actually the eastern terminus of the Atlas Mountains that extend across North Africa. It is hilly and obviously fertile because we saw many citrus groves, vineyards, and tobacco plantations. We also passed through fishing ports, and beach resorts.

The peninsula had a moment of fame during World War II. When the Allied Forces finally got their act together and learned to cooperate they were able to overwhelm the German forces under the command of General Rommel, known as the desert fox due to his ability to hit and run and his "Panzer attacks" . . . The German forces finally retreated up into the Cap Bon Peninsula where they surrendered.

But, lets return to Korbus—As I mentioned, we had been in Nabeul and decided to ride up to Korbus. In Korbus there are some Roman ruins. Well, in Tunisia it is not possible to travel very far without encountering Roman ruins. The Romans were very busy in many parts of Tunisia piling up various sizes of marble and other types of stone.

Korbus has been well-known for its thermal hot spring for thousands of years. Apparently it took the Romans to construct, of stone of course, a large bath-house. It has a reputation of being a thermal cure-all. The temperature of the water varies from 111-140 degrees. That seems a little too hot for me! It is a social gathering place, a center where people can relax and, "take the cure-all". My opinion is that the actual cure, if it takes place at all, takes place in the brain. The dance hall probably was not there during Carthaginian and/or Roman times. It is there now and it is very noisy.

When we were there all the noise was being made by French women and men. There were a few Arabs to be seen, very few. Most of them were working around the outside carrying out repair and maintenance work. There were so many French people of all ages that, when we arrived Emma asked me, "Where are the Arabs?" She knew that a question like that would set me off-

French vehicles, many of them expensive, lined the roadway. French, young and old, filled the bath house, the restaurants, the dance hall, and the beach. They gave every indication of having a great time. None of them gave any indication of being worried—About the country, the resistance movement, the Arabs, the declaration that

Tunisia will receive its freedom within a year. See, that is where I qualify as "strange". If I were a French person living in Tunisia today I would be worried about the events that are bound to take place when the Tunisians start to run the country.

Korbus is located right on the Mediterranean. It is surrounded by mountains. The white buildings with red tile roofing present a beautiful picture with the blue Mediterranean forming the background. The Romans knew where and how, and what to build. And the Carthaginians before them—And, no doubt the original inhabitants—the Berbers.

Carthage is next on our list of places to see. We hope to be able to spend a lot of time there poking about in the ruins. Good old Professor Guterman! He really loved to talk about Carthage and the Carthaginians. Emma and I think of him and we wonder if he was ever able to get over here. I doubt very much that he ever made enough money to permit such a journey. He was not the type man to ride a motorcycle!

Every time we rode over to Carthage we had to cross the ship channel on a small free ferry. It was always an interesting crossing. There were very few cars-but there were many two-wheeled carts pulled by donkeys and/or camels. Each cart had two huge wheels that raised the body quite high. How those poor men were able to get material loaded I do not think that I want to know! I do know that I would prefer not to be involved! They carried hay, straw, earthen jugs, furniture, and a lot of stuff that I was not able to identify or remember. We always looked forward to that crossing. We feel so sorry for those Arabs who have to load, walk to wherever they are going, unload, and return! (I keep calling them "Arabs" but I think they are a mixture of native Berbers, Bedouins from the East, and various other peoples who have invaded Tunisia.) Every time that we ride over to Carthage we have to pass through small, primitive, villages made of mud huts. They are small, made of stick frames covered with mud. Some are of mud bricks. I wonder what happens when it rains. We pass many women carrying heavy earthen jugs full of water on their backs. Some carry huge bundles of hay that they have cut or bundles of sticks for the cooking fire. Some of the women are veiled, many are not. We do not see any well-dressed people!

Carthage does not make a spectacular first impression. It is a large area strewn with stone rubble that has been picked over for hundreds of years. Various peoples have used the ruins as a quarry. If you look up on the hill you see a Catholic Cathedral—it was built of stone from the ruins of Carthage. The same is true of many of the buildings in Tunis. Mixtures of ancient Roman columns now support Arab Mosques.

Today Carthage is still inhabited. The inhabitants we see are children of all ages—some of them appear to be quite old. They are trying to sell anything that they are able to find, or dig up, from the piles of rubble. They all wear a uniform of rags. Some are better at it than others. They have not been a problem, we have enjoyed having them follow us around and show us various sights. Of course they are trying to make money but, they have not been pests—at least not to us and, not yet.

Many of the children are trying to sell "original oil lamps." For sales people who have very little command of the

English language, they are doing very well. Every time we visit the ruins Emma buys another lamp. That creates a minor problem—Space on the bike is very limited. Another factor, not an important one is that the "original Phoenician lamps" are very crude fakes. The children must run then off by the hundreds. They are solid mud or clay; there is obviously no container for the oil. If they ever have any value we will be rich.

Much of the original stone work has been carted away—and not all of it by the Bedouins, the Berbers, or the Arabs. Tourists, antique dealers, collectors from all over the world, and professional people and institutions have been very busy. Practically everything that is left has been defaced by Sheppard's tending their flocks with nothing else to occupy their time. The mosaics that have not been stolen by foreigners have been very seriously defaced by tourists. They chip away at the edges and collect the fragments. Only the entire mosaic makes sense—it relates a story in the form of a picture. The stolen chip is meaningless and has no value.

The ragged children delight in showing the "ancient tombs." We have little doubt that the tomb is authentic. However the contents are very much open to question. The strategy used is to escort the tourist or victim down into the tomb. Then they allow the "mark" to dig around in the dirt and dust. If he does not find anything the "guide" will assist by also digging through the debris. Surprise! A "human" jaw bone is found! If that fails to produce a gratuity of some kind the whole effort is abandoned.

All the tombs were thoroughly sacked within a few hundred years of their occupancy. But, the gullible tourist does not want to believe that. The Berber, Bedouin, and Arab children have been using the same standard tactics for many hundreds of years. We bought the "original, ancient, oil lamps—but absolutely no part of any mosaic. Those children are always there. We have arrived early and late in the evening and they are ready to transact business. They have no regular hours. Some of them may not even have a home.

It is not possible not to feel sorry for them—you have to be as generous as possible. Probably they do get some satisfaction out of "taking" the tourist—but they have really not done any harm.

If you are not an historian (we are not!) it is very difficult to separate the original Carthaginian ruins from the Roman ruins. The Carthaginian Civilization was first, starting about 1,000 BC. That ended in 146 BC, the date upon which the Romans defeated the Carthaginians and destroyed everything that the Carthaginians had created. The Romans next supported the nearby village of Utica, a former enemy of Carthage. However, after some time they came to realize that Carthage had the best location. They then constructed a new city on the site where the city-state of Carthage had been.

As you wander through the ruins and think about the history of such sites as Carthage you are almost bound to wonder if it all has any meaning. Carthage and Rome were both great civilizations with a great deal to offer the people of the earth. But they had different philosophies and each felt that it had to dominate. They were intelligent people and accomplished great things—But, neither side was able to learn the simple fact that nobody ever won a war. The nations of the earth have not yet learned that!

The Carthaginian civilization had existed for about 1,000 years. During that period of time it had come to dominate the entire eastern Mediterranean. The Carthaginians were Phoenicians; they were referred to by the Greeks and Romans as "Punic". Carthage was flourishing when Rome was trying to get organized. The first Phoenician settlers originated in Tyre, a city-state in what is now Lebanon. Legend has it that a queen had to escape from Tyre due to a struggle for power by her brother. At any rate, she left Tyre with an expeditionary force and located on the coast of what is now Tunisia.

The Phoenicians (Carthaginians) were great sea farers and astute business people. They established coastal trading centers all along the coast of the eastern Mediterranean. They built sea-going ships that could carry up to 100 tons of merchandise. Where they were not able to build warehouses they would dock their ships and conduct open-air markets. (Tell me-what is new?) The Phoenicians manufactured what the people needed and they produced it at prices that the common people could afford. (We could use that idea today)

Phoenician trading vessels went through the Straits of Gibraltar and down the west coast of Africa. There is evidence that they transacted business in what is now Nigeria. Some authorities believe that they might have circumnavigated the African continent! My memory relating to the history of the Near East is not very good. However, I do recall reading about a Greek, living in what is now Egypt, who estimated the circumference of the earth. He was only about two hundred miles off! That was around 400 BC and, at the time, the Carthaginians were trading all around the Mediterranean and the west coast of Africa.

It has also been established that the Carthaginians traded throughout the Sahara and south of it. They certainly could have negotiated through what is now Egypt and traded with peoples along the Red Sea and around the Horn of Africa, (now Somalis) and on down along the coast to present-day East Africa. It is quite amazing to read about Europeans "discovering" Africa during the eighteen hundreds.

After spending the day wandering around, and through, what is left of carthage (actually Roman Carthage), we are very hungry and anxious to return to the Hostel. The food is always very good. That French lady is really a fine chef. (Maybe I should have married her!!) After a good meal we are ready for bed. The bunks could not be called comfortable, but they are OK-and, we are so tired that it does not matter.

Today we were back in Carthage! All the "residents" there have gotten to know us. They act pleased to see us—and it is not because we are buying anything. We have no extra money and, no place to carry anything more than what we now have. I try to write up my notes every night before we go to bed. That way I think I am able to remember what has happened a little more accurately. It is very difficult to get to the truth. Every time the story is related it is done with the bias of the person doing the relating. (Hard to believe that I am guilty of the same thing!)

Well, today we met a Priest. We think that he is "stationed" at the cathedral up on the hill. They like to locate churches, synagogue, mosques, schools, etc. up on hills—That way the people have to "look up "to them. It is said to have a psychological effect. I do not think that it has ever affected me or the way that I think. Anyway, the Priest has, no doubt, seen us around there day after day and he wonders what we might be up to. Maybe he thinks that we are going to cart away that marble bathtub. It has been moved but it is so massive that a large crane would be required. The "sales people" have told us (sign language) that the best time to hunt for artifacts is after a rain. They did, one day, after a rain, show us where some old coins were. Did they "plant" them—we do not know. But, they were a gift, no charge!

The Priest was a very curious fellow. Lots of questions, and we answered all of them. Of course the conversation turned to Carthage, the Romans, and religion. He was critical of the Carthaginians because they believed in a series of gods. The original settlers brought their gods with them from Tyre. Although there were many gods they were presided over by the father of the gods. A goddess was the principle figure in the Phoenician Pantheon.

The number of Phoenician gods raised a serious question in the mind of the Priest. He stressed his belief in one, and only one, God. We were not able to resolve the issue. He felt that I should agree with him and I could not do so. I felt that I had to say, "They had many Gods, you have one, what does it matter? How to determine which belief is correct—if there is any truth to either of them?" That statement he did not like and brought up the opinion that children were sacrifices to the Gods, cremated, and buried in urns.

Again I had to say that the records are not available. The Romans burned Carthage, the fire burned for seventeen days-all written records were destroyed. The records that remain were written by Greeks and Romans—two cultures that clashed with that of Carthage and are thought to be biased. There are alternative theories that might explain the cremated bodies of the children buried in the urns. He gave every indication that he did not like my response, did not agree with it, and did not want to discuss the matter any further. On that we were able to agree!

Later, while we were looking around the Roman town, near the theatre, an Arab who spoke fairly good English came by. He showed us several mosaics, the baths, a store, and the marble tub which, he said, was for children. He also pointed out tombs that were supposed to be of Phoenician and/or Roman origin. We had no idea as to what the facts might be. We, once again, collected some bone fragments. He said that all the complete skeletons had been removed hundreds of years ago. That sounded right. He told us that "the White Fathers" up on the hill had removed large amounts of material including many mosaics.

The Arab (if that is what he was) said that he did not like the "White Fathers", that they and the French are not welcome in Tunisia. He said that it was not very long ago that someone preaching religion was stoned to death. Emma and I do not know much about the Moslem Religion. We do know that it rules almost every aspect of their lives. We know that many of them are quite fanatic. We have learned that, at times, when we attempt to take pictures. Knowing that, we feel that it is best not to get involved in trying to change their minds. The Arab said that he is not "just an Arab", he said that he is a leader. We assume that he was referring to the organized resistance movement in Tunisia. He talked to us in English—he also spoke Arabic and French. He said that he was never able to attend school that was reserved for the French children. Only a few very wealthy Arabs are allowed to attend school. He learned English during the Second World War when the British and Americans were in Tunisia.

While we talked the Arab explained why the Tunisians want the French to leave. He said, "Frenchmen hire only Frenchmen for the best jobs and the jobs that pay the best wages." He said, "Only hard-labor is usually offered or available to the Tunisians". The pay-scale is very unfair. For the same job, an Arab is paid 5,000 francs per day—for the same work a Frenchman earns 20,000 francs.

The man is, without a doubt, a full-blooded resistance leader. He became quite animated. He did not know who we might be and he did not seem to care. He went on—"The Frenchmen drive big cars and live in big houses, drink freely and have a good time." He explained to us that Arabs, in general, are not able to do such things. And, he went on, "This is supposed to be our country". He also mentioned that a Frenchman is able to buy a car on time-payment—an Arab is not allowed to do that—he must pay cash.

"So", he said, if the Beys representative returns from France without a guarantee that the French are going to get out, there will be a revolt, a revolution." About that time a big white train passed by. "See the train", he pointed toward it, if the French do not get out there will be no train, train will be kaput".

By that time Emma had become quite nervous. I did not exactly feel safe. Since we are not involved in the matter we did not give him any indication that he is not right. We returned to the Hostel with a lot to think about. Emma made an interesting comment. "Since 1776 no one in the United States has lived under the rule of a foreign power". I doubt that many people ever think about that. We take our freedom for granted.

But freedom is very fragile; it can die in a very short time if not properly cared for. I did my best to calm Emmis fears. I said, "Remember, we came here to get some movies. Let's concentrate on that." I do not think I helped very much—if at all.

Two or three nights ago, while we were shopping, we talked with a grocer. His story was interesting and confirmed what the Arab at the ruins of Carthage had already told us. "The Tunisians, Arab, Bedouin, and Berber, are all very agitated about the French taking over the country." "Now" he said," the Communists have evicted the French from Indo-China and, we want to do the same thing here." The grocer wondered aloud if the Bey has ideas of becoming King. He added, "He better think again. The French put him where he is and we are going to put him out once we get our freedom."

The grocer thinks that a man named "Bourguiba" will be elected president. "Bourgeba", he said, has been fighting for our freedom for many years. He has spent many of those years in various French jails." He does not think that Bourgeba will accept anything less than the complete withdrawal of the French. "Bourguiba", he told us, "laid out a plan for the freedom of Tunisia. He worked hard trying to get the French to accept it. When they refused he called for unlimited resistance and general insurrection.""That resulted with the French arresting him and putting him back in jail."

"Now" the grocer continued, "the French have elected Pierre Mendes-France. "He is in favor of giving Tunisia Home Rule. That is the first step toward our complete freedom. We are waiting for Bourguiba to return to Tunisia. We hope the French continue to cooperate with us. If they do not it will becomevery dangerous in Tunisia, especially for the French".

By now it was quite dark. We were in the Souk but we are familiar with the narrow passage ways and they do not seem as mysterious and dangerous as they did when we first visited. We wanted to hear as much as the grocer was willing to tell us. He certainly was not afraid to talk!

"Now", he continued, "Capital is no longer being invested in Tunisia. Investors are waiting to see what is going to happen. The situation is, at present, too "fluid". People who are able to get out are doing so, and they are taking everything that they can with them. That is not good for my country."

As the grocer talked customers constantly entered and left. They were all local people. I refer to them as "Arabs" but, as I have mentioned, the people of Tunisia are as mixed with respect to their genes, as we are in the US. He spoke Tunisian Arabic to all of them, switching back and forth from Arabic to English without any hesitation. We tried to tell him, as we left, how much we appreciated being able to talk, and listen, to what he had to say. He impressed us as a reasonable man, well informed, who just wanted his country to manage its own affairs. We could not see anything unreasonable about that!

After we left and we were making out way out through the twisting, narrow passages, we had much to think about. It was the same feeling of apprehension and frustration that we had after our conversation with the Arab among the ruins of Carthage. Emma expressed something that was going through my brain—"That "grocer", she said," may be a grocer but, he is also a lot more than that. I wonder what will happen to him if Tunisia fails to get its freedom and the French crack-down on such people." "And", I said, "What will happen to him if Tunisia does get its freedom? Will he continue to be a grocer or will he become an official in the new government?" We will never be able to find out—

Finally, after some wandering about, we located the bike and the little boy who was "guarding" it. Well he was still there so we felt he earned the few francs that seemed to make him quite pleased. As we rode back to the Hostel we paid more attention to the mud shacks along the road. It was dark and many of the people had little fires out in front of their "houses". It was very picturesque, yes, but, we wondered, how would you like to have to live like that?

The conversation turned to Tunisian freedom. What will happen if the country does manage to get the French Army (Foreign Legion) out, and all the French government officials? How will the living conditions of the poor people change? Will it improve? Will all, or any, of their expectations become realities ? We have the impression that the majority of the people believe that conditions can hardly get worse than they are. They want to have a hand in making their own laws, regulations, and mistakes.

Back at the Hostel our late dinner was waiting—as usual. We can not complain about conditions here or how we have been treated. The Frenchman is "distant", he never tried to talk, smile, or be pleasant. His wife is just the opposite. The food is excellent, the beds and the entire place is very clean. These people are under a lot of tension. They are French and they know that they are hated by the natives. They may have to abandon the life they have crested here in Tunisia, leave everything, and return to France.

Emma and I still would like to shoot a movie here in Tunisia. We have the 16mm film and a Pathe camera. What we need is a way to gain entrance, at least superficially, into the lives of some of the common people. The people are not unfriendly, they are distant. They are very suspicious of strangers. The country had a basic population of Berbers. They were here long before recorded history. The ancient Egyptians were aware of the Berbers thousands of years ago. Numidia's arrived, to be followed, about 1000 BC by the Phoenicians from Tyre in what is now Lebanon. They established trading centers along the coast and, as mentioned earlier, the Carthaginian Civilization grew up. Carthage was destroyed by the Romans and the Roman Civilization flourished for hundreds of years.

When Rome dec; the Visigoths, and then the Byzantines. The Byzantines set up the Beys in Tunisia. Through them they exerted very loose control and the Bey in Tunisia, as well as across North Africa became practically independent. It was under the Beys that the Barberry Pirates seized control of various ports across North Africa. Because of the Inquisition in Spain, resulting in the expulsion of the Moors (Arabs) and all the Jews, and the Crusades organized by the Pope in Rome, the Arabs had (have) valid reasons to hate the Christians.

The present population of Tunisia is the result of the mixture, inbreeding and gene-mixing, of all those various peoples over many centuries. Every time that Tunisia was invaded, many of the Berbers retreated up into the mountains, or, south into the Sahara which covers about the southern third of the country. When Emma and I discuss the present situation in Tunisia we wonder if that long history has not affected the nature, the attitude, of the present population.

When we attempt to approach the people that we would like to film they act afraid. They seem to feel that we are up to no good. The language barrier makes any communication impossible. I think that the situation is made worse by the constant presence of the French Foreign Legion. They are everywhere! They march through the streets of Tunis and along the main roads, they travel in truck convoys and we do our best to keep out of the way. I keep thinking, "How would we like a situation like this in the US?"

The culture of Tunisia is Arabic. When some people arrive in an Arab country they experience what might be called, "Cultural Shock". Emma and I have not had that experience. We try to keep in mind that, today, the Tunisians are Arabs. Their background, their history, and their culture are their own.

The lives of the people in Tunisia, those with whom we have had contact, seem to be rather uniform. The country is small; there is great similarity with respect to language and religion. Also, and we think most important, there is great unity of opposition to the French "protectorate". Small groups of Europeans, Jews, and Italians live in Tunisia. The French have exerted an influence, especially with respect to government, sanitation, schools, hospitals, and rail and road conditions. The new towns, built under the supervision of the French, make you think you are in France, and Western-style clothes are common, usually mixed with Arab hats and robes. The Tunisians educated in Paris certainly have been influenced, to some degree, by Western ideas.

Geography has had an effect upon the uniformity of Tunisian life. One day we rode up to a village called Beja where there are some Roman ruins. As soon as we left the plain on which Tunis is located we started climbing up into the mountains. The Atlas mountain chain extends across all of North Africa. In fact it is part of the Alps in Europe. The Atlas in Tunisia forms two branches, one extends over to the Cap Bon Peninsula and out into the Mediterranean. The other runs south and gradually slopes toward the Mediterranean on the east coast of Tunisia. The land in the valleys formed by the mountains and the coastal plain are very fertile.

The people raise cattle, sheep, and goats, depending upon what the land will best support. Along the coast toward the south, cereals, citrus fruits and extensive orchards of olive trees are to be found. During our travels around Tunisia we saw, as mentioned, wheat, barley, grapes, olives, olive oil presses, and date groves. The Sahara extends up into the southern third of Tunisia. There, in the several oases, large date palm groves are located

Tunisia has hot, dry summers and warm, wet winters. It can be very cold on some days during the winter. On the bike, early in the morning, we found it to be quite cold. One expert on Tunisia called it a country with a cold wind and a hot sun. We agree.

One morning I was doing some routine maintenance work on the bike. I spilled some oil on the front tire. Later that day we were in Tunis where there are trolley car tracks. I leaned the bike to cross the tracks and the oil spot flipped the bike and us up into the air! The bike righted itself and continued on down the street for some distance before falling upon one side. Emma and I each slid in different directions. We did not wear helmets but we were fortunate and did not land on our heads! We each slid for some distance, enough to tear some of our clothing off, produce some serious burns and burses, and smash the leg-shields and the windscreen. The leg-shields I was able to repair—but, not the plastic wind-screen. Neither could we locate a new wind-screen. The result has been that we are exposed to the full blast of the wind, rain, dust, and the hot sun!

Right now, Tunisia is in turmoil. We conclude that it is best to get as much information on the current situation as possible. From time to time we visit the American Consulate and visit with one of the officials. Recently we were in there and we were introduced to a local Arab who speaks English more correctly than we do. Obviously he is working with the French—at least that is what the French and Americans think. We ask the grocer's question—"They know more than we do?" Anyway we were invited to dinner.

The Assistant American Consulate was kind enough to give us some advice. The Arabs do not shake hands as vigorously as we do. Only men shake hands, if the woman extends her hand you touch it gently. If she does not, you bow your head in acknowledgement. At parties you are introduced to the women first and then the men, oldest first. Be sure to take pastries, nuts, fruit, cake, candy, or nuts to the hostess. No alcohol. You may be asked to remove your shoes. (I better check my socks!) Dress your best out of respect to the host. (That was a problem for us!)

Then he went into table manners—He said that we would not have to sit on the floor. Our hosts use table and chairs. The guest of honor sits next to the host. Before the meal is served a wash basin may be brought in. Hold your hands over while water is poured over them. Males and females usually eat separately but he did not think that would happen in our case. Do not start to eat until the host does. The food will be served from a communal bowl, eat from the section of the bowl in front of you. Normally, the food is taken in the right hand. It is rolled into a ball by the thumb and fingers and flipped into your mouth. At the end of the meal the wash basin and towel is passed around again.

I told him that I would surely have trouble with that maneuver! He laughed and said that in these Arab family knives and forks would be provided. He said to be sure to try to eat a little bit of everything. (I should have no problem with that!)

We were served a typical Tunisian dish of cous cous covered with a delicious stew of meat and vegetables. The host did not stand on formality and that made us relax, visit, and enjoy the food. The conversation was kept very casual—not much on the present situation. Later, Emma and I agreed that, from what we heard, it is not possible to determine what his position is.

The food was delicious, his wife ate with us, and it seemed to be very much European style. We tried to remember everything that the Assistant Counsel told us. I can not be the judge of how we did. I can say that we have not been invited for a return engagement—I wonder if that has any significance. Our next objective is the village of Sidi Bou Said. It is located over near ancient Carthage.

Jan 18 1955

No matter how early we get up, the warden's wife has gotten up and has our breakfast ready. She must have learned that Americans like to eat something for breakfast. She always makes more than toast and coffee. She is so much more pleasant than he is. Maybe it is because he was in the military He might have been an officer and is accustomed to giving orders. We do not know. If he was an officer it is quite a change from that to being a hostel custodian. Really, we have sympathy for him. He is a victim of circumstances just as the Tunisians are. The fault lies with the decision-makers in France and their policies driven by greed.

Well, anyway, we were up early and on the road to Sidi Bou Said. The crossing on the little ferry was Interesting, as usual. All the two-wheeled carts were lined up and waiting to board. Those little, high wagons have a long history. They resemble Roman chariots. Many of them, like the ones we saw in Sicily, are decorated with intricate geometrical designs. Each design has special significance according to the area in which it was made. (I probably do not remember the exact history.)

Well, anyway, we were up early and on the road to Sidi Bou Said. The crossing on the little ferry was interesting, as usual. All the two-wheeled carts were lined up and waiting to board. Those little, high wagons have a long history. They resemble Roman chariots. Many of them, like the ones we saw in Sicily, are decorated with intricate geometrical designs. Each design has special significance according to

69

the area in which it was made. (I probably do not remember the exact history.)

Sidi Bou Said is only about 15 miles from Tunis. It is located on a promontory overlooking the Mediterranean—a spectacular location. The village got its name from a religious man who lived there and is buried there (His name is so long that there is no chance of my getting it right!) The village now has a population of artists. There are several souvenir shops. Not all the souvenirs have any real significance so far as Sidi Bou Said is concerned.

A woman in one of the shops told us that the earliest record of the village goes back to about the 12th century. She said that in the 1920s Baron Rodolphe d" Erlanger originated the idea of painting the doors and windows blue and the walls of the buildings white. He had a good idea! The blue is very pleasant and restful; it matches the blue of the Mediterranean. Many people must agree, the Bey of Tunis has a home (palace) there along with many wealthy business people, expatriates, and political leaders. (We would have been receptive of any invitations—we did not get any.)

Sidi Bou Said is so pleasant, so quiet and relaxing! Emma thinks it would be a great place in which to retire. I think she could be right! We spent the day just walking around the village and enjoying the view. The homes are very attractive. The mosque and the cemetery were very interesting. We were not able to enter the mosque. Christians are not allowed to enter certain mosques but, it might have been closed for some other reason. The day passed very quickly. Carthage was close-by but we did not even consider going over there. As usual, it was late when we returned to the hostel—but, hot food was waiting for us !

While we ate we talked about our day in Sidi Bou Said. Emma said, "The harbor is so beautiful ! I wonder what it was like when the pirates were here." I thought that it probably was not quite as neat, clean, and well-kept as it is today. The village was there. It originated about 1200. The pirates did not arrive until about 1500 when the Ottoman Empire took over control of the area. We wondered what living on a pirate ship must have been like. We both took courses in entomology and parasitology. Emma offered the comment that it might have been a great place to collect human parasites, lice and fleas ! Those ships must have been infested with rats! On that pleasant thought I suggested that we go to bed.

On the way over to Sidi Bou Said we did see an Arab funeral procession. We were passing through the edge of Tunis. Emma said, "Look down that street, they are having a parade". I parked the bike and we walked toward the moving mass of people. It was an Arab funeral. It appeared to be a crowd carrying a bed, a wooden platform upon which a small body wrapped in a white cloth was lying. The body was completely wrapped, I was not able to make out any detail. Emma got up closer and said that she thought it might have been the body of a young girl. She said that the body appeared to flex with the movement of the platform. We were told that burial takes place very soon after death.

As the platform moved down the street there was a constant exchange of individuals carrying it. People rushed up and wanted to touch the platform. It is considered a great honor to assist in carrying the dead. There was a lot of color, especially red and a great deal of noise! Following the group with the platform was a contingent of trumpeters blowing long instruments. They were making a lot of noise.

My camera was slung over my shoulder and I moved it out, I had taken some distant shots but wanted to get closer. One man noticed the camera and shook his head "no". I did agree with him, many of the women were crying rather loudly and I thought that it did not seem appropriate to take pictures under such circumstances. We know that many Arabs do not want any image made of them under any circumstances. They feel that it might rob them of their soul.

Our next trip is going to be down to Kairouan, south of Tunis, in central Tunisia. Kairouan is located inland from the coastal city of Sousse. Sousse is a busy port; we did not stop there on this trip. We wanted to spend the day in Kairouan. When we did visit Sousse there was a great deal of activity in, and around, the port. I thought of the grocer in Tunis telling us that no one is investing any capitol in Tunisia because the situation is so "fluid". We can not be the judge with respect to that. We only know what we hear and see. It did seem to us that there was a lot of "capitol" moving into, and out of, the port of Sousse.

South of Sousse the road to Kairouan turns west across an expansive barren plain. It must have been a desolate area when it was founded by invading Arabs in 670 AD. Originally it was just a military camp, an outpost. As we approached the sprawling structure and the three-story, 100 foot high, tower came into view. It made me think more of a fortress in the desert rather than the 4th most holly place in the Moslem world.

The historical version of the founding is that it was a military camp. Emma and I prefer the following—

The custodian explained the founding as the result of a miracle. When the camp was first made a golden goblet was discovered in the sand. It was one that had disappeared from Mecca years earlier. When the goblet was exposed a spring gushed out! The water from the spring originated from the same source as one in Mecca! There were three miracles—the losing and finding of the goblet and the spring! Those miracles established the mosque in Kairouan as a special holly place.

From Kairouan as their first military base the Arabs started to spread out over Tunisia and eventually west ward to Morocco and the Atlantic. Over the next centuries Kairouan grew and became a cultural center. The Mosque was torn down, rebuilt, and continually added to and decorated. During the 17th through the19th centuries the area was under the control of the Turks. That is the time of the pirates and their control of the coastal areas. I do not think that Kairouan was affected.

The Great Mosque is laid out in the form of a rectangle. The courtyard is huge! When you enter and walk across it you feel very small! The walls are very thick and reinforced by towers. Along three sides of the courtyard are arched, enclosed walkways. Off to one side is a large prayer hall. The three porticoes surround the central marble-paved central courtyard.

The Arabs who built the Great Mosque were from the desert. They were uneducated and ignorant. They were

Moslem fanatics who knew very little, if anything, beyond what was told to them from the Holy Book, the Koran. Still, those desert nomads raided all the Roman ruins for many miles around Kairouan and, with them put together the mosque. I think that accomplishment might qualify as more of a "miracle" than the "finding" of the goblet.

The decoration of the mosque consists of designs created from ideas taken from pagan, Christian, Berber, Carthaginian, Vandal, and Arabic script. Arabic script lends itself to all kinds of interesting geometrical designs. The Arabs have been very creative in their efforts not to portray any animal designs. The whole structure is very impressive-especially when you consider, by whom, and under what circumstances it was constructed.

The Moslem religion dominates the Arab world. It does so just as the Christian religion dominates the world of the West, of the "Infidel". Kairouan made us think of the white domed tombs that we have seen in many places as we ride through Tunisia. Some are very plain, others decorated. They usually have a white wall surrounding the dome. They are the burial places of Moslem Saints. In life they served as healers and spiritual advisors. Originally they lived in fortified monasteries, they were warrior monks. Today many people worship their tombs and make pilgrimages to the burial sites. There seems to be an element of pagan ritual involved. And, I think, there is a similarity to all this in the rituals of the Catholics and the Protestants.

There are a lot of Roman ruins throughout Tunisia. I doubt that, in very many areas, you would not have to look very far in order to unearth artifacts. Emma and I talk about the condition of the ruins. Many people say that they have been dug up, exposed. No doubt that is true. But, we think, that, in many places the ruins appear to have been used as a quarry. Over the centuries, we think, the Arab Berbers, the sheep and goat herders, the Desert Nomads, have been responsible for a great deal of the damage to be seen today.

Then, in addition to the wear and tear of the weather, the sun, wind, sand and rain, there are the "collectors". "Professional" and private collectors. European "specialists" have done a great deal of damage in their professed efforts to "preserve" and "protect" the relics. Art dealers are among those collectors who have done untold damage in their efforts to make short-term profits. Shiploads of priceless relics were stolen by Europeans over the last centuries.

Before we left Kairouan we had one last question—well, we had many questions but we knew that it would not be possible to have them all answered by the custodian even though he was able to speak English quite well.

When we were finally able to locate him I asked, "If the Arab Bedouins swept out of the central desert in what is now Arabia and eventually all across North Africa and up into Spain as well as south of the Sahara and over into the eastern Soudan, what did they live on ? He said, "They were very destructive, they lived off the land and on whatever they were able to find". They did destroy much of the native Berber farm land and their irrigation canals. The Berbers retreated into the mountains and into available desert oases. Some authorities claim that North Africa has never fully recovered from that desert Bedouin invasion.

It is well-known that many Arabs are able to survive on some oil, a little meal or cereal, some olives, dates and some bread. Even so, the area around Kairouan was, and is, desolate. The invaders had to have supply-lines. They could not have advanced, survived, and built that Great Mosque by living, "off the land". He added, "Many Bedouins still eat whatever they are able to find—and, whenever they are able to find it". I am not quite sure that we ever did get a satisfactory answer to that question.

Out arrival at Bir El Bey was very late. So late that, for the first time, the hostel was dark, closed, and everyone was in bed. They did leave the dormitories unlocked and we were able to go straight to bed—very hungry! The food deficit was made up next morning at breakfast.

When we visit the mud-huts or watch the Bedouins working on their tiny "farms around their huts it is obvious that many of the men have several wives. Under present custom they are allowed up to five wives provided that they are able to provide for them equally. In most of the places that we have been able to observe the several wives are being provided for equally—they all appear to be equally poor and hungry! When a man puts five wives together, how does he avoid having one or more murders on his hands? Maybe I should ask—"How does he keep from being murdered?"

Some of the wives wear veils, some do not. It seems that Arab women still wear the veil. Berber women do not. Over the centuries the invading Arabs, Bedouins, and various other invaders, have mixed, cross-bred, with the original, native Berbers. Some Blacks from the Sahara have found their way into Tunisia and they have contributed their genes to the mix. As I have mentioned earlier, the situation is similar to that in the US, the population is the result of extensive cross, and, inbreeding.

A man with five wives must have a very complex social life. How does one man, if he has four or five wives, manage to keep track of each one or, all of them? We have not been able to learn much about that. However, a man with several wives must be able to produce many children, even if the mortality rate is very high. The first wife is said to have a certain amount of "seniority". We have the impression that the division of labor is rather "square" in favor of the husband.

In order to know and understand why these people live as they do it would be necessary to live with them over a period of time. During the day, out in the fields, the women seem to do much of the heavy work. The women work with one child slung over her back and several others in the area. As soon as they are big enough the older ones take care of the younger. Little girls carry "littler" ones on one hip. Little boys appear to be special—they spend the day playing.

The women do just about all the work around the house. They keep the area swept clean, collect wood and carry it great distances, they gather any locally available food and work in the garden. It is their responsibility to prepare and serve whatever food might be available. The women carry the water in heavy earthen jars or clay containers with pointed bottoms so that they stand upright in the sand. Of course, the women mend the clothes and probably make them if they have the necessary equipment.

After the trip to Kairouan Emma had to do some shopping. We went into the Souk and had another visit with the grocer. We had questions about the social life among the Arabs. He said that in a traditional marriage the young people may have never seen each other. The parents make all the wedding arrangements.

There has been considerable European influence, mostly, of course, due to the French "Protectorate". The society in Tunisia has been affected—and will be affected more in the future after the French are forced out. When any entertaining is done in a traditional Tunisian home, the women do all the work but, they are not to be seen. They prepare and serve the food, then remain out of sight. They do have special "peep-holes" built into the tile work through which they are able to watch and listen. When you visit such a home you really have to look closely in order to locate their "secret listening devices".

The Berbers living in their mountain strong-holds are little affected by the events in the cities. Berber traditions have survived, over the past several thousand years, the invasion of the area by many so-called "conquerors". Some, like the Carthaginians and the Romans, stayed for almost a thousand years. Others, like the Vandals, Spaniards, Ottoman Turks, and the Pirates, (And the French?) did not last nearly that long.

The most damaging invasion was that of the Bedouin Arabs who swept out of the desert from what is now Arabia. They spread out through North Africa like waves of human locusts during the 9th and 10th centuries. The exception was that the damage that they did to the farms, irrigation systems, the herders, and their pastures, and the social life of the Berbers was much more devastating than any swarm of locusts. The North African economy and way of life has never fully recovered.

On our ride into Tunis the other morning we passed a family of Bedouins with all their earthly belongings traveling along the road. They had two camels heavily loaded and several donkeys. Two very vicious-looking dogs and several children ran along with, and following, the pack-animals. The women's faces were not veiled; they wore a lot of loose clothing. As we passed them, we noticed that there were three women walking and one man was riding a small donkey. There were no sheep or goats to be seen and we wondered about that. Maybe they were on their way to a pasture area—the trouble is that we are not able to talk with the people and learn from them.

To get back to those Bedouin Nomads that poured out of the central Arabian Desert during the tenth and eleventh centuries—How could there have been so many of them ? They invaded North Africa over several generations, but still, there must have been thousands of people involved. If living conditions and sanitation was as bad as we are sometimes told, how could those people have multiplied in such numbers? Even if the life-span was very short, they still had to live long enough to have many children, and the children had to live long enough to reproduce!

They are one tough tribe, or rather, tribes. Blood-ties are very important. They are very superstitious. Many of them carry little amulets, containers with sayings written in Arabic of course, on strings around their necks and, or, wrists. Holy men and shrines are also extremely influential. They are free-living people and have been difficult to control but, as mentioned, they have accepted the Moslem Religion totally and without reservation. We have the impression that they are totally dominated by their Faith and are quite prepared to defend it to the death!

The Moslems do not have a monopoly with respect to devotion to a particular Faith. People all over the world are just as fanatic when it comes to their Religious Beliefs. Many Americans are very superstitious and carry many types of religious and "good-luck" charms. During the early evolution of man, before the development of science, belief in such things is understandable. However, under present conditions, and with the information now available, such beliefs are not comprehensible to many individuals. (That number is still far too small!)

While Emma and I were working in Michigan we attended several "Tent Meetings" in order to learn what was taking place with respect to certain "Mobile Evangelists". The experience was informative although I certainly would not classify it as "educational". It seemed to me that the evangelist noticed us almost at once. I got the impression that, to a degree, we cramped his style—but, only to a degree.

He certainly practiced what I would call, "applied mass psychology". He waved and pounded the Bible and shouted to the people that their judgment day was very close and that they would very soon be standing before the Lord. The audience was waving and shouting, some standing, some crying! He had a young man sitting by waiting for his cue—at the proper moment the evangelist hit him on the head and told him to get up and walk and he did! While the audience was still shouting, standing and some were jumping up and down—the evangelist directed several men to pass through the mob and collect donations.

While that process was taking place the people were admonished—"Reach down into your pockets, remember you are giving to the Lord—you are helping us do Gods work. I do not want to hear any change!" The comment about the change really got my attention. It is one of those things that seem to remain in your brain. I looked at the people around us—Most of them were poor, not well dressed, and hard-working. Still, they did reach down into their pockets; we did not hear any change rattle in the collection plates.

After making several passes up and down the road in order to get some pictures of the Nomads we rode on into the Souks of Tunis. The Souks, full of life, and color, never the same! We had to keep in mind that we were on our way to the grocers, Emma had to shop, and she has no way of keeping food fresh. There seems to be a never-ending supply of fresh vegetables in the market—we have never seen such big carrots! We did want to talk with the grocer, he has a great deal of information and he speaks English in a way that we can understand.

On this shopping trip he got onto the home life of the people and the influence that the French "Protectorate" is having upon the way they live, and their expectations. He said, "The people are not stupid, they see how the French are living. They want to live like the French. They want cars, clothes, and a home, and, they want to run their country themselves." In his mind he thought that they want the car first-and some of them have already accomplished that. Next they want clothes; they want to dress like the French. Then they want a home of their own, a decent place in which to live.

Our visits to the Souks indicate that the vast majority of the people are in no position to buy cars, clothes, and homes. We do think, from what we have seen, that many of the people are in need of better food, more of it, and clothes. They have little or no chance, of getting them as long as the French are here.

The Souks have just about anything and everything for sale. There are a number of shops selling European goods—probably imported from France since they have complete control of everything imported and exported. When one of the shop-keepers thinks that they have spotted a potential customer, they are not above moving out into the street and taking the person by the arm in order to steer or "escort" them into the shop. We have found that if you firmly resist such tactics they are quick to sense your attitude and you are left alone.

Winter is the slow season in Tunisia, the weather is unpredictable. Light rain occurs frequently and the wind can be very cold. When the sun comes out it is hot. That is why I have mentioned that Tunisia is referred to as a cold country with a hot sun. The shops are always open, regardless of the weather. Many of the streets are covered, protected from the weather. No matter, the Souk is always crowded, noisy, and full of life and activity. I get a little annoyed at times—the street is covered and quite dark, not an easy place to take candid shots if you do not have flash equipment.

The people enjoy getting together in small groups. They drink tea and discuss local and world-affairs. The groups do not include women. We have never seen a native Arab, Bedouin, or Berber woman in a coffee shop. I have mentioned the absence of sanitation several times so it should not be necessary to go into that subject again. I have to say that, after you have been here for a few weeks or months sanitation seems to become less of a problem. One Frenchman did say to Emma, when she insisted that the bread be wrapped,

"You dam Americans and your sanitation!" I am beginning to wonder, "Who is right?"

One day, in the Kasbah, we were watching a beggar woman and several children. While she was busy doing something one child indicated that he had to go to the toilet. Without stopping what she was doing, the woman patted the ground beside her. The child answered natures call and no one paid any attention. (Except us!)

The beggars work in groups. Each group seems to have its own territory. They appear there every day. Usually the unit is made up of one adult, a man or woman, and several children. They prefer to work a corner location. The adult is the "spotter". He, or she, points out each prospect and the child, or several of them converge upon the person. If the child is given anything it runs back and gives it to the adult. If "business" is not very good, they canvass the street. They enter each shop and beg from the customers. The shop-keeper chases them out and, a few minutes later, they are likely to return.

Apparently they wear the worst-looking rags that they are able to find. A pathetic picture is presented. A woman will sit, holding out her hand, with an expression that would get the sympathy of the most hardened person. If you give them anything you are remembered, probably as an easy mark. Some of the men are able to present physical shapes that are beyond my powers of description. They are so deformed that it

Borders on the unbelievable!

Today, Jan. 17th, we visited the bank and cashed a twenty-dollar Travelers Check. Out of that the government deducted 140 Francs! It would have been useless to ask why. Next, we checked in at the Consulate—Perhaps to find out if we still had representation in Tunisia. In talking with some of the American "officials" we have been amazed at their lack of knowledge with the country in which they are living. Obviously, they do not have any more contact with the natives than the French do. We wonder if they know the differences among the Arabs, Bedouins, and Berbers. (Maybe they do!)

(From the Consulate back to the grocer.) We wanted to tell him that the Consulate informed us that all is quiet in Tunisia and there is absolutely no reason to worry. He gave us his usual answer—"They know more than we do?" I think that he knows a lot more than he tells us. We suspect that the headquarters of the resistance movement is located in the Souks of Tunis. We are going to try to find out.

From the grocer back to the Hostel. Emma cooked up spaghetti and carrots. Our option was to order every meal at the Hostel or for Emma to cook it. She decided which way we should go. Either way, I never lost out!

About 3 PM we headed for Carthage where we were to meet, and did meet, our "revolutionary friend" We met among the ruins of an ancient Roman villa not far from Hannibal's Palace. Hannibal was the outstanding Carthaginian who almost put the Romans out of business. From Carthage he led his army across North Africa to what is now called the Straights of Gibralter. With his specially trained war-elephants he managed to cross the Straights, march over to Italy and, for fifteen years, defeat the Roman Legions in every major battle. The Romans took the war to North Africa and there by a false offer of peace, managed to lure Hannibal back into North Africa. Hannibal tried to fortify Carthage but could not get the adequate amount of support. The result was that in 146 BC the Romans destroyed Carthage and took over all their trading centers in the Western Mediterranean.

The conversation covered such things as the weather and several of our trips to various villages in Northern Tunisia. Emma bought several more "ancient, genuine, Carthaginian oil lamps". Our friend could only verify that they were manufactured locally—and quite recently. She also bought some additional "ancient" coins. How "ancient"? Who cares?

He told us that there was sure not to be any trouble for the next fifteen days. Mendes-France has told the representative of the Bey that fifteen days would be needed for "thought".

I suppose that the French do have plenty to think about. Maybe the French decision-makers should have done some serious thinking before they marched their army of 30,000 across the border from Algeria in 1881! He said that the message appeared in the local Arab newspaper that everyone should just wait for the fifteen days. He said that the local ten-man teams of Arab Freedom-Fighters would follow those orders.

Lately, we have not heard of any additional French Foreign Legion outposts being attacked. As I have mentioned, it is a bloody mess when they are. From what we have heard the Arabs prefer the cover of darkness and the knife over the gun!

As we talked we saw a long line of cars passing along a road some distance away. Our friend said that it was the Bey returning to his palace in Sidi Bo Said in Tunis. We left our friend in Carthage.

Back at the Hostel we had ordered dinner. As usual, it consisted of far more delicious food than we could eat. Let's see—Soup with toasted bread on it, lettuce salad, meat and potato chips, and plenty of bread! All that for 140 Francs each! That would be impossible to top, we think, anywhere in Tunisia.

We are still having a great debate as to whether we should remain here or return to Sicily. I am sure that Emma feels that we should leave. Since we came so far, and both looked forward to our visit here, I feel that we should stay. We still would like to shoot that movie on the everyday lives of the people—If we ever find a way to get into their mud-huts!

Of course, we are supposed to be on a vacation—if we are nervous and worried then, that is not a vacation. At this moment, as I write this, I do not have the slightest idea as to what we will decide tomorrow. Maybe it will rain and we will not have to do anything!

Bir el Bey Hostel Tunis, North Africa
Jan 19 1955

Last evening we were invited out. We visited an Arab and his French wife. They live quite near the hostel, in fact just across a sandy road leading into the hostel. The man's name is Habib. That is a popular and famous name in Tunisia. Habib Bourguiba has been the Tunisian freedom-fighter leader since the early nineteen hundreds. He is expected to become President of Tunisia as soon as it receives independence from France. (Which, as I have mentioned, is expected within a year?) To date, Bourguiba has spent several years in various French jails.

On our way into Tunis the other morning the chain came off the drive sprocket on the motor. It has been doing that frequently the past month or so. Always a greasy job, I was not in a friendly mood when Habib happened to come along. The conversation ranged over a variety of Tunisian topics and Habib invited us to his home for a visit that evening.

Habib's wife is a teacher in a local Tunisian elementary school. She teaches a class of about fifteen children. She is very pleasant—and very attractive. Unfortunately, we do not speak French or Arabic and she does not speak English. Habib has to translate everything. He was educated in Paris and speaks Arabic, French, and English—and a little German. He related some of his experiences, and his opinion of the Germans when they occupied Tunisia during World War 11.

Habib is obviously well-educated. He is very friendly, much friendlier than his wife. Emma thinks that she, his wife, does not quite know what to make of us. (No wonder!) We like her, she is OK—and, we think, a very good cook. She is from Sardinia—Tunisia is, as mentioned, the crossroads of the Mediterranean, and it has been for thousands of years.

Speaking of being friendly, at this time, I have the impression that Habib may be a little too friendly. When I sense that over friendly attitude I get a little suspicious. Anyway, when Habib heard that we wanted to shoot some movies of life in Tunisia he had many ideas as to what we might shoot. Of course, he is a native here and familiar with every aspect of everyday life. We know that he could get us into places that, otherwise, would be impossible for us to record.

When we arrived for the evening Habib said that his wife was not feeling her best. She had not gone to school during the day. However she was not so ill that she was not able to prepare a very fine meal! First, we had to have something to drink. We were offered ree different types of alcoholic drinks. None of them were familiar, and Emma never drinks alcohol—we just selected one. It was OK—as alcohol goes. Habib and his wife are Moslems but, they can not be very strict about it. We understand that true Moslems are not supposed to drink alcohol. Well, it was not very much—It had no effect on me—so far as I could detect.

The food included some kind of nuts and a peculiar type of candy. The main course was the ever-popular national Tunisian dish—cous-cous, a ground wheat grain covered with mixed vegetable stew. It was very well done, delicious. We could understand why it is a fact that a great many

Tunisians live on it. Habib's wife, as I mentioned, is French but, she certainly knows how to serve an excellent dinner of cous-cous!

The conversation covered several topics—life in various countries, education, and, of course, politics in Tunisia. Habib is well-informed, he is clever, and it is not easy to tell just what he is really thinking. On the "Tunisian Situation" he is very careful not to reveal his basic opinions. He does not sound at all like several other men with whom we have talked. He is more involved in the problems of education and politics in Tunisia than he is willing to reveal. Habib does not sound like a radical when the French are mentioned. He sounds much more reasonable. Later that evening Emma and I talked about him and what he said—we do not believe that he has told us the truth.

He did admit that the French, in Tunisia, have created a "captive market". The Bey and the puppet government that they have set up have no effective control. They have no power to exercise control with respect to local industry, jobs, or money. When people feel helpless, have no work or money, they get hungry—when that happens trouble spirals out of control. It sounds, and appears that, because of their greed to control almost every important aspect of Tunisian life, the French have driven a wedge between themselves and the people that they should be working with.

Habib and his wife stressed the fact that the poverty throughout Tunisia has seriously affected education. Poor people, hungry people, are not concerned about sending their children to school. First, they would prefer to feed them! The French have built, with Tunisian money and labor, some schools and hospitals. They can say that they have done something to improve the health and educational level of the local population. But, Habib and his wife, both involved in education, feel strongly that not nearly enough has been done. From what we have seen it would seem that they are right!

The French know that without a sound, effective educational system, there will be few effective leaders. That gives the French an excuse with respect to running the affairs of the country. The lack of schools and education creates a situation in which, the French hope, there is no way out for the natives. Of course, the system is bound to fail. Educated or not the locals are demanding that the French, "get out" or "get kicked out". Our feeling, at this time is that the exit of the French can be in one of two ways, the choice is theirs-they can leave in a peaceful "friendly" manner with some dignity, or they can get forced out after creating a bloody situation resulting in lasting hatred on both sides.

But, I would like to say, "People soon forget, on a historical basis the collective memory seems very short". How conscious are present-day Americans with respect to the series of wars that have been fought within the last fifty years? How many Americans know how many of their sons, daughters, other relatives died here in Tunisia? Have they ever even heard of the Kasserine Pass and the slaughter that took place there? What do you hear now about Pearl Harbor? It may be different in Moslem countries. We find that a great many Arabs are quite familiar with the Crusades organized, and blessed, by the Pope in Rome. But. I still feel that in one generation, people tend to "forget and forgive".

Right now, 1955, freedom is the most important issue in Tunisia. First, the people want to be free. They want to live their own lives and make their own mistakes. That is true for all peoples all over the world and at any time. It was true throughout history and it will be true as long as people exist, the date in not important.

But Habib said, "How are the people going to manage freedom if they have few educated leaders, no industry, no jobs, no foreign credit, very little to actually operate the country with." Some people, Habib may be among them, think the problems are insurmountable; they feel that it can not be done if the French do leave. Actually, with what would the Tunisians fight the French Army and Navy? The French have been and are being supported by the US! We give speeches about "freedom and democracy" and we support the French "protectorate" in Tunisia! The French warships are impressive in Bizerte and the Foreign Legion is ever-present in American trucks, uniforms, etc., etc.

The French were kicked out of Indo-China but, the situation was quite different. Tunisia is much closer to France; the supply lines are very short. The help does not seem to be available to the Tunisians that were available to the freedom fighters in that situation. There are well over thirty thousand, well-equipped French Foreign Legion troops in this country at this moment. The country is really "locked down" from a military point of view. But, of course, there is the pressure of "world opinion" and—can the French people support two wars? One in Algeria and one in Tunisia?

The French people? What are they thinking? It is now getting late in January, we just came down through France last November-December. During our ride through France we talked with a number of people-we heard nothing about "The Tunisian Problem". In fact we heard nothing about North Africa! Does the average Frenchman know, understand anything about what is happening at this moment in North Africa? We doubt it very much.

The situation makes you wonder about the government of a country and people—they are two very different things. As we see it, the French Government is sending thousands of young Frenchmen off to various parts of the world to be maimed and killed—for what? In the end, in the final analysis, all wars are futile. In a very short time, in this case, all the foreign colonies will be lost! No one ever wins a war! National governments just do not seem to be able to learn that truth. The government is apparently unable to process the concept of reasonable negotiation. Why not talk to your perceived "enemies"? Maybe it would be possible to understand his problem—while you have him talking and negotiating people are not being killed and maimed for the rest of their lives.

Another very important aspect of the problem is religion. As I read history, religion has been the root cause of more fighting, wars, and massive suffering, misunderstandings, than anything else—Christianity, for example, constantly parading under the banners of "love" and "peace" has, in reality, the bloodiest history of suffering and death ever recorded. It was the armies of the Popes that invaded Moslem countries time after time. They were armies of rape, murder, and pillage marching as Christian "saviors" into the Holy Lands.

On the one hand I believe that "the people" have short memories, they forget about a war that maimed and killed thousands of their friends, relatives, and neighbors in less than one generation. But here, even many of the small children have been informed about the Christian Crusades. The Arabs have not forgotten. The Crusades are still causing serious trouble. The native population of Berbers, and the Bedouin Nomads who invaded during the 10th and 11th centuries have all now accepted the Moslem Religion, in that respect they are Arabs and they believe what the Moslem Religion teaches, even though they have retained many of their original habits, customs, and beliefs.

We are told that the Moslems do not believe in Communism and will never accept it. The French government is therefore not worried about Tunisia going Communist. Interesting! As we rode through France and talked with various people, we think that the government should be more worried about the French people in France going Communist! In that event, what would happen in respect to Tunisia?

The Communists, like the Christians, are very good at causing trouble. Maybe the French should be worried about Russia offering the Tunisians assistance. It certainly would be most interesting if the Communist did take over in France. How would that affect our present crusade to stamp out Communism around the world? We did a dam poor job of it in Korea at the cost of about fifty thousand dear, young, American boys and girls!

Habib is, to us, a very good source of information. He is well informed with respect to both Moslem and Christian history. To me he is something of a problem. It is difficult to guess his age. He is not an elderly man. He is a little short, about five nine, and light of build, but muscular, and strong. He likes to demonstrate his athletic ability by climbing a rope hand over hand. One day, while we were swimming, he tried to get me to swim out into the Bay farther than it would have been possible for me to handle. That incident has made me wonder about his motives. But, my description—he is what I would call of dark complexion, has clear skin, and, I would have to say rather handsome. (Let me quickly add that he is not attractive to me!) Seriously, I do think that his manner and appearance would be quite accepted by most women. He visit's the Hostel, especially when there are young girls visiting. He is able to charm them from what I have been able to observe. He has mastered how to act and what to say—something that I probably should work on

As we learn from Habib, and, as we travel around the country, we find that every position of any merit is occupied by French people—male and female. I have to agree with Habib with respect to the French girls—indeed, they are, in general, very attractive. Maybe the Tunisian Problem could be at least eased to a considerable degree if more young French girls were shipped over!

With respect to the important posts being filled by Frenchmen, Habib always stresses the lack of attention to education on the part of the French. "Obviously", he says, "they want to keep the people ignorant. That way the people are less likely to get thinking about freedom, and operating their own country." We have to agree with him. We have visited schools, mostly in the country. They are poorly staffed and very poorly equipped. Basic supplies of books, paper, and pencils, are not available. We are not able to talk with the teachers because they speak only French or Arabic, probably both.

In general, the physical conditions in and around the schools are not good. As I mentioned, basic supplies are not available, and the desks, seats, blackboards, etc. are run-down or completely missing! The truth is that the schools we were able to visit, in and around Tunis, and in the south near Sousse, were in deplorable condition. That is true, in our view, of the facilities and the children.

With a few exceptions, the children were dressed in old and worn clothing. They looked ragged if judged by American standards. Many of the children did not appear to be in good health. They were quite thin, they appeared to be undernourished. Very few girls were present in any of the schools. The philosophy is that education is not necessary for girls. They can learn everything that they need to know at home. Well, that idea is far from dead in the United State! The emphasis is still on male offspring. Many fathers are quite outspoken about it—they prefer to have male offspring. Maybe they think that will carry on their name. What good that might do when they are dead I have never been able to figure out. Maybe one of them will give me an explanation some day that will make sense—it has not yet happened

Habib said, one day, that there is a rule, or law, in Tunisia to the effect that any male who has completed the requirements for the first diploma, need not, in fact can not serve in the military! That we fail to understand. We received no satisfactory explanation. I think that the more educated individuals would be wanted by the military. Maybe we did not understand what he said.

With a few exceptions, the children were dressed in old and worn clothing. They looked ragged if judged by American standards. Many of the children did not appear to be in schools. The philosophy is that education is not necessary for girls. They can learn everything that they need to know at home. Well, that idea is far from dead in the United States! The emphasis is still on male offspring. Many fathers are quite outspoken about it—they prefer to have male offspring. Maybe they think that will carry on their name. What good that might do when they are dead I have never been able to figure out. Maybe one of them will give me an explanation some day that will make sense—it has not yet happened.

Much of the Tunisian population is locked into a no-win situation. The vast majority is dirt-poor. They can not afford to send their children to school. They have so many children that the older ones have to go out and work or do anything to help feed and cloth the rest of the family. And, so long as they can be kept poor they will not be educated and qualify for worthwhile positions. And, of course. Without any education they are not provided with the facts required in order to think and reason. That way they will not be quite so ready, or prepared, to cause trouble. Their "protectors" are thinking ahead!

Americans have never had the experience of a foreign invasion. They do not know what it is like to have foreign troops constantly watching them. They have not yet lived under occupation forces, have not yet had the experience of "protection". They better be careful—it is a lot easier to lose freedom that it is to recover it once it has been lost !

Many Tunisians think that they are fortunate if they are able to get one meal a day! I suppose that I might be able to survive on that diet. I do not think that I would be very happy or have enough energy to cause much trouble. All my time would be spent thinking about food—how to get it. We have ridden out from Tunis in every direction—We see mud-huts, no conveniences, and abject poverty. A few of the people are living in the year 1955—the vast majority is still back in 18, or even 1755 !

Every day along the roads we pass Berbers and Bedouin Nomads heading in various directions. Some are looking for a better place in which to live and hopefully, find work. The Nomads are looking for fresh pastures. The camels, donkeys, and women, are loaded with all their belongings. Do they look "quaint"?

Would you not like to take their picture to show the folks back home ? See how the people lived during "Bible Times" ? Then the tourist gets back into the bus, goes into a plush hotel, has a few drinks, a fine meal, and then off to slumber land. After all he has to be well-rested for his journey back into history tomorrow!

Poverty and education—too much of one and not enough of the other ! It is easy to find someone to blame. But, that does not accomplish anything. The Tunisians, generally, blame the French. To a degree they were quite right. However, every time that we ride up to a group of mud-huts children of every size and shape swarm out like migrating locusts! There are too many French troops where there should not be any. However, the entire responsibility for the rampant poverty in Tunisia also has a local cause.

The people responsible are the parents of the children. It should not require much education in order for adults to realize that they should not produce more children than it is possible for them, or the land, to properly feed and cloth.

People in the United States are supposed to be educated—at least huge sums of money have been expended in an attempt to do that. But, at this moment people in the States are producing more children than the country can support. In the years to come it will get much worse. A few experts advise that the population in the States be limited to about 150 million. We are well over that and climbing at an all-time record! My point is that all the problems can not be blamed on the French, on lack of education, etc.

Organized religion also has to take a great deal of the responsibility. For example, the Pope advocating more and more children under such circumstances as I described along the waterfront in Naples. All religions advocate more "souls", they want more members. And, no doubt, it does create more jobs for the Preachers, Rabbis, Priests, Evangelists, and other such Bible-thumpers.

One day, on one of our wandering, exploratory rides around Tunis we ended up overlooking the garbage dump. (I may have mentioned it.) The scene made a lasting impression on both of us. There were literally swarms of women and children rummaging through the trash and garbage! I stopped in order to get a better view. I did not think of trying to get a picture. After a moment Emma said, "Let's get away from this place!) We moved on.

Many Tunisians have left the country. They are trying to find work, and a better standard of living. Most of them go to France, others migrate to various countries in Europe. France is the easiest country for them to enter. They form a cheap labor force. Some return as soon as they have saved enough money to support them here in Tunisia. Some return periodically, many never return.

The educated Tunisians do not like to go to Europe. In Europe they often hear, when they say where they are from—"Oh, yes, that is a French colony". The Tunisians do not like it when foreign diplomats visit the country and are received by the French Resident first, and then the Bey. Local natives tell us that they resent having to buy bananas from Madagascar, by way of Marseille. It does not seem very fair to them when they have to pay a 52% tax, if they buy other than a French vehicle. They do not want to sell the raw material for paper-making and then have to buy it back from the French when they are capable of making it here in Tunisia. They do not want to have thousands of men unemployed while, at the same time, the French will not allow foreign investment in Tunisia. They do not want to support more than 100,000 Frenchmen here in Tunisia and, another 300,000 in France while local Tunisians are unemployed and their families are hungry.

Many of the educated Tunisians do not want a complete break with the French. They want an equal partnership under which they have home-rule. They would prefer an arrangement similar to that of Canada and England. There seems to be little hope of their being able to get it. The Tunisians are very much aware that it required 6 years of bitter warfare before the French were forced out of Indo-China.

Tunisians are trying to avoid that here. But, we feel that they will do it if they have to. The French are here as "protectors". What the Tunisians want to know is, who are they being "protected" from? The natives know how, and under what pretense the French came into their country. What they want to know now is, how to get rid of them!

There are two opinions as to how to get the French out. The most desirable method was not helped when the US voted against Tunisian freedom in order to keep France from voting with the Communists when the problem was before the UN recently. Such behavior by a country that talks incessantly about freedom does nothing to inspire good-will and confidence by the people of the world. Educated Tunisians, and many who are not educated find it difficult to understand such two-faced action.

Not all, but many of the Tunisians with whom we have discussed the problem, feel that the US has not been even-handed in respect to dealing with Tunisia and France. One man said, "The United States has, over the years, poured millions of dollars into France, an empty barrel". It is a fact that the French have accepted our assistance and at the same time critize us for not doing more! The American voters have seen fit to elect such decision-makers. France is, at this time 33% Communist. Does the US really think that France would fight the Communists? One Tunisian said, "France is for France, and only France!"

This AM we jumped on the bike and made it over to the Bardot Museum. It is always an interesting ride. There was the usual mix of Berbers and Nomads moving along the road. We sympathize with the women, all the hard labor falls upon them! Anyway, it was a pleasant morning, sun, no rain, and the chain did not come off! The museum is full of ancient art treasures. Many beautiful sculptured pieces, mosaics, pottery, lamps, beds, and sarcophagi are to be seen. The building itself is a masterpiece of architecture. The Arab Civilization certainly has been, and is, creative.

Three civilizations are represented—Phoenician, Roman, and Christian. There are spectacular tombs of the Romans and Phoenicians. In one area is displayed the treasures from a Greek ship—it had carried a cargo of statuary, pottery, gold currency, olive oil, many other things. The displays are very well done. Casts of many of the sculptures are available at reasonable prices. We feel that it was a great experience to be able to see such priceless treasures. Emma made a remark, she was very impressed, and she said, "Too bad that we do not have enough background to appreciate what we have just seen." She is right (as usual) but, at least we did get there to see it—It gives us some concept of the abilities of what we, too often, refer to as the "ancients". We are "stealing" the ideas of the "ancients" in so many areas—art, literature, architecture, etc.

It was on our way from the museum back to the Hostel that we got lost-again! I thought that I knew a short-cut that would avoid the traffic and congestion in parts of Tunis. By accident we rode right into a beehive of activity! Many, I have no idea as to how many, women and children were all over the area sorting through the material. There is a main street that runs through the center. It had started to rain and the street was treacherous for a cycle. It was wet, and strewn with all kinds of garbage, mud, and manure. A thriving population of flies and rats ! There were very few men to be seen. As we watched we noticed that no one paid any attention to us. They were so intent on what they were doing, they were oblivious to anything taking place near-by.

There were many filthy puddles of water through which some of the children ran and played! There are stores and houses, such as they are, here and there, scattered about. All the buildings were in terrible condition, unpainted, we have no idea as to what they might be like on the inside. Some people were just loitering about—they were sitting outside on old wooden benches and chairs, and on the ground. Here, I think is an area in which sanitation does not exist. How do those people continue to live there? The people must live very short lives. There were several fires burning and plenty of smoke—As I mentioned briefly, earlier, Emma was not able to stand it for very long, she said, "Lets get out of Here !)

Our advantage was that we could, "Get out". The people we were looking at could not get out! How would they get out? Where could they go? They have less than nothing! With what could they start a new, better, different life? Think about it. When a man is down and out, how does he get up? If you have never been there, you just can not tgrasp how terrible the situation is—

We are just passing through. Although we have seen the situation and deeply sympathize with the people—what might we be able to do to really help them ? We do not have any answer. It would take a lot of money, many workers, food and housing, schools and hospitals—and sincere determination. That is one tough list !the resources now being wasted on preparations for unending, futile wars, would accomplish a great deal. Well, I know that I am just dreaming—

103

Let's talk about a lighter subject. The other day in Tunis Emma wanted to buy a loaf of bread. She had me take her from one store to another in an attempt to locate bread that was wrapped! Finally, even Emma had to give up. In Tunis, so far as we were able to discover, bread is not wrapped. It is baked, loaded into carts, trucks, into side-saddle baskets on donkeys, etc. In the shops the bread is displayed—naked. The flies are the first to sample it—they walk about in the street filth, then on the bread where they have the habit of vomiting up some of what they last tasted before checking the bread.

The flies cover the displayed bread, cakes, muffins, candy and sandwiches. When one is purchased, the flies have to move over to one near-by. When bought, the clerk might wrap it—but not usually Emma "flames" the bread over the gas stove before we eat it. Then she feels much better.

Yesterday we were walking around Tunis watching how the traffic moves—or does not move! There are few regulations of any kind. The driver gets into the vehicle, starts the motor, grinds it into any gear, presses the accelerator to the floor and releases the clutch! He might start to blow the horn. From that point on it is every man, woman, child, camel, and donkey for himself. Accidents are very frequent—the amazing thing is that there are not many more of them. Pedestrians are at risk on the sidewalk, if there is one, and trying to negotiate across the street is a very dangerous venture. Still, there are many old people still walking about.

Emma went into a candy store to buy some chocolate. The open displays look so good—it is difficult to not pick up a few—until you see the flies. After some time she found a Nestle bar. The clerk insisted that the bar be wrapped!

Practically all of the food eaten by that clerk is handled by the dirtiest hands and covered with flies—but she rewraps the already sealed bar! If only it could be possible to discover how the brain works!

When we returned to the Hostel, it was locked! It was the Wardens day off. His wife and the "domestic", as they call him, went into town. The old fellow; hurried us out at seven and closed up the place. He acted as though he was late for a top-level international meeting. Later we learned that he was here all day with the doors locked and the shutters closed. What he found to occupy his time in that locked and shuttered building we have not been able to figure out. These people are fortunate to be here so close to a beautiful white, sandy beach along the blue Mediterranean bay—we have never seen them outside!

They seem to reflect the typical "French attitude". They seem not to be able to relax and have a good time-except with other French people or, if money is involved. Our experience has been that they will not offer assistance, many times even when it is requested. When the chain comes off on the bike, or when we ran out of fuel, the French vehicles passed without any thought of stopping. It was the locals, the Arabs, Italians, or Berbers who would attempt to assist us. They do not react as do most of the Germans, English, Austrians or Belgians. Emma and I try to understand them—is it because they once had a world-wide "Empire" and now realize that they are losing it? The British do not react that way—or the Dutch—

I never did report what we had for dinner at the Arabs home the other evening. First we had some drinks-I have no idea as to what we drank. With the drinks we had some type of circular pretzel tied together with string. I had a little trouble with that! Then some nuts—they were good! It was then time to sit down and eat (by that time I was really not hungry. The main course included olives, sliced radishes covered with oil and wine, followed by a huge piece of boiled rabbit cooked in vinegar, bread, no butter, and finally desert consisting of whipped cream, jelly, and something else that I have not been able to identify. It must have been digestible because, so far as I can determine, I am still alive.

It was a very fine meal. The man said that he shot the rabbit that afternoon while hunting with his dog. It seems that even the Arabs have to economize. His wife served the food and was very pleasant. It just seemed strange to us that she did not sit down and eat with us. But, that is their custom. To me, she seemed more like a servant than his wife. But, when in Rome, do as the Romans do. I have to say that it made me feel uncomfortable; I just did not feel at ease and welcome—that is because I have trouble accepting customs with which I am not familiar.

Our hosts had a nice, though quite small, two-room apartment. It consisted of one bedroom and a combination kitchen and living room. The furniture looked OK, not expensive, but practical.

Bir-El-Bey Tunisia North Africa
January 22 1955

We spent all day yesterday working out the movie shots that we thought we still needed and what I might say when they were being shown. Tempers flared at times but we did manage to write down some sort of script. We need some good weather if we are to get the needed scenes. The past several days have been very cloudy, no rain. Two nights ago we had some very heavy rain. I slept through it. Emma gave me the report in the morning. As I mentioned, the sexes are separated here. The girls on one side of the main building, the boys on the opposite. Is that a strange thing for the French to do? Some nights I frustrated the best efforts of the warden to keep the sexes separated—after the light went out I would sneak past the main building where the warden and his wife slept together (I think) Anyway, I wonder if he ever saw me? He never seemed to miss anything that happened in, or around the Hostel.

Once again we have decided to return to Sicily. On the surface Tunisia seems quiet. In Morocco and Algeria there is much fighting and killing. Last evening, with the aid of a French-English dictionary, we were able to read some of the news in a local French news paper. It did not make Emma feel more secure. One report indicated that in a skirmish nine "rebels "had been killed and over one hundred taken prisoners. That happened just over the border in eastern Algeria. The paper was full of bad news relating to North Africa. Emma is quite nervous and I do not think that it would be wise to try to cross Algeria to Morocco at this time.

The plan for today was to get some pictures of some Nomads camped in their black, goat-skin tents not far from here. The men seem to go into Tunis every day looking for any type work that is available. The women and children work around the tents. They collect anything edible in the form of plant life, carry water, and sweep the area. If a child is able to walk, it is able to do something to help around the camp area. They keep the area neat and clean. Babies are either carried in a sling-like cloth on the backs of the mothers or placed in hammocks strung between tent supports. Whenever a child or mother passes the hammock it is given a push so that it swings back and forth a few times.

Bir-El-Bey Tunisia North Africa
January 27 1955

Once again we went south to the Sousse area. The Arab who helped us when the cycle broke down invited us to visit his home near Sousse. We thought that it would be great for us to get inside an Arab home, see what it is really like and get some pictures. It was an experience to live in an Arab home in a remote village for a few days. It was more of an adventure than we expected.

As I mentioned, the man's name was Habib. I am not trying to follow Arab custom and ignore her by not mentioning her name—I do not remember it and can not find it in my notes. We rode down, the four of us, in Habib's new car, a French 2CV. He did not want to pay the exorbitant tax that would have been required had he selected any other make. The 2CV is small, not much power, but has great suspension and economy. Along the way many small mud-hut villages dotted the landscape. Two-wheel carts, donkeys, camels, and ragged shepherds were to be seen in many places. There were vast olive tree groves owned by French non-resident "farmers", being worked by local Bedouins and Berbers.

Serious erosion of the land is obvious. With the expanding population something will have to be done, and quickly! The land that supports the people is being washed, and blown, away. If the French do leave next year the Tunisians have a lot of hard work ahead of them. The south of Tunisia is Sahara Desert—if action is not taken to prevent it, all of Tunisia will soon be Sahara Desert!

The village in which Habib was raised, where his mother still lives, and where his father was a teacher, is located some distance from the port city of Sousse. The village, south-west of Sousse, is named "Motmir" after his father. As we approached the little village of Motmir conditions deteriorated. The road turned to rutted dirt, then a mix of mud and manure. Conditions of the mud-huts became even more basic primitive might be a better description. No windows, no doors, very narrow twisting streets crowded with people, sheep, goats, and cows. Water from known, and unknown, sources formed puddles of mud and manure. Bare-footed women and children, and men on donkeys made their way through the stinking mess. A few of the structures were painted, most were rather run-down, dilapidated. The centrally located Mosque was well cared for, like the churches, mosques, synagogue, cathedrals, etc., in the US.

Habib's home was located near the Mosque. The entrance was framed by the typical key-shaped arch so common in Moslem areas. The ancient-looking wooden door was narrow and so low that I had to stoop in order to enter. The outside mud-brick wall was partly white-washed, needed repair, and was quite high. A ladder would be required if one wished to get over it. Emma looked at me. Neither of us said anything. I thought, "We made a bad mistake by not coming down on the bike."

When we stepped inside it was like entering a different world! The reception area or hall was very large, tile-floored, rather poorly lit, with almost no furniture. The hall entered the central, open, patio. The patio must be thirty feet square, surrounded by the various rooms of the house, completely walled off from the outside world. It is open to the blue sky, the floor and walls covered with tile having very attractive geometric designs. The effect of the blue and white tile is, I found, very relaxing. All the rooms of the house open only onto the patio. There is only one opening to the outside, the front door.

In a "working" Arab home I assume that each wife would have her own room. They would all meet, work, and gossip on the patio—and be exposed to the fresh air and sun shine. I did notice what I assume are small, eye-height, and "peep-holes" from each room onto the patio. That would make it possible for anyone in that room to watch and listen to everything taking place on the patio. There was one such hole in the room that Emma and I occupied.

In the center of the patio there is a drain. Very heavy rain is possible in the area. The result of that rain is the extensive erosion that we saw. In one wall an alcove enclosed a well complete with a long rope and a tin bucket. The kitchen was located off to one side. Food was stored on shelves along the walls and in numerous earthen crocks and jars on the floor. All the cooking was done on the floor of the kitchen and outside. All the bed-living rooms are the same in design. There were several, each T-shaped. The horizontal bar of the "T" ran parallel with the patio. The entry door is covered by a cloth drapery having an attractive geometric design. In each arm of the "T" was a bedroom containing a very high bed, at least three feet from the floor. The bed was surrounded by heavy drapes. The room was tiled and the heavy drapes, the woodwork on the bed and surrounding it created a pleasant atmosphere. The bed was set in an arched cove. There is a table and chairs, at this moment I am using the table and one chair for writing up my notes.

Our bedroom opened, on one side, onto a private, walled, garden, planted with various decorative bushes and flowers. Maybe this is the "master bedroom."

The whole building gives the impression of spacious, open-air, and living. And, at the same time, you are protected by high walls, curious eyes, thieves, etc. It is all very different, foreign, to us. We like the over-all plan—would be a good idea in many locations in the US. For dinner that evening we had more rabbit. Almost every time that we are invited out rabbit is served. There might be different reasons—not much cash for meat, too many rabbits, our hosts like to hunt rabbits—we never got an answer. The rabbit was served with coos-coos, the national Tunisian dish. It was delicious! Habib's mother prepared the meal with the help of several women servants. I probably should say that she directed the proceedings. No matter, in this case, it is the result that mattered to me.

But, that coos-coos was made Arab-Tunisian style! It was very, very hot, full of many spices. Habib was very understanding, he had one of the maids work on cutting it with additional coos-coos. It was very good, we enjoyed eating "Tunisian Style", sitting cross-legged around a low table on a beautiful hand-woven carpet that was created locally. It must take a lot of time and labor to make such beautiful carpets. Habib tells us that each geometric design represents a different locality.

During dinner the conversation covered many topics—mostly about conditions in Tunisia and the French "protectorate". The situation is difficult to understand. It is the result of the actions of many people over a very long period of time. The country is very poor, and getting poorer every day under the "protectorate". All the blame should not be attributed to the French. Looking back only a few years, it is clear that the Bey made some serious errors. When Emma and I talked about the situation later, in private, we asked ourselves if Habib is not taking advantage of the local people. Obviously Habib and his family have money and influence here in the Motmir area. The village carries the Motmir name. The Motmirs own olive orchards and herds of sheep. Many local Tunisians work for the family. How much are they paid? We could not find out. We feel that, when you are a guest in a foreign country, you should be cautious.

We were traveling through Mexico recently and stopped at a service station for fuel. While we visited with the attendant an American drove in with a huge American vehicle. He was, to me, loud and boisterous. Of course there were many children about trying to make a few pesos any way that they could. Two of them started to wash our new car with dirty water carried in an old leaky bucket. Emma paid them not to wash it. Anyway, when the American received his change, he threw it around in the sand. He really enjoyed watching the poor kids scramble through the dirt trying to find the coins. I strongly advised him to get into his vehicle while he was still able.

After he left the Mexican attendant told us something that we have always tried to keep in mind—"When you are a guest in someone's home, do not spit on the floor." It is our opinion, and experience bears it out, that very many Americans need to learn that—And put it into practice!

Well, right or wrong, that is what we believe. Probably we do not ask enough questions and so we fail to get valuable and interesting information. Back to the Tunisian problem—It is clear that the French are taking out far more than they are investing. In a word they have been, and will continue to be greedy. We think that the collective opinion of the Tunisian people might be that, if they must be taken advantage of, then they prefer that it be done by Tunisians, not Frenchmen.

At this time, 1955, in Tunisia, there is little industry, sanitation standards are minimal, there are no schools in many villages, no teachers and no school supplies, too many people are dressed in rags, many are fortunate to get one meal a day, and on and on—We like to eat coos-coos because it is tasty and different. Most Tunisians eat it because it is cheap to buy.

Habib's cousin visited one evening. He is a local school teacher. He verified some of the things that we had already figured out—too few schools, not enough teachers, very few high schools and universities, no school supplies, local people must, in many instances, build and furnish their own schools. There are no local doctors, no medical care for the children. As a result of the chaotic situation, attendance at school is very irregular. And girls are, for the most part, just not sent to school. The opinion is that they can learn everything that they need to know at home!

Of the children who do manage to attend school, 10 % are able to start high school. Education for girls is considered, in general, to be a waste of time. When a girl reaches 10 years of age she is considered an adult, she is "mature" and is expected to work at home. If the government changes and education is stressed, then education will become more widespread. As I have mentioned, the French will not encourage education—educated Tunisians will be able to run their own country and also, educated people in an occupied country will only be more likely to cause trouble!

All the rural schools that we were able to visit were badly in need of supplies and improvement of physical conditions. Desks are very crude, windows and doors need paint, repair, or replacement. There are no facilities provided in the school yard. The kids have to entertain themselves, and we noticed that, they do.

Just in back of one school that we visited lived an old man. When we made a tour of the grounds he got our attention—he thought that I might be a doctor. One glance made it obvious that he certainly did need a doctor, and a good one. I think that my bald head made him think that I might be an MD.—I never wished more that I were. The teacher explained that he would have to have 1500 Francs in order to have a doctor make a home call. He would never be able to make it to a doctor's office. There is no chance that he will ever be able to see a doctor.

When we see a situation like that—and so many other such situations almost everywhere that we go, it is frustrating and depressing. There just is no way that any individual would be able to help so many needy people. The people and the government must work together if the problem is to be solved. And the system must generate the required money—not possible when a foreign power is in control and making off with the profits.

The following morning we had breakfast at Habib's home. It consisted of bread, and very strong coffee. We also ate some very sticky, sweet food—we have no idea what it might have been. That stuff must be popular in Arab homes.

After breakfast we visited the village of Monastir, an ancient, walled city on the coast of the Mediterranean. Monastir is not far from Habib's home in the south of Tunisia. Such a walled city or village appears to be very romantic in stories relating to life in "olden days"—that, however changes when you are there. Of course we see what we want to see. Pictures do not show the reality of a situation. It is my impression, after visiting quite a few castles in Europe and here in Tunisia, that life for the average person during those days would not be pleasant. Probably a little better for the "upper class "citizen.

Walking through the narrow streets, through the souk or market place, reveals the usual collection of dirt, water, mud, manure, and black masses of swarming flies. The flies travel back and forth from the filth in the street to the bread, cakes, meat, etc., exposed for display on the counters, shelves, and meat hooks. Many of the open, especially sweet foods are completely covered with flies!

Emma thinks that it would take some time and effort to educate the people so far as sanitation is concerned. I agree. The process would have to start in grade school. When I think about it, we have been educating people in the US for quite some time—almost any visit to a market, shop, restaurant cooking area, or especially a restroom will indicate that we have a lot of work in front of us.

Visiting all the streets and narrow, dark, twisting passages, there are doors and low openings into numerous shops and living quarters. We wondered how customers are able to find such places—they are small, dark, and tucked away in corners and under old stone arches. But there is activity in every one of them—many very young children are to be seen doing all types of craftsmanship. In every souk that we have visited the children are seen doing all types of work. All the machinery is operated by hand and/or foot power. When those children work all day in such places, how much time is left over for education? They have to work if they, and their relatives, are to eat. It is a no-win situation.

Well, the situation has existed for many hundreds of years—most people would claim thousands! It is going to take time, money, education, prosperity, to change it for the better. And, again I have to repeat the fact that, unless we all learn the simple fact that the resources will only support a limited, and fixed, number of people, the population will outstrip the ability of the environment to support that population. The final adjustment will be made by nature and, it will not be pleasant. I know, I have said that before—

From a distance the walls, towers, ramparts, and minarets of Monastir are very impressive. If you have an active imagination, you can see the village as it must have appeared during, say, the 16th century. The people, the activity, the carts and donkeys would surely be as they are today. The towers would be manned 24 hours each day, and the guards would be walking back and forth along the ramparts. Sailing ships loaded with all the various products needed and being produced would jam the harbor—as they still do to this day! Local transport by sailing vessel constantly travels up and down the long Tunisian coastline. We did not see any sea-going Arab Dows in port when we were there but we know that they do sail between the coast of Africa and ports in Arabia, and India. During ancient times Chinese Junks also visited.

After a visit that was much too short, we had to move along. Habib was able to get us into places that we would not have visited without his assistance. We appreciated that, I was very anxious to get as much of Tunisian daily life on film as possible. I have been very preoccupied with making the movie. But Habib is a nervous traveler, he likes to keep moving, we prefer to stop, look, smell, and listen to what is taking place around us. As we traveled back and forth through the souks the merchants began to recognize us. Of course our manner of dress made us stand out and they are very astute business people—they are able to smile and act very friendly if there is a possibility of a sale.

The visit to Monastir was very pleasant. The village is picturesque, the setting by the sea unique, the harbor a treasure trove of possible pictures, the people very friendly—What more could a visitor want? Tunisia has been visited by all types of people since man originated in East Africa. It is even possible the early man slowly, over many generations, migrated up through what is now Tunisia, over through Sicily and Italy and up into Europe. Tunisia is the crossroads between the Eastern and Western Mediterranean Sea. Every generation of what is now called Tunisia has been exposed to a constant flow of foreign "visitors." That is especially true of those people living in the port villages, and the fishermen living in many tiny villages along the coast.

Not far from Monastir Habib stopped along the road. There were the graves of five Tunisian Patriots. They had been shot by the French Foreign Legion in Monastir. The shooting was meant to send a message to any other such individuals. Such action on the part of any foreign power does nothing but exacerbate the already unpleasant situation. Now the men are National heroes. They are buried in a special location in marble coffins. A marble placket tells the story.

We were stopped at the gate by a group of Arab boys. One of them said, in a very unfriendly manner, "No French allowed in here". Habib explained to them that we were American visitors, not French. They smiled, acted friendly and went on their way. The incident gave us a feeling of how the young people feel, their attitude toward the French. Had we been French—I wonder what would have happened? Those young Tunisians made no attempt to hide their feelings—they did not show any sign of fear.

To the French occupation forces, those Patriots were rebels, to the Tunisians they are heroes. The only answer is for the French not to have invaded a foreign country. In my view, the Europeans weren't given any mandate to "save the worlds peoples". Their ego, their greed, over ruled their common sense. Practically all the European powers are guilty—they should have enough to do if they work on solving their own problems, and they have plenty of them!

When we talk with the native Tunisians, some of them are very philosophical about the present situation. Habib interpreted what one elderly man was tying to tell us. He said, "The French will leave. The Romans, the Vandals, and the Turks were here-now they are gone". The man knew his history—at least that part of it. We were surprised. You can not determine what a man might know by looking at him.

When we met that man he appeared to be just an elderly man sitting in an old upright wooden chair taking in the bright Tunisian sun. (I should mention that the sun does shine almost every day—I tend to stress the "bad" weather because of our attempts to get the pictures.)

We have been told many horror stories. We have no way of knowing the truth. What are we to think when the following incident is related—The Legion frequently fails to use legal means of prosecution. Some Legionnaires who had been drinking abducted a local Tunisian citizen and threw him into jail. In jail, over a period of an hour and one half he was tortured and finally died. His bloody hand-prints still can be seen on the walls of his former cell.

One Tunisian, known to advocate a French withdrawal from Tunisia, was shot in his car as he drove toward the Beys palace. That incident appeared in a local paper (Tunisian) published in Sousse. It was probably not a "legal" paper. The story is that the man was shot in his own car. He was shot a second time as he tried to get into a passing vehicle. He was then taken by the Legion and later found dead along the road.

Such stories, true or false, unite the Tunisians. A deep-seated and all-consuming hatred is created. As we rode back to Ber-El-Bey we had many things over which to ponder. We had to be careful about what we said to Habib—we knew how he felt. He could not be expected to think objectively. It is his country and he wants the French out. Why? Well, he is educated and he is almost certain to be given an important position if, when, Bourgeba takes over. I think he knows that it will just be a matter of time.

There are many serious problems facing the Tunisian people. Will they be able to form a new government without the assistance of the French? Will the French leave without a fight? If the French refuse to leave and the Tunisians attempt to force them out—with what will they be able to fight? The French have all the modern fire-power—with the help of the Freedom-loving Americans. How badly do the Tunisian people want their freedom? In what way do they want to move if given the opportunity? Maybe they are satisfied and content in their tents and mud huts. Are they able to govern themselves or will they fall prey to a local dictator?

Life in Tunisia, under present conditions has been described, no need to repeat it again. Those conditions have existed for hundreds of years. How strong is the will to change? And, change to what? If the country does become "free" and "modern", will the people be better off—will their future be more secure or will there just be more of them? I am not even suggesting that the French should remain here. I am trying to think of the problems that they have created and will leave behind.

Bir-El-Bey Tunisia
January 30 1955

Today we rode over to Carthage—twice! Not the first time—it is a short ride, and, always an interesting one. People of every type are constantly on the move—seems that those in the north want to get to the south, and, of course, many in the south have reasons to be headed north. Most of the people have to ride camels, donkeys, or walk.

There is always something to photograph in the Carthage area. This time we wanted to get pictures of the Catholic Cathedral and, more of the ruins. Also, more shots of the amphitheater would be nice. Immediately, a contingent of Tunisian young boys joined us. They are very cooperative—they will get into the scene only when asked to do so. A Boy Scout Troop came along while we were shooting. They too joined in and cooperated. One young fellow was very willing to act—and not for money. He showed Emma what he claimed was an "ancient tomb ". They both dug around in the "tomb" and finally found what are supposed to be human bones. Before we left, and without any request for payment, the little fellow gave Emma what are supposed to be Roman coins and another "genuine oil lamp".

When we arrived back at the Hostel we were over an hour late. The friendly French warden announced that everything was "finish". We were quite angry and left. When we returned later, he and his wife tried to be very friendly. As I keep saying—She is a very pleasant woman, and he is a dam old grouch.

From the Hostel it was back to Carthage again. Those kids know us and probably think that we are here to stay. We will never finish photographing the Carthage area. Every piece of marble, beautifully engraved, is a picture. No doubt—they were the best artists and stone masons that this planet will ever see. While there our "revolutionary" friend appeared. We are certain that he either lives in one of the ruined villas, or near-by. He has calmed down. He believes that within a year Tunisia will have its freedom. He is very sure that Bourguiba will be the President. He is far from alone, many people have told us that Bourguiba is there leader and that, if he will accept it, the people would make him King of Tunisia!

A group of Catholic orphans came along and proceeded to crawl all over everything in sight. They were old enough to have been taught more civil manners. The contrast between the Tunisian Boy Scouts and those orphans was very obvious. Our "revolutionary" friend did not miss the opportunity to point it out to us. Today, there were many visitors about, more than usual. They were spread out so that we did not have any difficulty getting shots of a Roman paved road of large, hexagonal, flat stone. When horses pulling a chariot raced over that rough pavement it must have made enough noise to drive any pedestrians off the street but into the first available shelter! No horns needed! I took general shots of the ruins, close-ups of some columns, and, one of the boys "selling" Emma "original" oil lamps. I noticed that she did hand out some Francs—they know that she is an "easy touch". We returned to the hostel about five thirty.

The air really gets chilly here when the sun sets. I have my winter underwear on and I still get cold! Emma is also cold—I am not permitted to record any details relating to her underwear. We understand why the Tunisians wear those heavy robes, if they have one. If they do not they wear a collection of any old rags that are available.

The hostel was full last night, and today. A group of young men and women from Tunis and the surrounding area were here. They seemed to have a fine time. There were a couple young Tunisian young people with them. They appeared not to mix to any degree. I tried to talk about Tunisia with one of the young fellows who spoke some English. Either he did not know what the problem is or he did not want to express any opinion. I have mentioned, and still wonder, if many of the French people know that the Tunisian problem exists?

One problem here in Tunisia is that all the hostels are staffed by the French. Since this is a Moslem country it has occurred to many Tunisians that, at least some of the better paying positions, should be staffed by natives. Half the wardens should be Tunisians. If they can not staff a few of the hostels with natives, how are they going to operate the country? The French have created many of the problems. They have very little respect for the Moslems. I suspect that much of their attitude is created by their religion.

Last evening we were over to Habib's for dinner again. He invited the Director of the local school system. The Director does not speak English. First we talked of things in general and, at times, lightly insulted each other. He is the Director in this area, a rather important position. He is supposed to be a Tunisian—but he sounds more like a Frenchman. Habib gave us the impression that he is taking a position in the middle. He wants to be on the winner's side. The Director thinks like a Frenchman—if Habib translated the conversation accurately. (Of that I can not be certain.) The Director is connected to the UN. I have the impression that the UN is made up, mostly, of people who like to travel around the world, meet in elaborate places, and talk. Their accomplishments are few.

Few men can be French, be in the UN, be in touch with the situation here in Tunisia, and still have sensible ideas knocking about in their heads. During the evening very little of value was said. We did not hear any new or worthwhile ideas. And, I am beginning to wonder about Habib. I have been under the impression that, in reality, he is an active member of the Tunisian Resistance Movement. The Director sounds as though he believes a lot of the Socialist, and Communist, ideas. We have heard all those ideas and we agree with many of them. We do not think that Democracy is the best, and only, possible system of government. We think that each of us has been brain-washed by the system under which he grew up.

Everyone gives lip-service to the idea of "equality". I think that everyone is not equal, not equal by a dam site, and never will be. And who would really enjoy living in such a society if it could be created. The poor want to be "equal "to the rich, the dumb want to be equal to the intelligent. What a hell of a mess that would create!

The Director seems to want total equality—work for all, equal pay, government control over everything! "Why", the Director said, "could the US Government operate the Ford plant?" "Why not have the government operate all plants?"

If Habib gave it to him as I said it, he now knows that the US Government has never created any capitol, never made a nickel in profit, all it is able to do is spend more money than it has coming in from taxes.

The Director and I argued throughout the whole evening. He believes the Communist and Socialist propaganda—I question it, just as I do the American "Democratic" bunkum. Habib acted as translator.

Bir-El-Bey, Tunisia
January 31 1955

This morning we were up at 7:30, had our breakfast of bread, jelly, tea, and cheese, perhaps an odd mixture but, better than nothing when you happen to be out of cash! We ran out of money on Saturday and have had to be very careful over Sunday so as not to run out of gasoline.

We made it half-way into Tunis this AM and we did run out of gasoline, ("Petrol", it is called here, and in Europe. There was not a petrol station in sight and, if there had been, we had no money! We began to push the cycle toward Tunis. The sun was bright and hot and I was very sorry that I had not taken off my heavy underwear. Heavy underwear is fine on a bike at 40-50 miles per hour—but it is not so comfortable when you are pushing a bike. We pushed and walked and sweated. As we did so several Frenchmen, in vehicles passed us like freight trains passing bums. After some time, an old man on a small motorbike came putting along. He could not help us—he had no petrol and we had no money. Next, several fellows on an old tractor came along. They offered to let me hold onto the back of the tractor—that idea did not appeal to us.

After pushing the bike a short distance some Tunisians in a car stopped. A young man riding with them had a bicycle—they sent him down the road to a petrol station for a liter of fuel. None of them spoke English; we were not able to communicate. By sign language we got the idea across that we would stop on our way back and pay them for the petrol.

While we were waiting for the petrol to arrive an old man on a bicycle stopped. He had noticed the tripod on our bike, he kept pointing to himself and saying "photo". We had only the movie camera with us. It would be too complicated to set it up and, even if we did, how could we ever get a "photo" to him? He left, only to return in a few minutes with his red hat on his head. After considerable conversation, one of the men got him to understand that we could not take his "photo". He got on his bike and left. Our petrol arrived, we got the bike started and headed for Tunis.

Life in Tunis was, as usual, being carried on at the usual frenetic pace. Every driver was blowing his horn, every cop his whistle, everyone in the street was yelling at everyone else, the carts were clattering, and the donkeys were joining in by braying! The situation was "normal".

Emma tried to ask an elderly man where we might find a bank. As soon as he realized that she did not want to buy anything displayed on his two-wheel cart, he ignored her and moved away. Several Frenchmen either ignored me or gave me the usual, "non-compri". Eventually a woman wearing a veil and covered from head to foot, except for her eyes, realized what we wanted and pointed down the street.

As we were about to set out for the bank, along came a short, fat, pudgy-looking man who said in English, "You want bank? Exchange? You American? I give you very good exchange for green American dollars". We informed him that we had only American Express Travelers Checks. They have no value on the "free market". His next idea was to show us where the bank is located. In spite of our obvious attempts to dislodge him, he insisted upon showing us where the bank is. When we arrived at the bank we knew that no checks would be shown, or cashed, in his presence. We talked to the cashier, he was like a leech, we decided to leave and return later. The leech gave up and vanished into the melee along the sidewalk. He may have heard us mention ten dollar checks and thought it a waste of his valuable time to stay with us.

When we returned to the bank the cashier said that he was very surprised to see us with such a disreputable person. He said, "He is a very bad person, the police have had much trouble with him." We decided that he was unclean in appearance—and in character. His clothes were dirty and "rumpled". His body-language sent a message—"watch-out!"

It required some time to cash a ten dollar Travelers Check—and a lot of paper work on the part of the cashier. He obviously knew the complicated procedure and went through it as quickly as possible. I still wonder, 'Does anyone ever look at all those records—where do they go? Into a thick heavy steel vault?" Finally we were able to get out of the bank and out into the street—where the noise of the constant horn-blowing is enough to drive one out of the country!

After all that time conducting our international finances we thought it best to check on the bike. If anything happened to the bike we would be in big trouble. Buying anything here, under the French tax system would be just about impossible! We do not understand how the Tunisians are able to buy the bicycles and motor bikes that they do have. When we left the bike we thought that there were several strange-looking fellows standing around—but, we tend to be suspicious of almost everyone. The bike was OK so we headed for the Post Office.

At the Post Office we mailed eight rolls of color film. The film had to be mailed to Dr. Cantral, a professor at the University of Michigan in Ann Arbor where we had worked before leaving on this trip. He was our Biology Professor during a Graduate Field Course in Insect Ecology—and he was a very good one! He was our teacher and our friend. We also mailed several rolls of 16mm movie film. I do not expect anyone to believe me—mailing the film out of Tunisia to the US was more complicated than cashing a Travelers Check! That steel vault must be a very big one!

By the time we were able to escape from the Post Office it was noon. Emma had wanted to shop but there was not time enough—we had to be back at the hostel for lunch at 12:30! We still had to stop and find our friend who had given us the liter of petrol. When we returned to the bike several locals were just standing around looking at it and talking. We have not seen another BSA bike here in Tunisia. We have wondered what we would do if we needed any parts?

This time the attraction was not the bike—it was that French women, driving a Citroen vehicle had backed into the bike and bent one of our fender braces. It is not anything that I can not repair myself and so we decided not to attempt to do anything about it. However, if we had wanted to peruse the matter, one of the men standing there had her plate number written down—we think he was hoping that we would make an issue of it. As the crowd started to grow larger we decided it would be best for us to get out of there.

When we got onto the bike we were approached by one of the men who had been standing there. "Money", he said. "Money?" I answered, "For what?". "Guardian", was his answer. That made me angry. I got off the bike and, in a loud voice said, "Guardian? All we have is a bent fender-brace, guardian-pay for that?, never !" We left him standing on the edge of the sidewalk. It is important not to be intimidated. If some of them think that you are afraid, then you are in trouble. On the other hand, it is best not to push too far!

Through the usual maize of traffic and noise, we headed out of the city. The bike needed to be filled with petrol—usually a complicated affair, especially with the language-barrier. The attendants just do not know that motor oil must be mixed with the petrol, well, almost everything is a hassle

Along the road, on the way to the hostel, we stopped and gave the young fellow 100 France for the petrol. He paid 40 francs but we felt that he should make something for the road-service. He did not react—just took it and said, "Good-bye". I got the impression that he had expected more. We told him that we would return after lunch to take the old mans photo—I wonder if he bothered to tell him. (I wonder if he is a Frenchman, down on his luck, living in a mud-hut.)

Back to the hostel we roared, at 40 MPH to have lunch—meat, peas, gravy, and, more noodles! Much more than we could eat! (The French lady does make much stew!) Price? 145 francs each. After lunch we headed back to photograph the "old man on the bike".

When we arrived at the mud-hut village where we thought that he lived the area was "covered' with children of all sizes, shapes, colors, and ages. There is a rather long row of huts and we had no idea as to which one might be his home. None of the kids spoke any English. An older boy called out two middle-aged men—they did not understand any more English than the kids did. The men called their wives in another futile attempt to figure out what we were saying. Habib had warned us to start speaking English if we were stopped for any reason probably a good idea in many cases but, not in this one!

From every hut in that long row flowed a seemingly never-ending stream of children. Most had on some type of clothing—but, many of them had on very little. There is every shade of color in those huts from very black to almost white. A few of them were quite clean—most were not. More and more women arrived and everyone talked, yelled, and laughed. They all seemed to be having quite a fine time. Some of the women were completely covered, with veils, most did not wear a veil. Some were rather plump, some were very thin.

As we moved down the row of huts in our effort to locate the elderly gentleman, the huts varied in size and condition. Most of them are in run down condition. A few are white-washed and, in that setting, appear more prosperous. There is one hut built of cement blocks—that one seems to be the most permanent. Some of the huts are inhabited only part of the year—the rest of the time the people are our in the fields with their cattle, sheep, or goats. Some of the families are in the employ of the French or, the more prosperous Arabs.

By the time we reached the end of the row of huts a very large crowd had accumulated. How many people live in that row of huts? We would never even try to guess! How could a census be taken here?

Just as we were about to give up, a boy, perhaps 15 years old appeared on the scene. We were so tired of saying, "Parley English" that we almost failed to ask him. We were shocked when he answered, "Yes, a little". He did not understand what we were saying so, I showed him the camera, then bent over and limped away. That brought out a tremendous roar of talking, yelling and laughing on the part of the audience.

My act must have been very professional. The young man joined in the laughter but he also ran into one of the huts and emerged with the old man and a donkey in tow! When the elderly man saw us he knew why we were there and sent for his wife. She emerged with four children! That made me think that the old fellow was not as old as I thought or, he had some help in the village. His wife appeared as a typical Nomad—she wore colorful flowing robes and a great deal of jewelry. That jewelry appeared, to us, to be the genuine thing. How those women get into those robes and keep them from falling off I am sure I will never know. To me they appear to be a yard wide and fifty feet long!

Anyway, we had finally located the old fellow and he was there with his wife and children. Taking the photograph was next. He informed us that he would not charge us for the pictures if we sent him some copies. That was accomplished after some time and much "sign language". We tried to have the boy who had helped us locate the old gentleman get his mailing address. Emma provided the paper and pencil and he did his best but, it was hopeless. There is not any address to write down. The old man is probably a Nomad, no telling where he might be next month, or next week.

A real problem surfaced! Too many people wanted their picture taken. It would have been impossible! We would have been there for days and the cost of the film we could not afford. The people we were with at that time may be Moslem, but, they have no objection to being photographed. Emma and I have the impression that they are, in fact, Moslem, but religion rests very lightly on their shoulders. We did notice that, as soon as we finished photographing the old man and his wife, he sent her back into the hut. Was that being Moslem or being jealous? We are very sorry that we do not have a Polaroid camera, film, and enough money to operate it.

The crowd kept increasing in size and we began to get nervous, it might turn into a mob! The decision was made to wave good-bye and leave. It was not easy to leave, they were friendly, if only we could have exchanged ideas with them! Most of them were not well-fed. They had no facilities of any kind and no hope of any medical care. Anyone who would not feel sorry for them and want to help them would have to be hard-hearted indeed! (Or French?) It is going to require a lot of time, energy, devotion, money, education, and resources to improve the situation. The population must be controlled. The French can not be expected to take on such an expensive, extended project.

The past few days have been quite busy. We have been trying to get shots of various people and places here in Tunisia. It has been interesting but, it has been work. Most of the sites are easy enough to photograph—the people can be a problem. The people in the mud-hut village that I just described were cooperative but, we have no way of communicating with them. Quite a number of people here do object to being photographed. Well, back in the States, religion is not a problem, still, many people object to having their picture taken. There must be a psychological reason for that—I wonder if it is because they are superstitious? Many people still believe in spirits, ghosts, angels, and other such nonsense.

Last evening we were invited by Habib and his wife to accompany them to an Arab Music show. The theater building was beautifully decorated Arab style, with geometric designs. Many people were there, some had to stand in the rear. The audience was made up of almost all men, very few women. One man brought his three wives. I always wonder how I would be able to handle such a situation. (Should I have said problem?)

It was an interesting and enjoyable experience. Arab music has a quality that is not present in our music. I certainly do not qualify as a critic. Perhaps I enjoyed it because I found it so different. The music seems to represent the Arab people, their long history, even their patience. Habib explained that an old song was being performed, then several modern ones, a poem was read, and finally a musical comedy. The performers did not have a conductor such as we have. The closest thing to a leader was an elderly man who sat behind the two rows of players. All the players sang as they performed. At certain points throughout the performance a quartet of two men and two women sang. Two women sang solos. One woman performed alone. One man did a comedy act while a young and very shapely girl sang.

The "belly dance "was very well performed—might I describe it as "moving"? She was an able performer, she was able to move different parts of her anatomy at different times and separately. It was interesting to know that all the parts fit together so perfectly! I was doubly surprised—the audience was, of course, Moslem, second, she had very little on in the way of clothing. (During her performance I thought that it got quite warm in the building!) What she did have on seemed to keep slipping down—I was afraid that she might take a chill! It must require excellent coordination between the nervous and muscular systems to wiggle like that. The mostly male audience appeared to enjoy her performance very much; however, their response was quite restrained. I was quite stimulated.

I wonder if the response reflects the prevailing attitude of the men toward women. I have the impression that they feel, basically, that women should be in the home—not out performing in public. However that may be, they definitely believe in sex, there are so many of them! The women are generally kept at home, not given much freedom, except to work! They are allowed to do that with complete abandon!

The performance lasted from nine until about 12:30. We were very late returning to the hostel but were able to get in due to the fact that we made previous arrangements with two hostlers from Switzerland. The Swiss had no problem with the plan but it almost went awry—we think that the warden was aware of the fact that we were not there. He could have given us trouble—maybe he just decided to make believe that he did not know about it. In some dealings with the French, especially if they think that they have a little authority, I reach the tentative conclusion that they are born without any common sense and that the condition gets worse as they age.

The French people here are faced with serious problems. They are, to a great extent, victims of circumstance. The warden was, no doubt, sent here by the Foreign Service. He is retired and, no doubt, receives a very small pension—he has to supplement it. It must be difficult for he, and his wife, to have to live here where they are hated. They, nor the local Tunisians, really have any control over what has happened to them—nor what is about to happen to them!

Yesterday we tried to shoot several general views of the city of Tunis. It was possible to make it up to the roof of a rather tall building. No one who saw us asks any questions but, we are certain that they had some in mind. It is necessary to carry everything with us when we shoot—camera, extra film, large and cumbersome tripod. The two of us transporting, and setting up, all our gear makes a picture in it's self.

The view was worth the effort. Mosques dominate the landscape. But, there are many other interesting things to see. The edge of the lake, Lake Tunis, looks far more picturesque than it smells when you are there. People are up on their flat roof-tops throughout the city, most of them are quite colorful. There are all kinds and types of skylights! Many are open, many are broken. What happens when it rains? The buildings are very close together—in fact I think that they are all holding each other up, more or less. Tunis is a very old city and parts of it are very much in need of repair. A great deal of the plumbing is in need of repair, replacement, or installation in the first place. The electrical system appears to be anything but a system! There must be untold, unreported, electrocutions.

The view from aloft is, overall, beautiful! Tunis is the "original" melting pot of human varieties. The mixing has been taking place for several thousand years. There has been cross-breeding to a very great degree, and still, there are very definite, separate and pure, ethnic groups. One would think that students of the human race from all over the world would be here. Maybe they are.

A couple days ago we were able to get some good shots of what appeared to be, a farmer and his wives workin on a large field of grapevines. Two of the women had small babies slung over their backs. It was difficult to see the babies due to all the flowing, long, robes. The women were working, and working very hard! As we watched, one woman shifted the child around to the front and nursed it as she kept working! The vines had to be properly cut and the cuttings placed in large bundles, probably to be used for cooking fires. They were, no doubt, working for an absentee French land owner.

The large packs of cuttings were bound together in what had to be very heavy loads. We watched them for a very long time un-noticed. It was possible to get several shots through our 6x lens. The Pathe is a fine camera but—only 10 % of the available light is reflected into the eye. That can make it difficult to get some shots. Anyway, when the bundles were ready to be carried away, each woman hoisted a pack onto her back and started to walk off the field. Those with babies shifted them to the front—for safety! The "shot of the day" was this—The man picked up a very small bunch of cuttings, tucked them under one arm and followed the three women.

This morning we went into Tunis and tried to get some shots of the entrance to the Souks. Almost any kind of photographer should be able to secure interesting shots throughout the Souks. The possibilities are endless. The constant activity of the people in all types and colors of clothing, the endless parade of carts, donkeys, and back-packing peddlers and porters. Then there are the tiny shops, sidewalk markets, and stalls of children operating complicated machinery without and protection and, no doubt, very little pay. For pictures the possibilities are endless. Many of the streets are covered. In some places the "street" becomes a very narrow, dark, hallway. Such places create feelings of the unknown and possible danger. But, people are going about their business completely unconcerned and we did our best to follow their example.

The lighting is wonderful! In places the "roof" is lattice over a framework that supports it. The pattern of light created is really spectacular! It is possible to get pictures in such places with the 35mm camera but, it would be too complicated to set up for movies—and only movies with sound could possibly give anyone anything like the experience of actually being there ! The statement may be over-used, but, I have to use it again—You have to be there!

While we were shooting in the Souks we accidentally got into the area where bodies must be temporarily held. There were several stretchers on which the dead are carried to the grave yard. The place is not very popular so we were able to take all the pictures that we wanted. We have been told that the dead are simply wrapped in a white sheet and buried at once. It was noted above that, during the procession we saw and heard a great deal of crying and the blaring of trumpets. We do not mean to infer that there is not a formal ritual carried out following the death of every individual.

From the Souk we rode down Carthage Avenue and into the "modern city". It is much like any city in France. It presents very little of interest to us, especially after just having been walking through the Souks.

We shot a couple street scenes, an Arab restaurant or coffee shot complete with Arabs sitting around, some smoking water-pipes, and all discussing the present situation in Tunisia. The word is that it is safe to move about when the locals are busy talking. We think that may be true. It is a fact that you can learn a lot more as to what the current situation is on the street, not in the American Embassy. The information given out at the Embassy must have to pass through Washington, D.C. We have formed the impression that the men, in general, do their best at talking, the women do the work. You know, just maybe, having three wives is a very sensible idea—if you happen to be a man.

After taking the pictures we rode on through the city and into Belvedere Park where we had lunch. Emma also made tea since we happened to have our blast furnace Swedish stove along. That stove makes so much noise that it attracts attention, even outside in the park. When those Swedes make a camp stove, they make one to be used outside. The lunch was very pleasant, not like yesterday when we tried to have lunch in the same place and it started to rain!

From the Park we rode back through the city, past the Souks Entrance, and out to Bir-El-Bey. We passed the entire afternoon talking. It was pleasant sitting under the flowering Eucalyptus trees, not far from the sound of the waves along the bay of the Mediterranean. It is no wonder to us that it was one of the favorite resting places for the Barbary Pirates! At times I wonder about the amount of free time that Habib has.

Every time we talk with Habib we learn something new. Of course that is to be expected when one is as ignorant as I am with respect to Tunisia. Now, too late, we realize that we should have talked with Dr. Guterman about Tunisia. As I keep mentioning, that Professor was a fountain of information when it came to world history. Well, Habib's "lecture" this afternoon was on the Tunisian flag. The red flag has a crescent moon and five-pointed star on it. The shape of the moon represents the shape of the Arab Empire when it included all of North Africa and much of Spain. During that time both much of Spain and Portugal were in Arab hands. It should be added that the Arab Civilization in Spain and Portugal flourished. Scholars from all over the Mediterranean World flocked to universities in Spain and Portugal. It was the activity of the Arabs in Spain that held back the middle Ages and kept Spain in the vanguard of learned progress. That period ended with the defeat of the Arab armies by the Christian Knights, sent and blessed, by the Pope in Rome. The Arabs and the Jews were expelled and migrated across North Africa where they continued their efforts to the benefit of the civilized world. (And, that did not include Europe at that time.)

The stars five points represent the five major tenants of the Moslem religion. 1. There is but one God—2. Every true Moslem must make at least one pilgrimage to Mecca, if he is able—3. Everyone must donate at least 10% of his wealth to the poor—4. Everyone must fast from dawn until sun set during the Holy Month of Ramadan—They may eat and drink after mid-night—5. They must pray five times a day facing Mecca, the Holy City.

Not every Moslem is able to keep all those Commandments. Not every Christian does a perfect job either !

They are goals toward which true-believers are supposed to strive. In my opinion, great numbers of Moslems and Christians fail to even attempt to strive toward such lofty objectives. Many great thinkers have questioned each such goal, and many have sincerely questioned all of them. Many Greek scholars questioned the tenants of Christianity. I suspect that many Moslem scholars entertained similar doubts.

For example, the Greeks had many Gods and they must have venerated each of them as much as Christians do their single God. When there is a Pantheon of Gods, each one is more or less of a specialist. No one of them carries all the responsibility for everything that takes place. Maybe that is a better arrangement—The responsibility, the blame, as well as the praise are shared by all.

Turkey once held Tunisia. The Bey was appointed by the Turks. When first appointed, I think that the Bey came from Turkey. As the years passed the Bey originated in Tunisia and the influence of Turkey waned. Finally the Bey was independent, he was the equivalent of a King.? Originally the two flags were very similar. The original red moon and star were "white-washed". The white circle was dropped. For all practical purposes, Tunisia became independent. The Bey was the King of Tunisia.

Today is Friday. On Monday we plan to ride down to Sousse and visit Kairouan and, maybe, El-Djem if we have the time. If not we will return to the hostel and make it down to El-Djem the following day. Near Sousse we will stay with Habib's cousin in a little village. We should be able to visit Kairouan and El Djem from there. On Monday Habib will come down and we hope to photograph his home, his Mother, their servants, and anything else that might show up. Habib tells us that he might be able to gather up authentic Arab dress in which we can be photographed. Of course we also hope that we will be able to get some local village scenes. There is a small village school in Motmir and we would like to get that on film.

The film is a constant worry. What shots can we get ? How can we get them ? Where ? It is not possible to have the film developed here—the processing is done very poorly, no quality. So, we shoot and hope the exposure is correct—then we worry !

143

I need some new clothes ! Emma does her best with what I wear but, some of it needs to be replaced—not washed and put back on. Our budget is really tight. We have to be prepared for any possible emergency.

We do not buy anything that is not absolutely essential. Probably, we are carrying the conservatism just a little too far ! If we could both ease-up, relax, and enjoy a few minor luxuries, we would feel better. That is much easier to say than to do.

People have told us that there are many Americans in Tripoli, Libya. An American base is located close to the Tunisian border in the south. The idea of visiting Libya has been discussed. The Partisan Tunisian Fighters are being trained in Libya. The French know that. Going over there might be easier than getting back into Tunisia. As we travel south we see more Legion trucks loaded with troops. Habib has been urging me to go over alone—I do not want to even think of leaving Emma here and crossing the border into another country that is as restless as this one. Is he trying to get me shot ? I told him that, if I go over there and try to shoot film, maybe the Partisans will shoot me—if not, when I try to return, maybe the Legion will shoot me ! "Oh!", he said, "I did not think of that ". I think that maybe, he did.

Emma is not very enthusiastic about going over to Libya. She is getting more nervous. Tunisia is a very different country populated by a variety of very different people. The Arab culture is strange and foreign to us. It is not easy to relax—we all know that the war against the French never stops. French Legionnaires are being killed, especially in outposts, almost every day. Bombs are thrown into crowded restaurants where the French are known to visit. I am preoccupied with trying to make the film—I know that I am not doing enough to ease the tension that she feels. Emma is just holding on—she is homesick. It is February, Emma has been shopping, cooking, living, in a two-man tent—she has been riding on the back of that loud, BSA through Europe and now North Africa. That has been a six-month journey and over ten thousand miles to date!

Bir-El-Bey Tunisia, North Africa
February 5 1955

This morning we went into Tunis with Habib. First, the bank, then try to buy a camels-hair brush and some blue bulbs for indoor shots. I would think that camels hair brushes would be common here—not so ! No one seems to have ever heard of such a thing. Maybe I should try to go to the source ! The bulbs were very difficult to locate, but, we finally did it. I also bought a new French ball point pen. It will not write ! Perhaps it is designed to write only in French !

Last evening, on the BBS, we heard that the government of Mendes-France fell. That means the negotiations with Tunisia might have to begin all over again. It could mean that the Partisans will become more active. That makes me feel more uneasy—and, it sure as hell will not do anything to help Emma!

Habib seems to be a "moderate"—at least on the surface. But now, even he says that the war might heat up.

He says, "Maybe the French will have to be forced out. That means more bloodshed."

At this moment we are trying to sit in the sun along the beach here by the hostel. We are having real trouble ! Our air-mattresses fold up, snap together and make "chairs". The problem is—the flies ! They are so bad that I can not write. That means that there is garbage near-by. There are

146

no sanitation laws in this country. We suspect that it is the Warden, but, it could be Habib. Flies will travel for miles on the prevailing winds but we think that these flies are local—they do not appear to act tired, they are all over us ! On our clothes, face, hands, everywhere! We have to go inside, they are not so numerous inside.

Bike in front of Hostel—N. Sahara

Habib shaking hands with Ted but thinking of Emma

The Souks were busy and exciting

The meat had to be well cooked—it was covered with flies

We were arrested for taking this picture

Emma checking bones in tomb at Carthage

Ted collecting locusts

Well used for irrigation and drinking

We furnished the food for a Bedouin family

The Cous cous was prepared on the ground

Caravan of Bedouins

Ted filming rugs

Bedouin boy in front of tent

Habib's house in the South of Tunisia

Central area in Habib's House in Southern Tunisia

Emma was given a tour of the village on a camel

Circumcision celebration

Ancient Apartment—Southern Tunisia

Potter in Northern Sahara

Raft like ferry to Djerba, that almost capsized

We met Habib when the chain broke at the entrance to the Hostel

Emma having lunch with Habib's Wife and Mother

Ted driving bike through sand storm

Bike at Hotel on the remote island of Djerba

Only one hand spray to fight the locusts

We used our air mattresses to lounge along the Mediterranean

Gabes Tunisia North Africa
February 9 1955

At this writing we are in the south of Tunisia—on the east coast, near the port-city of Gabes. We rode down the main road through Sousse and Sfax, also port cities, and through the extensive groves of olive tree orchards. A narrow strip of land along the east coast is very fertile, it is the main farming area of Tunisia. The locals call the coastal area the Sahel. When you reach the Gulf of Gabes you have passed through the farming area and you are entering the northern stretches of the Sahara Desert that is slowly encroaching upward, toward the north. One thing that the Tunisians need to do first is attempt to slow the relentless process of erosion. The topsoil is washing away in the infrequent torrential rains—the population is increasing—the approaching crisis should be, but apparently is not, obvious.

All along the coast are small villages, the olive orchards, fishing ports, and small mixed farms. The Sahel is only about twelve miles wide. The shallows, in places, along the coast produce quantities of salt that the locals bag and sell. The fishermen collect Tunney, sardines, octopus, and sponge. Here and there are located oil presses and fish canneries. The village women produce beautiful gold embroidery, basketry, and woolen material. The Romans seem to have planted and established the first olive groves. Thousands of trees were planted, no doubt by slave labor.

The olive tre is a small tree, native to the coastal areas of the Mediterranean. It is an evergreen that rarely exceeds 8-15 yards in height. The oblong leaves are small and silvery green. Small white flowers are formed. The olive tree goes back in history to an era long before records were kept. It is mentioned by the Greeks and the Romans. Olive leaves have been the symbol of abundance, glory, and peace.

Olive oil has long been considered sacred. Kings were anointed with it and athletes in ancient Greece. It was burned in sacred lamps and in the "eternal flame" of the original Olympic Games. Olive oil is still used in some religious ceremonies.

Some olive trees live to be very old. There are claims of ages reaching 1600 years ! In Italy some olive trees date back to Roman times. One tree in Crete has been dated at over 2,000 years by tree ring analysis. That date certainly seems to be accurate. A tree in Croatia has been estimated to be about 1600 rears old. That tree is still producing fruit.

The first authentic records of olive tree culture date back about 3,000 years BC. In Crete. The olive tree may have been the source of wealth during the Minoan Civilization the tree is not only a source of oil, it provides fine wood, olive leaf, and olives for consumption. The plant and its product are frequently referred to in the Bible, the Book of Mormon, the Quran, and the earliest recorded poets. Olives are now grown in South Africa, Chile, Australia, Israel, Palestinian Territories, and California.

Today thousands of cultivars of the original olive tree are produced. In Italy there are about three hundred. Only a few are grown to any extent. Farmers in the Sahel tell us that the tree will only grow in calcareous soils. They tolerate drought very well—they have to along the Sahel. The root system is very extensive. Cuttings and layering are the most common means of propagation. Olive trees grow very slowly. That is why the French plan to establish olive farmers failed. They require constant care and attention. The French would not make credit available to the farmers, and it was necessary in order to tide them over until the first crop could be harvested. The farmers wandered away looking for work and the plan, to a considerable degree, failed.

Today most olives are harvested by shaking the boughs or the whole tree. Some are harvested by using ladders and climbing the trees. The olives are gathered into bags tied around the waist of the worker. Olives allowed lying on the ground produce inferior oil. The olive can be 60-70% oil. I think one farmer said that a tree can produce about 8 pounds of oil per year. Along the Sahel entire hillsides are covered with trees for miles. Tunisia produces about 500,000 tons of olives each year.

It should be reported that the flies in and around Sousse have been as numerous as they were up north. Maybe this is the season—or an unusual outbreak? They really are a dam nescience.

Before we left the hostel we had to pay the Warden 15,000 francs. That made him happier than we have ever seen him. We did notice that he charged us for some gas that we did not use. Neither of us said anything—his wife worked hard and fed us very well. In Tunis we were told that it was too dangerous to camp in the south. Here in Gabes the Wardens wife says that there is no danger—at present! What does that mean?

Finally, we arrived in the little village of Motmir where Habib's mother and cousin live. Here we learned that the cousin went to Sousse to get a haircut. He is supposed to take us to Kairouan and El Djem. While we waited his five children put on quite a show for us. They played games and spun tops and talked to us constantly. They could not understand that we did not speak Tunisian Arabic.

The oldest girl went for a friend about her age, eleven, who is able to speak English. They made and served us coffee. The coffee was very good and they were most considerate. They were not accustomed to foreign visitors, but, they did a great job—we enjoyed trying to talk to them.

While we waited one of the women in the house, probably a servant, called Emma out. She motioned for Emma to come out from a protected spot where I could not see her. There was to be a wedding in the village and the women were celebrating. Musicians and singers were practicing by going from house to house and performing. Of course, the women and men celebrate separately.

Emma received quite a shock when she entered the kitchen. Several women were seated, on the floor, around a large bowl of sour milk. Emma was handed a spoon. She was expected to sit on the floor with them and dip into the bowl. When she hesitated they brought her a chair and a separate bowl of sour milk. Emma reports that the bowl and spoon were not clean and the living and dead flies floating in the milk failed to increase her appetite. She tells me that she felt obliged to at least taste the milk and that it did not taste very good. She was able to keep it down by eating very slowly and, I gather, without gusto!

While Emma was enjoying her bowl of sour milk, the girls brought me a bowl. I took one look at it and decided that I was really "stuffed" and could not eat another thing—especially chunks of sour milk floating around with dead flies in dirty water. The girl who spoke some English understood what I said and removed the milk.

Next, the girl brought in some very old books printed in English, from London. They were revival books written by a man named Smith. Obviously, according to the books, Smith was a hard worker and a dedicated soul-saver. He had my complete attention until Habib's cousin did, finally, return. (I really wish that I could have made-off with at least one of Smiths books>)

As soon as the cousin returned he rushed us out of the house. The educated men feel that they have to minimize the cultural differences. The women acted natural, we appreciated their efforts—we are in Tunisia and we would like to see how the native Tunisians live.

Before Habib's cousin arrived the women had invited Emma to the wedding—she accepted. She was curious, she wanted to see what happens during a wedding.

We left Motmir in a very small French car—the cousin, two of his children, Emma and I. Such an experience gives you a feeling of "togetherness". We decided to visit El Djem because of the time available. On the way to El Djem the cousin had to make another stop. While we waited we drank another cup of very strong coffee. It was served in an Arab restaurant in water glasses and, it was not only very strong, it was very sweet! Several Tunisian men sat around tables smoking Turkish water pipes, the type pipe in which the smoke bubbles through water before being drawn through a long, flexible tube and into the mouth. The smoke smelled aromatic, we have no idea as to what was actually in those pipes.

Arrival in El Djem followed lunch in Sousse. The restaurant was pleasant, but not clean and not as interesting as the coffee shop had been. It is a real Tunisian restaurant—not another woman in the place. Tunisia, I think will remain a man's world for many years to come. The glasses, the water, the cutlery, and the restroom were about equally unsanitary. Sousse has a freshwater problem but, we doubt that that is the real problem. Anyway, the food tasted good and we had no trouble keeping it down. When we have to eat out, we think of that. In true Tunisian—style, we washed our hands after we ate, not before.

The coliseum is another Roman masterpiece! It was constructed over a period of about 100 years by slave labor. We could learn nothing relating to the architect. He could have been a slave, some of them were able to rise up through the society to become very important. We thought that the Coliseum in El Djem looked better than the one in Rome. It is smaller but, the surrounding area is much less cluttered. In fact, you see the coliseum from a great distance as you approach across what can only be called desert.

The coliseum alone is worth much more than the effort to get there. However, we were very impressed by the underground road that runs from the coliseum to the edge of the sea. The distance is about 25 miles! Stone for the amphitheatre was transported from Mahdia, several miles up the coast. It was then moved through the underground road to the building site.

The tunnel through which the road passes is about 20 feet wide and 12-15 feet high. Every 10 yards there is an opening to the surface about one by two feet that allows light and air to enter. The tunnel was constructed for several reasons—it made transport of building material much easier, it allowed passage from the seaport which then existed to the coliseum in safety, escaping rain, hot sun, and the constant wind that blows across the desert.

The city of El Djem was built, like almost all Roman cities in Tunisia, on former Punic settlements. The climate is thought to have been less arid at that time. A definite indication, I think, that the Sahara is moving north. At that time, in the 2nd century, the port was important for the export of olives and olive oil.

It was also the seat of a Christian Bishop—which is still occupied by a Roman Catholic bishop today. The coliseum was built during the 3rd century. A revolt began in the city in 238 AD. Roman troops were sent in to restore peace, they destroyed the city and it never really recovered.

The amphitheatre seats 35,000 people. The coliseum in Rome seats 45,000. The amphitheatre was used for gladiator shows and chariot races. The structured remained untouched until the 17th century when some of the stone was used in the construction of El Djem. Some of the stone went into the construction of the Great Mosque in Kairouan. The two structures are only a few miles apart. At one time, during the Turkish occupation, the Turks used cannon fire to flush out rebels. Drifting sand is said to be preserving the original city, the market, and many floor mosaics.

The size of the amphitheatre indicates the fact that the area now called El Djem was during Roman times a large center of activity. It was a busy port transporting agricultural products to Rome. Many thousands of people must have lived and worked in the area. Today it is practically deserted! No longer are the cries of martyrs and suffering beasts, their blood, and that of the gladiators to be seen and heard. What thoughts went through the brains of spectators, and near-by residents who inhabited the area? Well, what about the suffering and cruelty of present-day wars? "Human" nature has not really changed.

From El Djem we motored to Mahdia over some very rough roads. There we visited the quarries from which the stone was transported to El Djem. We passed one village after another. Every one of any size had a Mosque. (Like every village in the States.) Animals of every variety wandered freely. Along the streets, plain solid walls of stone, or mud-bricks form the front of every home. Entry doors are small and low. Groups of men sat around doing what they do best—drinking tea, smoking, and talking.

In Mahdia we walked along the coast where the ancient port was located. Only scattered stone fragments remain and, it looks as though the sea has moved out a little. Overlooking the port on a rocky outcrop is the old Arab Fort. It still gives the impression of strength and stubborn resistance. Most forts and many castles do not appear friendly to me. They create the impression that the people were afraid, that they expected an invasion at any moment.

The Youth Hostel is located in the old fort. While we were there we went up to check with the Warden and his wife—we wanted to know if the hostel would be open on Tuesday when we expected to return. We thought that we might be coming up from the south.

It is never a certainty as to where we might be or in which direction we might be traveling when we are on the bike. The freedom to take off in the morning at a moments notice is a real privilege—we appreciate, and enjoy not having to constantly be here or there at any specific time. That is why we want to go out into the bled in the south of Tunisia. The back country is referred to as the bled. That is where the nomads set up their tents, out in the open, windswept, "wild" country.

The nomads travel north in the spring and south in the fall. They are constantly on the move seeking better pasture for their livestock and any type of temporary day-work that might be available in the olive orchards or grapevine fields. They are willing to accept just about any type employment so long as it is not permanent. We admire, and feel that their life-style should be respected, not looked down upon.

The nomads pack everything that they have to have on their camels and donkeys—and wives. The girls are very attractive when they are young. Hard labor and most of the daily responsibility of keeping everything operating makes them old, wrinkled, and bent over very quickly. One day we were watching a nomad family moving along the road. All the animals were fully loaded including the women. The single man was riding a tiny sad-eyed, ever silently suffering donkey. The women were walking, one of them carrying a baby slung over her back as is usual. Emma commented, "No wonder they have the custom of having several wives. When the first one gets old and worn out long before her time—they take on a new, younger wife to do the labor".

How did that life-style originate? It probably started in the Arabian Desert among the many tribes that have wandered there for thousands of years. I have never read an authoritative report on the subject. My brain does, during rare moments, go over the pros and cons of trying to establish the custom in the states!

(Just kidding Emma—honestly!)

Well, we are in Mahdia but I have wandered, in my thoughts out into the bled with the nomads. I have to add here that I wonder about the numerous, dedicated, "do-gooders" from the States who sincerely believe that they are doing the best thing for the nomads when they attempt to force them into our way of living. They have brains and the ability to think quite clearly—they can see the life-styles of different cultures. Allow them to make their own choices. Everyone should not have to practice the same mode of life. We believe that the so-called style of living in the States calls for great improvement. How free is the typical American who has a great deal of material "stuff", none of which he really owns and—he must be a slave to his job in order to keep making the payments?

At this moment our life-style is very similar to that of the nomads. We have chosen it without ever having heard of the nomads. Maybe that is why we are able to sympathize with, and respect, them. Emma and I have all our belongings on a motorcycle, I think that we can understand their way of life because—we are modern, motorized, nomads. Many Americans would like to be nomads—they go camping, buy expensive trailers and motor homes—but then, they have to stay home and work in order to pay for them!

Again I have wondered away—I know that we are physically in Mahdia even if I am, mentally, out in the bled with the nomads. Let's get back here to Mahdia.

The recorded history of Mahdia begins in the 9th century. During the m is located as "Africa". It was during the 9th century that a Moslem missionary converted a tribe of Berbers to one branch of Islam. The history of Mahdia is very much like that of North Africa following the introduction of the Moslem religion. Massive wall, in places said to be 25 yards thick was built across the narrow neck of the peninsula. That was begun about 900 AD. For the next six hundred years the village of Mahdia was impregnable. Not that it was allowed to go uncontested-it was attacked rather frequently but, without success. In 1500 the corsair Dragut, a pirate, made the village his center of operations. In 1550 the Spanish stormed the town, before they left a few years later that blew up the walls.

After 1550 things became quieter—except for routine pillaging by Spanish pirates and the Knights of Malta. The history of almost every town and village along the extensive coast of Tunisia is one long story of intrigue, pillaging by pirates and crusaders, or outright attacks from the sea or from the land. It is the familiar story of fighting and bloodshed! In the final analysis, it was all for nothing. Present-day nations are doing the same thing, repeating the same mistakes, and for the same worthless reasons. If our leaders can not learn the mistakes made throughout history, then they will repeat them. (Of course, if they are unable, for mental reasons, to read history, then we have another problem!)

After we left Mahdia with our host, he ran into an old friend who insisted that we visit his home (if only for five minutes). It was a long five minutes. There we had to try a gin drink. It was strictly Arabian and very strong. We wondered, but did not question, an Arabian gin drink. We just drank it! Very fine coffee followed the gin—maybe to sober us up?

After the visit we headed for "home",—Motmir. During the drive back to Habib's home in Motmir everyone listened to the news on the car radio. It happened to be the BBC News in English. The Americans and the Chinese were into another squabble over Formosa. Habib's cousin did not speak English very well but, well enough to give us the ides that he has the opinion that America, "Talks big but acts small". He is not alone. Many Tunisians have told us that they do not believe that the US would be able to defeat either Russia or China if it came to that. One Tunisian said, "The Chinese and Russians have the United States scared". My own opinion is that the American people would be more prosperous and happier if the government avoided distant foreign entanglements.

Habib's mother, or her maids, prepared a delicious meal for us. Meat, cous-cous, vegetables, cake, it was a feast! And, we were very hungry. These people are able to go all day on practically nothing. If I do not eat something I get a headache. Habib tried, without success, to get us to drink some sour milk. It must be a favorite dish in Tunisia. The milk looked, and smelled, the same as it did the first time around. Habib was too insistent. I do not like it when the host tries to force anything upon me when I am a guest.

Not long after dinner we went to bed. There was available a "modern bath", complete and without any running water. No toilet—a pot under the bed. The sleeping bags were opened and we slept well in a bed with a mattress almost three feet off the floor—and no ladder!

In the morning I caused a disturbance. I made it known that I needed a toilet, and soon. The facility was available but difficult to reach. One had to pass through the kitchen and, before that could be done by a man, all the female maids had to be given time to "escape", or "hide", or get out of sight, whatever they do or wherever they have to go. That required some very valuable time ! Finally, I was given the all-clear signal and was able to reach the bathroom toilet which consisted of a hole about four inches in diameter in the middle of the floor. That was accomplished, just in time!

Personally I wondered about the accuracy and trajectory involved—It is not, in my considered opinion an easy maneuver. On a wooden table a beautiful pitcher glazed and embellished with Arab design, full of cold water is provided. That is to be poured over the left hand-the one to be used while in the bathroom. Similar facilities were available, and used by us, in France. I wonder which nation was the first to invent such a simple, trouble-free facility. Sometime in the future, I must conduct some extensive research on that topic. At present we have more pressing problems.

One such problem, at the moment, is plumbing and sewage disposal. In Motmir there is no central sewage disposal facility. Remember? The well is located in an alcove on one side of the central tiled patio. The hole in the floor is not more than forty feet away, across the patio. Where does the toilet pipe go with the sewage? I did not ask and I did not mention it to Emma. I did not need to, I noticed that neither of us drank any water that had not at least been heated. Travel in many countries requires a good strong gut able to handle many species of foreign organisms!

During breakfast the milk problem was presented—again! And with the same result. Sour milk in dirty bowls, complete with living and dead flies is just not one of the foods that Emma and I prefer. I have studied, and am very interested in all species of insects, they are essential to life on earth—that does not mean that I would like to eat them. I suppose that I might get interested in a research project concerning the ability of flies to swim, and survive in a bowl of sour milk—but not at this time!

Now Emma tells me—It was camel's milk! Well, I doubt very much that it would have made any difference in so far as I was, or am concerned. We understand that no part of the camel is wasted. When it is no longer useful for carrying heavy loads or riding, it is slaughtered. Years of service are not considered. Retirement for the camel, like the owner, is not a possibility. The urine is used, when necessary, as an antiseptic for cuts and abrasions.

After breakfast of the usual, bread and strong coffee, we headed toward Kairouan. The mosque is located in the center of a completely treeless, barren plain. The location must have been chosen with safety uppermost in mind. It is about 25-30 miles inland from the sea. That makes any attack from that direction unlikely. It is about as far from the mountains making it fairly safe from attacks by the Berbers. The sandy, rock-strewn track crosses the desert in almost a straight line. The Great Mosque suddenly comes into view, it seems to rise up out of the sand and stone. On the road the decision was made not to visit Kairouan first but to stop at El Djem. El Djem is southeast of Kairouan but, it is located in a similar environment, a desolate stretch of the bled, the remote hinterland created by human folly.

Traveling over the bled toward El Djem and Kairouan, numerous Nomad tents sparsely littered the desert. Some of them were on the move because it is spring and they start to move north. A few of the caravans were quite large, they were strung out for over a quarter of a mile. The camels and donkeys, and the women, were loaded just as we had seen them earlier up north. The tents, made of goatskins sewn together, are rolled and packed onto the camels along with the tent-poles. Firewood, iron cook pots, shiny tin cooking pots, food, carpets, and earthen water containers are loaded or hung onto the suffering animals. When a Nomad family abandons a site, nothing is left. Even the dried dung is collected as it is in transit. Waste does not seem to exist.

A poor family forms a short caravan consisting of perhaps one camel, a couple donkeys, several goats and a few sheep. And, of course, the man and a variable number of wives running along behind the donkey upon which he is riding.

A large caravan might extend for over half a mile. It might consist of the oldest headman, several of his sons and their wives and families. There are many more camels, donkeys, even horses, sheep and goats, wives and uncountable children. Most of the children, with, or without any clothing, trot along, as does the ferocious-looking white dog that is tied by an old rope to perhaps, a huge, old two-wheeled cart being pulled by a snarling, miserable-looking, camel that seems to be constantly trying to dislodge something that is wedged between his dirty, corroded, uneven, teeth. I do not think that we ever encountered what could be considered, in any way, a pleasant, let alone a happy camel.

Everyone, adults and children, are thin, most of them very thin. I do not remember seeing loaded horses but, I saw plenty of very thin ones. The saddle and bridal has polished, brass, buttons. The old cart might be painted red or blue and red. The women carry one small child slung over their backs—any that are left over are packed onto the camels with the rest of the household goods. The donkeys deserve great sympathy. Their large dark eyes look so sad—their long, straight ears and tiny hoofed delicate-appearing feet. It would be tempting, but not practical or possible, to buy them all and allow them to retire on a luxurious farm with lots of food and water. Along with the larger caravans there are herds of bleating sheep and goats. It can be quite a large, long, and noisy procession.

I have said that we admire the Nomad way of life—that, at the moment, we are living and doing just about what they do. That does not mean that we would want to join one of those caravans. The required adjustment that would be required would not, in my opinion, be possible for us to make. We know that it has been done—it would not be possible to begin to understand the Nomad and his life-style without actually living with them. I wonder—if it would be so difficult for us to adapt to their life-style, would it not be just as traumatic for them to accept ours? Everyone should be free to make that choice freely, without pressure or force on the part of the present government. Nomads are considered a problem by present-day political, so-called "leaders". In the history of the Nomad any current government is a temporary one. But, they do have the ability to destroy an ancient way of life.

The Bedouin nomads are not a separate race. Some are light and blond, some are very Negroid. The Bedouin nomad, to us, represents a race, a different, unique, life-style. As I mentioned the men tend to be tall and thin. We have never seen a fat one! The women have their foreheads tattooed. The women's dress never changes. It is made up of a long piece of cloth draped around the hips, over the back and shoulders and finally fastened in the front—often by a beautiful piece of silver jewelry made into the shape of a pin.

(I hate to admit that I did not get that information first-hand!)

The wealth of the nomad is represented in the jewelry that his wife wears. In good years it can be a considerable amount. In lean years it must be used in order to secure essentials. The caravan camps when dusk overtakes it. I think that they have made the trip so many times that they know where they are going to set up for the night, or, for a few days. If possible, near a well or other source of water. The women gather brushwood for the fires and for cooking—they pick up anything that will burn during the days march. In the evening, whatever they have that is edible is eaten and they go to bed. We have heard, rarely, what we think was flute music but, we think that, after the days travel, riding or walking, everyone is ready to go to bed. Day or night, it is very unwise to approach a tent or mud-hut if one of those white dogs happens to be on duty!

The young Nomad women are, as I have mentioned, very attractive. Their eyes are very striking. They have tattoos on their forehead, chins, and cheeks. The marks have tribal significance. We have never seen a veiled Nomad woman in a caravan or camped on the bled. Habib, his cousin, no one with whom we have talked seemed to know very much about the Nomads or the details of their lives. Emma and I have reached the conclusion that the Arabs in Tunisia are no more familiar with the Nomads than the average American is with the Indian (Native American) tribes in the States. I think that they might be afraid of the Nomads, do not try to understand their way of life, in fact, with respect to the Nomads and the Berbers, the Arabs are ignorant.

Emma is as curious with respect to the various life-styles here in Tunisia as I am. We are aware of three major ethnic groups—the Arabs, the Berbers, and the Nomads. Emma collected some information while she was with the women in Motmir celebrating the wedding. A young girl joined the group who was able to speak a little English. We think that some of the Nomads, if they are able to locate permanent jobs, settle in the villages. Anyway, the girl told Emma that, on the wedding night, the groom is expected to beat his bride. She also related the information that all the Nomad children gather around a woman who is about to give birth—they watch the infant being born. We have no way of knowing if that information is fact or fiction.

When I wandered off over the bled with the Nomads we were on our way to see the coliseum in El Djem. As you approach the spool-shaped structure, it seems to rise up in the sandy wasteland that surrounds it. There are a few stunted olive trees and some prickly-pear cacti scattered about. Some mud huts are to be seen and several Mosques. The elderly guide (it is required to have a guide) told us that a market is held near the coliseum every week. The amphitheatre (the proper name) is 120 feet high and 485 feet across.

The current population of El Djem (or El Jem) is about five thousand, give, or take, a caravan or two. The population when the Amphitheatre was constructed is estimated to have been over fifty thousand. The original, Roman, name of the town was Thysdurus. The amphitheatres were built about the year 200 and have been referred to as the single most impressive Roman monument in Africa. During the Roman era El Djem was the center of an extensive wheat growing and olive oil production area. It was so prosperous and the people became so wealthy that Rome levied very high taxes on the people. That led, eventually, to a revolt. The revolt was put down by the Roman Legions but, it spread to other regions and led to the down-fall of the Emperor Maxima.

To us El Djem appeared to be a Bedouin village. There are encampments of nomads scattered all over the place. Almost everyone within walking distance tries to make it in to market day. Present-day El Djem is not even a shadow of what it was during Punic and Roman times. That prosperity was spread across North Africa, but if came to a very sudden halt!

The political complications leading up to the sudden crisis are somewhat complicated—the results relatively straightforward. The local rulers shifted their allegiance from their original rulers, the Fatimites, who had moved to Cairo, to the Caliph of Baghdad and angered the Fatimites in Cairo, the Arab rulers of Egypt. The punishment was severe and diabolical. Cairo had been having trouble with certain desert tribes in the north for years. They made a deal with the leading tribe, known as the Hilialan, the leading tribe of Upper Egypt. Cairo promised the Hilialians and their followers a sum of gold and free pillaging rights if they would leave Upper Egypt, attack North Africa, and never return. A bargain was struck.

For the next ten years the Hilialians and their followers swarmed out of Egypt like a plague of locusts. Wave after wave swarmed across North Africa. They raided farms and villages, burned orchards, cut down the olive trees, stripped the grape vines, destroyed the gardens and wheat fields, and most destructive of all was their damage done to the irrigation systems. It had required centuries of labor and planning to construct the aqueducts carrying water from the mountains to the villages. The destruction was so complete that Tunisia and North Africa have never recovered. It was leaders of one of the leading religions of our time who accomplished that disaster—just as the Christians later carried out the Crusades and the Inquisition.

The Bedouin of today live on the desolate landscape, the bled, that their ancestors created. And we, no matter where we might be living, live in the environment that our ancestors created. We are now in the process of creating the environment of generations to follow us—and, I think, doing a dam poor job of it!

The games held in El Djem were the same as those in Rome. They were equally as cruel and bloody. The circus shows were the opiate of the masses. They were put on, and encouraged, by the rulers to occupy the time of the people and keep them happy. TV serves the same purpose in our society. The programming is dreary, the intellectual level about fifth grade and the content as destructive and bloody as the laws allow.

Gladiators dueled to the death. Often they were criminals with nothing to lose. As in Rome some of them were famous, like our boxers and football players. Roman rules applied—the wounded gladiator raised his left arm if he wanted to plead for his life. The ruler, from his special box, looked at the cheering mob, if the majority gave the "thumbs up" sign, the ruler usually did the same and the man's life was spared. The "thumbs' down" signal resulted in the downed victim being summarily dispatched.

The problem with the games and gladiator contests was that the mob wanted to see more and more blood-shed, more and more human and animal slaughter. The level of brutality was constantly increased. Wild animals were in good supply and they were pitted against each other, against criminals and gladiators, and against unarmed victims. I mentioned earlier that, on the day that the Coliseum in Rome opened, more than five thousand animals were slaughtered in the most inhuman ways that could be devised.

It must have been a weird scene—the night before the games, banquets would be held during which the gladiators would be feasted and, the victims scheduled for death the following day, paraded. How the citizens must have relished such events! It has been recorder that human life was cheap and, in some areas, Christians were in good supply. Conditions have not changed very much. On our way to Kairouan and the Great Mosque we made the stop at El Djem. From Kairouan we planned to pick up our cycle and return directly to the south.

Kairouan is located in a more desolate area than El Djem—if that is possible! The fortress-like Mosque rises slowly out of the desert upon your approach as does the Coliseum at El Djem. I have already described the general location of the Great Mosque. Some mud huts and nomad tents are scattered around and, some of the huts huddle close up to the walls of the mosque. No doubt the people feel closer to Allah when they are in that location. We wondered what they are able to find to eat. When they die there is a graveyard nearby, close to the walls. Caravans arrive, frequently carrying bodies to be buried in the holy ground.

Several miracles are said to have occurred when Kairouan was founded only forty years after the Prophets death. Water suddenly came to the surface that certainly must have seemed like a miracle! Also a golden goblet, lost in the Holy Land was found at the site! In deed, another miracle if there ever was one! Well, anyway the village was started and it just happened to be at the crossroads of caravan routes—another miracle!

Kairouan is one of the most holy cities in the Arab world. Pilgrims visit it from everywhere. They arrive on foot, horseback, camels, donkeys, and vehicles of every type and description to say nothing of condition. A certain number of visits to Kairouan equal one visit to Mecca. Special attention is paid to Allah and very little to sanitation—the streets are covered with dust and garbage, the place stinks. On the much more attractive side are the beautiful rugs. They are produced locally, we were told, by the women, after many hours of labor. The design is geometric, no animal figures. We have seen designs that seemed to include fish, I wonder about that? The flies are all over everything! We do not think that fly swatters are made in Tunisia—it would not help if they were. We saw one man walk down the street with a swarm of flies buzzing around his head!

The guide tried to explain that there is one tomb named the tomb of the barber. In that one there are three hairs from the beard of the Prophet. That makes me think of the numerous vials, all over Europe, that contain some of the blood of Christ—there must be far more than five quarts of it! The Great Mosque is open to the public, so far as we know the mosques of Tunisia are not, the reason for that was not explained.

The Great Mosque of Kairouan was founded as a temporary military base about the year 670. Over many hundreds of years there have been five or six mosques built, or rebuilt, on the site. It became one of the most holy cities in Islam (after Mecca, Medina, and Jerusalem). Not long after 670 the Arab forces drove the Byzantines out of what is now Tunisia. During the centuries that followed Kairouan became a center of learning. The sciences, literature, and the arts flourished as it did in the Middle East. Construction, building, and re-building of the Great Mosque were carried out. Many wealthy Arabs, and new converts, contributed to the Mosque and it became extremely well endowed.

After the eleventh century other centers grew up in North Africa and Kairouan slowly lost its attraction as a center of learning. However, it continued to become more important as a holy city. The mosque became a magnet for pilgrims as it is today. The present Great Mosque is in the form of a rectangle. The sides measure 242, 229, 410, and 406 feet. The enclosed space contains a prayer hall, a huge courtyard, and a soaring minaret. The enclosing wall is contains several buttresses and two stone towers. As mentioned, it makes you think more of a fortress than a holy place. The courtyard is enclosed by three porticoes the roofs of which are supported by a series of reused Roman arches.

The minaret is 103 feet high and about 34 feet on each side. It was built in 724. Vegetation and geometry are used in the designs. The basic material is stone, marble, pottery, and wood. The designs created are very ingenious, original, and artistic. The ideas originated with the pagans, Christians, and Berbers. Arabic writing is, in itself, very decorative. I appreciate the decorative value of Arabic script but when I see it I realize that I would never have the intelligence to understand the meaning. I have trouble with the fact that when we write it is backwards and as one Tunisian said, "No! It is you who writes backwards and also, you start to write at the back of the book!

The raiding, wandering Bedouin Nomads who founded Kairouan were intelligent, that is, I believe true. However, they were religious fanatics, believed hardly anything not in the Koran, their Holy Book and they were ignorant, not educated. They had no machinery with which to work, only their animals and their own muscle-power. In spite of those limitations, they collected the abundant ruins lying all over the landscape, combined it in a very haphazard way and ended up with a Mosque.

Over the centuries since the first structure was scraped together, the building has been torn down, rebuilt, and constantly refurbished and additions constructed. As I remarked above, I got the impression of a fortress. Under the first environmental conditions the builders probably did the right thing—they needed a fort in order to deal with some of the local Berber tribes.

While we were visiting we encountered men and women from Europe who were enthralled by the Mosque. One man informed us that he was "speechless"! He went on to rave about the tile work, the courtyard, the minaret and, especially, the prayer room, a very large, semi-dark, room set off to one side. The prayer hall, built in the ninth century, is 123 feet deep and 230 feet wide. I did my best to console him and agree with his impressions as best I could. I was hoping that his emotional state would not get out of hand and he would have to be carried away physically—as he obviously was emotionally. I found it very difficult, after listening to him, to believe that he was, in fact, "speechless"!

The building impressed us. It does not create the feeling of the Tosh-ma-Hal in India. To me it is not the Alhambra. I think that the appearance of the Vatican is more impressive or the Cathedral in Venice. My lasting impression of the Great Mosque in Kairouan is one of a religious fortress.

That is my impression, I do not expect anyone else to agree with it—they are entitled to form their own opinions. The truth is that piles of stone stuck together, no matter where they are located or who did it; fail to make a lasting impression on me. But if you are talking about the piles of stone in the Rockies, the Alps, or the Atlas Mountains, or along the Mediterranean, well then, I am impressed indeed, impressed to the point of being very emotional. I have great respect for the ocean and the desert; I love the experience of traveling across such vast, open, free, natural areas. But, after writing all that, I can hardly state that such places and experiences leave me, "speechless!"

Not much probably should be said about the streets and the souks that we visited in Kairouan, It might have been a bad time or, maybe I failed to see the place in the right light. We found the area unclean. The garbage and litter needs to be properly disposed of, not left strewn about for the fly maggots to eat.

The Moslems, and/or their fanatic converts certainly enjoy constructing domes. And Kairouan is no exception. White domes are to be seen all over Tunisia, especially in places that are just about physically impossible to reach. The more difficult and treacherous it is to reach a high point, the more likely it is that you will find, or see, a white dome there. It is the same with the Christians and their crosses. The goal seems to be—get to a remote, inaccessible location and put up a cross! The higher and larger the cross, the better!

Many of the domes are, really, domed tombs of popular Islamic saints. Maraboutism began in the 13th century. It is a flourishing devotional cult. The marabouts were, originally, warrior monks or sages who lived in fortified monasteries. The marabouts were healers and spiritual advisors. The people who sought their services practiced a combination of Pagan and Moslem beliefs. The same is true today. Pilgrimages are made at certain times to the tombs of the saints. Many of them are specialized—they are believed to heal only specific diseases or conditions.

A man told me, "If you believe it, it is not a lie".

From Kairouan Habits cousin drove us back to Bir-El-Bey. There we picked up our bike and headed back toward Motmir where we were supposed to meet Habib. He is going to arrange for us to get some shots of domestic life in a small village.

The ride south went well until we returned to Kairouan. We thought that the distance would be less that way. It looked shorter on the map. South of Kairouan we suddenly ran into a combination of wind, rain, and blowing sand! The road was OK but it was too far inland. The weather probably would have been milder along the coast. But, we were not along the coast! By the time we were south of Kairouan it was getting dark. I tried to hunch-down behind the wind-screen as much as possible. Emma had a little protection behind me—but not much! The wind drove the sand and the drops of water, into our faces and into our clothing—and into the air filter of the bike.

The road was quite good and, in spite of the weather, we made our way through Gabes and on into Motmir. One fact is clear enough—on the open bled there is no protection. No matter how slowly you travel, you are still bucking the wind and, it hits full-force!

By the time we reached Motmir it was dark and getting late. The weather seemed to improve. Habib had obviously talked to his mother and the maids. The house was cleaner and more comfortable. We enjoyed a late dinner and interesting conversation. Most of it relating to Tunisian problems but, also, on the topic of shooting scenes and trying to set up the blue bulb that we found in Tunis. There were six 100 watt bulbs. Every time that we tried to light all of them at the same time the lights went out. There is one fixed main breaker that can be easily reset but not replaced. The circuit will not allow more than a couple lights.' They probably feel fortunate to have electric light at all.

The inside shots at night were impossible for us to get with the basic equipment that we have. The only answer seems to be to shoot in the central courtyard tomorrow—and hope for sunshine. The sun does shine here in Tunisia almost every day. Unfortunately, that was not the case during our recent ride down. The project was abandoned and everyone went to bed.

At seven the following morning everyone was up, ready for breakfast—and ready to start shooting. Habib could not have done more for us or worked harder. He was all over the place—acting as interpreter and director. He offered many good ideas.

During the day we were able to get shots of everyone eating "Moslem style". It was necessary to set up the low table in a corner of the patio because of the lighting limitations. Habib rounded up authentic Moslem clothes for us. The clothing was very old and very beautiful. Emma wore family jewelry handed down through the family over a period of many generations. Emma, in those clothes looked very attractive indeed! We have been out in the sun and weather a great deal and she has a dark tan—with her naturally darker skin tone and those slightly slanted eye she could easily be accepted as an Arab—as long as she would not have to answer any question in Arabic or, the Tunisian dialect! May I add here that in the costume I was given, I did not look too shabby as an Arab? Habib photographed us and, from his reaction, I think that he was impressed. (No doubt mostly by Emma.)

At this juncture, Habib suggested that we step outside. When we did we found one of Habib's men waiting with a beautiful light-colored camel. When the man saw us he had the camel get down in that awkward-appearing, slow, resentful manner that they have. It must be the camel's genetic nature to appear to dislike and resent anything that they have to do. The animal finally did agree to get down and Habib assisted, and directed Emma as to how to mount it properly. She did so well, I was surprised! The man, I guess that I should refer to him as a guide, he managed to get the camel back on its feet. He then took Emma on a tour of the entire village. The camel appeared to be in much better condition than the guide. The camel certainly made a better appearance. The poor man was dressed in the most decrepit gathering of rags that I have ever seen. He had on an old jacket that was literally in shreds. A combination of rags formed his hat and his shoes were held together by ropes. What was that mans pleasures? What did he ever see, do, or accomplish by living? He must work for Habib—what is his salary? Is his present condition completely the responsibility of the French "protectorate"?

Phones do not exist in Motmir but an excellent system of communication does. Emma tells me that as she was led through the streets many people came out of their houses. They must have been very surprised to see an Arabian Princess riding a camel through their village. Upon returning, as the camel knelt down I was afraid that Emma might be thrown forward over the camels head—she dismounted perfectly!

We then returned to the house patio and continued to shoot various scenes of household activities—entrance and eating, grinding corn, making cous-cous, and making and baking bread in an outside, beehive-shaped oven. It was a little exasperating at times because I could not speak their language. However, Habib was always right there, ready to interpret and help direct.

Because of Habib we were able to get shots of the women carrying out their every-day activities—doing what they would normally do. My lack of experience in making movies was very evident—also the lack of equipment. We were too interested in what we were trying to do to worry very much about anything else. When we started the women were very shy—some of them covered their faces when I looked at them or tried to give directions. After a little time and a few miss-takes, and some friendly laughter, everyone relaxed and enjoyed the acting and shooting. We thought later that the women enjoyed the attention. One of the maids put on Emma's shoes—a real Tunisian act of friendship and appreciation.

After some time, and walking around on the rather cold patio tiled floor, Emma had to appeal, through Habib, in order to get her shoes back. She told me later that she is very sorry that she could not have allowed the maid to keep them. Those minor, sad incidents are bound to occur, especially when you have to deal with such poor, hard-working people. They actually have very little to look forward to in life. They work very hard, never have any genuine free time, very low wages, if any and, no place to go if they did have any money. (I could really expand here on the subject of the Americans being just plain lucky and not appreciating, or protecting that great, good fortune.)

It required a little time but, we were quickly accepted by everyone. Emma was very well accepted by all the women including Habib's mother. It was obvious that it was not easy for her to accept the company of very strange, and foreign, people. However, as the time passed I saw her looking at Emma and smiling, finally she grasp Emma's hand and held it for just a moment. I was very pleased; it seemed to me a genuine gesture of acceptance on her part.

Everyone agreed that Emma looked much better in Arab dress. I have to agree, she did, indeed, look very much like an Arabian Beauty! It is quite possible that the Moslems have developed something better than we have with respect to dress. Probably the motives on the part of the men are to protect their women and also to prevent other men from looking at them and wanting them. However, it is human nature and curiosity, when anything is hidden from view, to want to see what it is. When a woman is completely hidden by those flowing yards of cloth so skillfully draped and pinned, I certainly wonder what they might look like. Then my imagination takes over! On the street, a bare ankle or lower part of a leg catches the eye, maybe both of them! I might have mentioned that, some of the women, if they think that they are attractive, will lower, or pull back the veil for just a moment. It is what I have to imagine that gets my attention. A Tunisian female, properly dressed, can be very attractive.

When we finally, and reluctantly had to leave Habib's mother and the other women it was sad. They hated to see Emma depart. Habib's mother motioned for us to wait, one of the maids ran and returned with four eggs and Habib's mother presented her with an old, and I am sure, valuable gold pin. What can I say?

We thought that it was too bad that the day had to end—we had such a great time! From breakfast to the end of the day everything went perfectly. Even the camel came close to cooperating—but refused the piece of cactus that Emma offered, he selected his own.

There is a custom in Tunisia among the men and women of kissing each other on each cheek when meeting and leaving. The custom can be confusing for foreigners. It was for Emma. I did not have to take part in such antics. A woman came upon the scene; Emma responded in Tunisian style and kissed her on both cheeks. The woman was obviously very pleased. When Habib appeared he said it was one of the maids. Later that day Emma found an elderly woman in the entrance hall. When the woman extended her hand Emma grasp it and followed through, again in formal Tunisian style, showing her good manners, kissed her on both cheeks. Once again Habib happened upon the scene a little too late. He gave the beggar woman a few francs and sent her on her way.

We felt it best to leave Habib and his family. We had been living there several days and did not want to stay too long. We do look forward to returning and getting more pictures but we do not think that we should attempt to get everything at the same time.

After leaving Habib's we rode over to Gabes on the Gulf of Gabes. The gulf is an indentation of the east coast of Tunisia about 60 miles long and wide, an excellent harbor and an important port of commerce, now, as it has been for hundreds of years. Gabes is unusual in that it has rather high tides—as much as seven feet during spring tides. We were able to walk along the docks and see the sponge and tuna fishing boats. Such areas are always picturesque and interesting. The dock areas were quite clean—well cared for.

Gabes was a very important city when Carthage was dominant in the north. After the Second Punic War the area was taken over by the Romans. In the 7th century it was the Muslim conquest followed in 1881 by the French—then the Germans in 1940 and back to the French in 1943. During the Second World War the port was bombed, only to be rebuilt in 1945. In 1956 it was returned to the Tunisians when they became independent of France!

Gabes does not have much attraction for us. It is in the process of growing and it promises to be an industrial center. Factories provide jobs and an increase in population density—and the very great possibility of serious problems with pollution. I have the impression that the laws with respect to pollution are not very strong or effective here in Tunisia, if there are any.

We paid a short visit to the souks in an area called Jarah. We thought that they seemed to be cleaner that the souks of Tunis and better organized. It is not easy to judge, every souk has its own characteristics and we enjoy all of them. Gabes has some extensive beech areas but, if pollution from the factories is not controlled, those beach areas will be unusable. It reminds me of the soil erosion that we see almost all over the country. We understand that the French did not care about pollution and soil conservation but, the Tunisians had better take a more serious approach to those problems.

Gabes is in a special geographic position—it is on the Mediterranean Sea, fairly near the mountains, an oasis, and the desert. That is quite a combination of factors. It gives the area great potential—providing that the future growth is controlled. It is a short distance from Gabes to Matmata, a very attractive, scenic part of the country. I am naïve in many ways but, I am not so naïve that I believe the pollution problems will be prevented. The Tunisians are as greedy as the Americans—first they will create the pollution problem, then they will make some ineffective, feeble attempts to correct it.

All our wanderings up and down the east coast are not necessary but, we do not seem to mind the wind, rain, and sand from time to time. We enjoy the scenery, the people traveling along the highways, and the fresh air—we get plenty of that!

The other night we were back in Mahdia. We have stopped there several times. The warden has not said anything but, he must be wondering about our mental state or, maybe, just how lost we are. We like Mahdia, as I have mentioned it is a quiet Tunisian village located right on the coast and not far from Kairouan, the Great Mosque that we recently visited. We enjoy seeing the fishing boats and, we think, that they might do some sponge-fishing. The fishing boats appear very picturesque but, from what we have been able to see from the docks, we would prefer not to spend much time on one. When the plague was killing about one third of the people in Europe it was imported into one of the Tunisian ports along the east coast. It wiped out most of the population in the port city but did not seem to spread inland, probably because of the sparse population and lack of transport for the infested rat-carrying fleas. The desert was just too much of a challenge to them!

It was mentioned earlier that the hostel in Mahdia is located in an old Moslem Castle. It also appears picturesque, located on the high ground over-looking the village and port. When you enter you must pass through very old, very thick wooden doors that were hand-carved, probably several centuries ago. Then along dark corridors and into a large open courtyard. Everything is enclosed and protected by enormous, thick walls. It is a real fortress. We did not learn anything about its history but I am certain that it would be interesting—and probably full of bloodshed. Here we were in a great place to visit, like the fishing boats, but, we would prefer not to live here. Does it sound too American to wonder about sanitation, potable water, lice and fleas, and garbage-disposal? Imagine the castle under siege and most of the people from the village trying to exist in such a relatively confined space—all the enemy might have to do is wait for disease and/or starvation to do the job—

We ordered our dinner and breakfast. The bill was 570 francs. That paid for dinner for two, a nights lodging, and breakfast. Well, breakfast consisted of bread or buns and coffee. The atmosphere suited us just fine—we were, for the moment, out of the wind, blowing sand, and rain!

Each hostel is, of course, different. Each has its good and bad points. Much depends upon the traveler and what he expects. The hostels are not hotels and they do not claim to be the most lavish facilities available. If that is desired then there are plenty of hotels. We are comparing the hostel facilities with camping out on the ground in the weather whatever it may be.

Next we head for Gabes—again! The objective will be the oasis just inland from the village and the artesian wells that supply the water. Shots are needed of the oasis, any activity that might be seen in the area, some of the people, and the aqueducts that transport the water into the palm groves and farms. From Gabes we hope to be able to make it to Madenine where the gorphas are located. The gorphas are supposed to be very primitive and unique mud huts built on top of each other. We are very anxious to see that.

Gabes Tunisia
February 10 1955

Today was spent trying to see part of the oasis of Gabes. It is beautiful, yes, but it does not, at present quite live up to the pictures in the tourist folders. Not many places do. The expansive water surface shown has, perhaps evaporated in large part due to the desert heat and wind.

While searching for the location shown in the folders we had the opportunity to ride up and down the narrow lanes that run through the oasis. They are really beautiful, shaded by the tall palms and the over-arching foliage casting sharp shadows on the sandy tracts. We stopped to inquire of a small boy where we might find the expanse of water. After showing him the picture he offered to take us there. We knew that we had to be careful and avoid the emphasis being places upon, "take us"! We rode slowly and he walked.

Another young man was encountered and he joined the party.

The attempts at communication were as confusing as they usually are. There was not any common language. However, the one fellow, older than he appeared did understand, and speak, more English than he admitted. We reached a point at which we could not use the bike. The understanding was reached that one boy would watch the bike and the other would act as our guide.

At that point we thought it best to settle the price of such an arrangement. The negotiations required a considerable amount of time. Time they seemed to have plenty of—The negotiations indicated that they both understood more English than they admitted and that it was not their first experience. They refused to set a fixed price until we strongly indicated that, if we could not agree on a price the deal was at an end. At that point the "guide" asks 250 francs and the "guard" 200. We started to leave. When I kicked over the starter everyone quickly agreed that the "guide" would accept 200 and the "guard" 100.

The cycle was locked and we were off to see the beautiful oasis (we thought) we walked some considerable distance. Along the way were several huts constructed of palm branches. Again I must use the word "picturesque". In the setting along those narrow, sandy paths closed in on both sides by palm-leaf fencing, set in the shade of the tall arch-forming palms, picturesque is, I think, the right word. To us it is a different world. How could we ever understand those people, their problems and life-style? How might we comprehend how they think—and what they think about?

The "typical tourist" might walk through there (if he bothers to walk at all), snap a few shots to show the folks back home how "primitive" these people are—maybe even "dangerous"! Then back on the air-conditioned bus and back to the hotel for a few drinks, a hearty dinner, and a warm bed, not infested by bedbugs, lice, blood-sucking bugs, and flies. We have not had the pleasure of watching tourists here in Tunisia; no doubt the danger of the war is keeping them away—for the moment. Next year, when Tunisia gets its freedom, we are sure that they will swarm in.

The life-giving water is carefully conducted through man-made channels into reservoirs, and out into the fields. It is a complicated system that is constructed as the result of back-breaking labor over many generations. The system requires constant attention and repair as well as extension. In some places the water was conducted over the path, in other locations it went under the path in tunnels.

Finally we climbed up to a high point from which we were able to look down into the water pool of the oasis and out across the barren desert. At that summit the wind was very strong. The blowing wind and fine sand made it difficult to take pictures. The scene of the pool of water surrounded by the stately blowing palms does make an outstanding photograph—and a lasting impression. Our "guide" did not appear to be very impressed. He very well could have been bored, there were no other people there are no tourists or Europeans in the vicinity. The contrast between the oasis, full of life, and the desolate, wind-blown desert was, we thought, most impressive. Water is the life-blood, not only of the oasis, but of the planet earth and every living thing upon it.

The return walk back through the narrow paths and past the palm huts was most pleasant. In the oasis we were completely protected from the wind and to a considerable degree, from the sun. From that windy summit it was like entering a different world. All the space in the oasis is used for the production of crops. The protected areas under the palms are cultivated. Nothing is wasted, especially not the water. From the main water lines smaller tributaries branched off—many closed. They are only allowed to be opened at certain times. Even though it is an oasis, water is in short supply and is under strict control. Wide roads through the oasis would be considered a terrible waste of valuable space that could be used for growing crops.

The crops that are produced make up quite a list—apricots, pomegranates, henna, tobacco, bananas, and alfalfa. Some of the plants grow very profusely. Some crops can be harvested several times each year. The source of the water in the oasis is underground springs. The real source of the water is probably the mountains a few miles inland. Gabes is located in a narrow corridor between the mountains and the sea. It is a great location for producing luxuriant crops but, not a safe place in which to live. Many invaders have passed through this corridor on their way to other places—like North and West Africa.

The invading Hilalian Desert Nomads from Upper Egypt were, as I mentioned earlier, induced by the Moslem Caliph to invade Tunisia and all of North Africa by passing through this corridor. The most recent destructive invaders were us—yes, during the Second World War, the Germans, British, the French, Italians, and their American partners, all passed through here. With respect to the degree of destruction, they were equal to, or surpassed the tenth century invasion of the Desert Nomads. We supplied the heavy guns, tanks, other armored equipment, and the aerial bombing that destroyed much of Gabes. Once again the locals were the victims of foreign wars carried out on their soil.

Emma and I had our picture taken with our two "guides". They cooperated and we all enjoyed each others company. If there was any resentment concerning the charges, it was well-hidden. During the day we wandered back and forth through the oasis and passed them. They were very friendly, waved and shouted.

The village of Gabes has serious water problems. Every day, while we were there, the water was turned off from about three in the afternoon until seven the following morning. That creates very serious sanitation problems. No doubt, many people do as the warden does—they have barrels and tubs which they try to keep full for use during those hours.

The present and past, in so far as fact and fiction can be separated, in and around the oasis of Gabes would provide more than enough material for a movie. The history of Gabes goes far back into the mist of pre-history long before any written records were kept. Herodotus was the first of the Greek Historians to record information relating to the peoples along the North African coast. Much of what he wrote was, at that time, gathered from oral legends mixed with the tales of Mediterranean sailors. He writes of the various tribes found along the coast—of Lake Tritonus, now a salt marsh, of Athena, a popular Pagan Goddess, born of the lake and Poseidon. Herodotus thinks that the Greeks copied the dress of the Libyan women and used that style to adorn their statues. Some of his "history" is ancient legends, but, much of what he recorded can be verified by present—day geography and customs still practiced by the people.

As we rode toward Gabes we thought that we were entering the northern area of the Sahara. The sun is very hot and the nights can be very cold. No wonder that, if they can afford one, the burnoose, the heavy woolen robe is so popular. In the desert, during bad weather, a man can be seen as a dark, rounded object protruding out of the rocky, monotonous, featureless, wind-blown wasteland. How they are able to get enough oxygen completely covered by the heavy burnoose, is a mystery to us.

In the area of Gabes underground springs reach the surface. The contrast is so impressive that, I am sure; I might mention it several times. It is like entering another world! Anthony, in his interesting book on Tunisia describes the area very well. He wrote—"Gabes is an oasis by the sea. Gaffs is a mountain oasis. Jerba is an oasis in the sea."

We rode into Gabes the first time from the north, later from the south. From the south the contrast between the desert and the oasis is even sharper. It is great to experience both worlds. We enjoy being on the bike and riding through the desert—but it is very consoling to know that we will not have to spend an unknown period of time there. In spite of the sharp contrast, there is a similar feeling experienced when you are out on the ocean, or out in the desert.

An entire day was spent trying to get shots of daily life in the oasis. We doubt that it is possible for the majority of these people to ever leave the oasis. I doubt that many have the desire to do so. They probably have little information relating to the world outside. How would they ever be able to accumulate enough money to travel any distance—if they did have the desire to do so?

We were able to shoot scenes of women washing very colorful clothes in the streams flowing through the oasis. In the same water, children were playing and, beyond that area, people were collecting water to be used in their huts.

We must be the only people in the oasis who even think about sanitation. The scenes are picturesque; they are full of color and human interest. After the clothes are washed they are draped over bushes and rocks to dry. Stubborn stains are pounded out by hand and foot—the item is draped over a rock and beaten with hands and/or feet. We were not able to get a good shot of a woman jumping up and down on a piece of laundry. When they are finished, the clothes are clean.

There are very beautiful waterfalls in the oasis; the clear water sparkles as it reflects the bright sky and sun. Shepherds bring their flocks of sheep and goats in to be watered, and, we saw a few camels—but no cattle. The narrow paths lined by dirt-embanked palm fronds and the shadows cast upon the sand by the trees make sharp, and attractive patterns to be recorded on film.

We ere very impressed by the great variety of crops grown under the palm groves. I probably mentioned that we were able to identify a variety of plants—apricots, pomegranates, henna, tobacco, bananas, and alfalfa. I know that I mentioned them earlier but the variety and the productive capacity of the soil is very impressive.

The genetic mixture in Gabes reflects that found throughout Tunisia. Various ethnic mixtures have passed through Gabes since prehistoric times—and each one has made a contribution with respect to genes. The water and ease of growing crops would have been discovered thousands of years ago. People entered Gabes from all directions—from the land and the sea. Nomads from the east and the west have migrated back and forth since man evolved in what is now East Africa. And, it is important to mention that Gabes was the terminus for the Saharan slave trade for many centuries. The slaves were sold at regular auctions and transported on European and Arab Dows to various parts of the world. The conditions on those ships for those slaves, and the slaves were supplied from a variety of locations and included all races of peoples; those conditions were, no doubt far beyond description or imagination.

From Gafsa it was a short ride over the desert to Medenine located to the southeast. Nearby is the village of Matmata. It made sense to have a look at both places. Habib's mother's home was located in the area but we did not think it a good idea to go there when Habib was not present to act as interpreter. The language barrier was a constant problem.

First we went to Medenine located out in a remote, desolate area of the desert. Anthony referred to Medenine as a "monument to fear". In so far as Emma is concerned, he is quite right. Emma became more nervous as we rode farther south—I do not know why. By the time we reached Medinine she was very upset and could not adjust to the complete desolation. (She made me nervous.)

The village made me think of the mud cells built by mud-wasps on the sides of old, weathered, abandoned sheds and houses. The mud-rock cells are piled up against each other in rows and then on top of each other to heights of three or four stories. They were used as homes and storage places by the original builders. They are damp and dark inside. We were only able to glance into one or two on the first, or ground, level. There are many places that most people might not want to live—Perhaps Medenine would rate high on that list. It was hot, very hot, but the desert wind was very cold! I thought I saw some fleas—we did not see any people, not even a stray dog! What did the fleas live on? I was very certain that Emma did not want to wait around until I found their source

The upper levels were very difficult to reach, and dangerous! Wooden ladders are still in evidence and narrow, mud steps lead to the upper "floors". Neither of us even thought of trying to go up those steps. The cells are called ghorfas. In some places the steps are made of stones stuck into the mud walls. There are no windows and the "doors" are tiny openings through which a fat person could never gain entrance. If there were any fat nomads they did not live in any of those cell-huts. In our experience here in Tunisia, we have not seen any fat Bedouin nomads. That does not prove that they do not exist. If they do, we hope they do not ride on those little donkeys! How would they ever get through those low, narrow doors?

The ghorfas are strictly utilitarian. They were built as places in which to hide—from enemies and from the elements. Do you wonder why the people lived there, why they built those cells? We did. We all tend to stay where we were born—or return to that location before we die. I do not think that statement answers the question. We did not see anything in Medenine that would make us think that it was a town or village—maybe we missed it. There were no streets, no mosque, and no "business section". We think it was a temporary shelter for nomadic people and a place in which to store some of their food and "things" that they did not want to carry when they traveled with their flocks of sheep and/or goats and camels.

It is thought that when the various invaders were passing through, the locals took flight into the mountains! In Matmata they literally went underground. Huge pits were dug—it had to be done by hand and with the aid of the ever-suffering donkeys. The area seems to be made-up of jagged cliffs and soft rock. The area that we were able to ride into over a rocky and sandy track was composed of mixture of broken rock and sand.

In that region we did see people, donkeys, sheep, goats, and a few camels. None of them were numerous. If an accessible cliff face was available, then a "cave" was excavated. The front seemed to be walled off and the usual tiny door installed. It was not possible for us to enter any of the living places and I knew that Emma did not want to. The area was just desolate and seemed to be unfriendly. No one paid any attention to us; no one waved or gave any indication that they even saw us. To me it seemed like a very bad place in which to have trouble with the bike or run out of fuel.

We walked to the edge of one of the numerous pits that had been dug into the level plateau of rock and sand. The crater was about square, with what you might call a central courtyard or outside living area. In the walls "cells" had been carved out, walls erected, and the small doors installed. There were several women doing something in the courtyard—they all looked up and then went back to their work.

Emma's comment "Let's get away from this area!" I did want to get the movie camera out and try to get a few action shots and maybe some pan-shots. It would have taken some time to set up and might have attracted attention. It was the "attention" part that had me a little worried. We left. It is too easy to look back for me—I will always wonder—should we have stayed and taken the pictures? I did not get what I wanted—well, it was not the first time! At times, I have gotten what I thought I wanted—only to find out that I really did not want it!

A variety of different ethnic groups are found in this area. Some are dark-skinned, probably from the weather and are in Bedouin type dress. Others are quite fair-skinned, with blue eyes and red hair—they are Berbers. The people found across North Africa were known by a variety of different names during the Egyptian Dynasties, and by the Greeks and Romans. Now it is known that they are all Berbers—that is the light-skinned, red heads, with blue eyes. Egyptian wall paintings, 1400 BC are said to show Berber warriors with white skins, light beards, and blue eyes. The Egyptians called them "Libyans." Berber troops served in the Punic Wars. Europeans, today, are impressed when they see a blond, blue-eyed Berber. They are certain that there has been cross-breeding or even, maybe, abduction! Relax!—They are original types.

It was not possible to get Emma's attention, let alone keep her in the area, by mentioning that there have been some very interesting archeological finds near Matmata. Actually, the Cro-Magnon skulls were found near Gafsa, an inland oasis in the mountains about 60 miles west of Gabes. That would place them in the Paleolithic Period. Cro-Magnon man was far enough "advanced" that, it has been said, if you dressed him western style and he wore a hat, he would not draw attention in our present-day society. Well, the way some people dress I doubt that he would need the hat—and, maybe, not the shirt and shoes!

Some authorities' theorize that Cro-Magnon man might have migrated, over many generations, up through what is now Tunisia and across a land-bridge that existed between Cap Bon and Sicily. Then up through Italy to spread out in Europe. Might some of those ancient people spread out across North Africa and become the ancestors of the Berbers?

The French refer to the Berbers as a people without a history; maybe not a written history. Every group of people has a history, so does every person. Not every people have kept a written history—that does not mean that they have none! It seems to me to be a derogatory statement—typical of the French who's relatively recently written history leaves very little, if anything to brag about.

The French might ask, "What contributions have the Berbers made to civilization?" The Berbers, as a people, go back into the mists of history. They developed their various ways of life many centuries before the "French" were ever thought of. Berber caravans traveled across the Sahara for thousands of years. The Berbers adapted to living in every type environment that North Africa has to offer. They are to be found from the high Atlas Mountains, into and across the Sahara into what is now West Africa, and to the edge of the Atlantic and the Mediterranean. The Berbers were probably the first to explore the edges of both the Atlantic and the Mediterranean. That is just for starters!

The Berbers developed their own brand of religion. They had several Gods; the leading God was called Athena. So, they practiced polytheism. They had a pantheon of Gods long before the Greeks—maybe before the Egyptians! Pagan religions were not exclusive. As I mentioned earlier, with polytheism responsibility is spread out among the various Gods. The worshipper has a selection and does not place all the "blame" or the "praise" on one deity. Every people should have the freedom to worship, or not worship, as they desire. Not too bad an idea?

Every nation that now exists has more internal problems than it is able to solve. The French nation is very far indeed from not being on that list-neither is the United States. It is a dream that a few of us entertain that each country would offer assistance, when they are able, to other countries and stop at that point. It is not necessary that any group of people set themselves up as being "superior". In fact, that is what starts wars! Most missionaries should be promptly deported, upon their arrival in a foreign country.

Gabes Tunisia
February 14 1955

The weather was very pleasant this morning. We were out early and the ride through the oasis and out into the desert was scenic and inspiring. The air seemed cool and unusually clear and the sky was an intense blue. The only problem was the noise made by the bike! For such a small, under-powered machine, it creates a terrible racket. Many people were up and at work—none of them appeared to even notice us.

The ride out into the empty desert was also a pleasure. We passed one small caravan headed out to what seemed to us nowhere. The object of our ride was to get some shots of us riding across the desert by using an automatic shutter release. "Automatic" was not the correct descriptive term for that device. It either failed to start the film or did not stop the camera at the set time. If you would like to have one, you might be able to find it somewhere in the sands of the North Sahara Desert, a few miles west of Gabes. My anger due to frustration subsided quickly as we rode through Gabes, out to the port and along the beach. At that location there were a number of available, interesting shots to be taken. We did not set up the camera because we were not quite sure that the material would fit into a film on native life in Tunisia. The bathers ranged from wearing strings in place of swim suits to not wearing the strings at all! It was a group of young French boys and girls relaxing and having a great time on the beach. None of them appeared to be worried about the war or that they were cavorting in a country that has no written history.

Emma said that she wanted to visit the port and look at the ships and boats. I was quite content on the beach looking at the waves—but I decided to go along over to the port. Peacefully resting on the calm water of the port was an old sail boat loaded with a colorful collection of pottery. The boat, and the pottery piled high right to the gunwales, was reflected in the calm clear-blue water. It was the type scene that will remain in your brain as long as it is functional—but it would have been very difficult, maybe impossible to get it on film, that is movie film. I became frustrated but Emma had the presence of mind to take a few shots with the 35mm Exa camera. I should have been satisfied to have seen it.

As we wandered about the port two men stopped us. One claimed to be a French soldier. He had only part of his uniform with him. The other man spoke very broken English. The idea was that they could take us on a trip around the port and along the coast. They appeared unkempt and, I must say, rather dirty. We looked at each other and I knew that Emma thought it too risky. I agreed, then, and now. We both got the distinct feeling that it was just "not right", and we went with that gut-feeling. With no idea as to whom they were, where they came from, what they might have had in mind—it just did not seem "right". Now we wonder if we were too cautious.

It was well past lunch time so; we rode back out into the desert. Lunch consisted of a can of sardines and an orange. The oranges here in Tunisia are delicious—and the price is right. There are groves scattered along the tracks and it is easy—and very tempting to stop and sample one! Sitting in the sun out along the desert track with a continuous parade of nomads with their donkeys, camels, and trailing wives, the sardines and orange tasted very good. It always impresses me when I see a man riding a donkey and his wife, or wives and many children, run along trying to keep up with him. There is another custom here in Tunisia that I like very much—during dinner, if the man desires service he simply claps his hands and his wife, or one of them, comes to his side and takes his request. I have carefully pointed that out to Emma and patiently explained the custom to her—without any sign of success. These are life-styles that American women are not likely to adopt. There were many donkeys, mules and carts, all types and kinds of combinations passed along the track. Some of the camels carried what appeared to be huge and heavy cargoes. All types of things were lashed onto those camels including, in several instances, small children, a

young goat goats and chickens.

After lunch we continued to ride on out into the desert. Our information indicated that another oasis is located some distance inland from Gabes. We never reached it. Along the track a French soldier stopped us and requested our passports. We had left them at the hostel. He was very pleasant about our not keeping them with us—and, he was right. We were able to understand him but it was obvious that he was not at all comfortable about speaking English. He was riding a big, beautiful, and powerful bike—just the thing that we needed to get across the desert in much less time. The incident reminded me of the Indian Motorcycle in London with the side-car for Emma—The one I failed to buy!

The weather was very pleasant—a clear blue sky, no sand blowing, and not too hot. In a desolate hollow we came upon an Italian cemetery. Until their defeat during the Second World War, the Italians had dreams of an African Empire similar to that of the French, English, Germans, etc. The Europeans were hell-bent to help the Africans no matter how many of them they had to slaughter! There were very serious World War 11 engagements in North Africa. This one is one of many cemeteries full of young men who had their lives blown away long before they had any opportunity to live. For what? The desert sands are slowly covering their remains. Some people actually believe, and say, that the insanity of war is necessary!

When we were in Medenine I was checking our maps—they are French Michelin Maps and we have found them to be very accurate. I had done some reading on Ghadames, a village at the tip of southern Tunisia. The lines on the maps of Africa were drawn up in Europe by people who knew very little, if anything, about the actual conditions at the borders created. Those lines on our maps mean nothing to the tribes living in the area. Ghadames is really out in the Sahara and it is visited by the "blue men" the Tuareg Nomads who controlled the Sahara for the past several thousands of years. They acted as "guides" for the many caravans that wanted to pass through "their territory". If you wanted to get through alive, it was best to hire them. The Tuareg ruled the Sahara until 1903. At the Battle of Tit they were defeated by the French who had superior fire-power and the assistance of a desert tribe known as the Shamba. The Shamba migrated into the Sahara from Syria hundreds of years ago. The accepted way of "pacifying "an area; or settling a difference of opinion, is to slaughter as many of them as possible.

Following the killing of most of their best fighting men, known as "nobles" the Tuareg spirit was broken and their way of life destroyed. There were only about 40-50,000 originally. It is true that they were the pirates of the desert. They lived by plundering travelers and other tribes, and by collecting locally available foods, plant and animal. Slaves tended their flocks of camels, sheep, and goats. The Tuareg are Berbers. They are not "lost" crusaders. There were six classes of Tuareg society. It is a matriarchal society—they claim descent from a queen. Inheritance is traced through the mother. The women are not veiled, the men are. The veil is protection against the sand but, it is never removed in public, not even to eat or drink.

In an area such as Ghadames the camel is an essential animal for many reasons—not just for riding and transportation of materials. The camel is thought to have been introduced into North Africa from Persia sometime during the 5th century BC. It made crossing the Sahara possible as well as living there. The split, wide, spreading feet of the camel gives it the ability to walk across soft sand. The long legs hold the body mass above the surface of the desert where the heat is most intense. The animal can be induced to regurgitate water that is drinkable—That is probably done only in cases of emergency. Pieces of fat can be removed from the hump without endangering the life of the animal. Camels produce milk and the urine is reported to be antiseptic. Its dung can be dried and burned and finally—the meat can be eaten and the skin used in a variety of ways. Not bad, what?

The camel made trans-Saharan travel and trade possible. Caravans transported all types of materials in all directions—north to south, east to west. Indeed, it was, and still is, the ship of the desert! The captured slaves had to walk. The caravan route leading north with the slaves in bonds and no protection from the sun, must have been littered with human skeletons.

It would have been a fascinating destination but, it was only a dream. The police in Gabes advised very strongly that we not attempt it. The road, they said was "primitive". In fact it would be necessary to cross into Libya and then go south. That, even I knew, would not be a good idea. The route south on our map indicated that the road was "passable". "Not on that little motorcycle", one of the officers said. It was time to give that idea up.

One morning we were riding along the edge of the desert just outside of the oasis and we ran into a "light" swarm of locusts. It was not a large swarm. We stopped and I collected a few of them. They looked like the migratory form of the desert locust to me but, we went on and forgot about it.

When we returned to the hostel the warden and his wife had company. Emma had done some shopping so, we put the food away in her room. The cycle had been parked so we decided to walk along the river that runs through the oasis. Two women were washing clothes—they have to do a lot of that. They wore dark red dresses with bright red and yellow scarves and "hats". As usual the washed clothing had been dried over near-by bushes. That added more red, blue, and yellow to the scene. Wherever we go in Tunisia, whatever we photograph, it is the women who are doing practically all the work. We do not know much about Moslem society—only what we have been able to observe and what we have been told. Personally, I would like to know how that custom was decided upon. It had to be a decision made by men. No matter how "open minded" I try to be, that practice disturbs me. It is popular throughout very large areas of the world—maybe it is our society that is off the track!

Djerba North Africa (Ile de Djerba)
February 15 1955

This morning we were up at 5 AM and on the road by 6. The ride took us along the coast and through the cold desert air. When you are cold, it seems like a long time for the sun to rise, but finally, it did but then a heavy cloud bank rolled in and the cold air again took over. The track from south of Gabes was sand and rock. The rocks made it a little difficult to handle the over-loaded bike. The track was supposed to be a "short-cut", I should have known—they never seem to turn out that way for me.

It was an interesting track because it ran along the coast and made it possible to see something of how the natives live. The huts were constructed of palm fronds with grass-thatching on the roof. They are very picturesque along the edge of the sea—and great places for insects and rats. The track passes through a village called Sekhira and to the port of Djorf. The so-called "port" consists of several rough-sawn planks arranged so that the over-sized boat can come alongside. Across the gunwales planks were fastened to form a platform long enough to accommodate a normal sized vehicle. Both ends of the vehicle extend out over the water. It was not a problem getting the bike aboard.

There was a large, and ethnically mixed, audience watching as we boarded. Some of the women were completely covered with a slit for one eye. My question, not asked, was how do they ever manage to navigate? One of the women, completely robed had the head of an angry chicken protruding. The camel was much angrier, at least it gave every indication of being very disturbed about the entire procedure. It had to be prodded and pushed every step of the way and, when the boat moved the situation got worse. Several men were required to get it aboard and back to the stern where it finally knelt down, having objected to everything. The boat was quite low in the water and the camels head, held erect, seemed to be observing the entire scene—and disapproving of it.

After we boarded and the camel was pushed, prodded, and carried on, it was time for the baggage and the people to get aboard. The cargo included a full-sized mattress, a couple goats, a mixture of bags and boxes, many tin pans, and several rolls of carpeting. After the cargo the people started to board. I have no idea as to how many but, as they piled aboard the boat sank deeper into the water! I could tell that Emma was very nervous—she did not say anything. If I said that I was not more than very concerned, it would be far from the truth.

We cast off and the boat settled into the water with only a few inches of clearance. Fortunately the bay was calm. When the motor was started Emma and I just looked at each other—it was too late to say anything. The motor made noises that I had never heard from any type of internal combustion engine. It hissed and sputtered, and back-fired. After it warmed up it ran a little more quietly but my confidence in the thing had been shattered. And I had been concerned that the camel might decide to act up! After about 30 minutes the island came into view and we docked. The entire procedure was replayed in reverse. Everyone knew what to do. Even the camel seemed to object a little less strenuously—but only a little. The charge for our crossing was 400 francs. I thought that, perhaps we paid the passage for several of the passengers, including the woman with the baby slung over her back. She shifted it from back to front so smoothly that we concluded she had a lot of experience. How do they do that with all that material draped around their bodies?

The Island of Djerba is a different world. You are aware of the calmness and peace as soon as you set foot on the sandy shore. It seems not to be a part of Tunisia. Our landing was at the port of Adjim and rode over a meandering road through forests of palms, extensive patches of cacti, past palm huts and along fences of palm fronds. There were several small mosques, many little donkeys and as many bicycles. On a flat island a bicycle makes sense.

The hats worn get your attention at once. They are wide-brimmed with pointed crowns. Made of straw, they are unique and give the men and women an individuality that they would not otherwise have. The hats give the entire island an oriental atmosphere and the idea might well have originated from boats that came from Asia and/or China. Mongoloid skulls have been found in North /Africa. Many of the men leave the island to seek work on the mainland or in France. When they have saved enough money they return. The men working on the mainland are usually referred to as "the grocers".

The road took us to Houmt-Souk, the market place located on the north western edge of the island. It was afternoon and everything was closed, there was no activity of any kind. Everyone must have been taking his afternoon siesta. Many of the souks are roofed, probably for protection from the hot sun. Anything that you might need is available—and many things that you do not need. There are shoemakers producing the heel-less soft yellow slippers, jewelers selling very artistic original creations, and piles and piles of colorful blankets and carpets. They were all closed. The old Spanish fort had plenty of room but it was not possible for us to camp there. The fort appeared to be very well built, low with several round towers, but, not too comfortable. The first priority of an invader is the building of fortifications. Nations have not changed—they are still investing more in arms and offensive and defensive killing machines than they are in bettering living conditions for the people who are paying for the weapons. A place to sleep was needed. Since no hostel existed on the island, we went to the "Hotel du Lotus". Four hundred francs for a room—it was our "400 francs day." Our room was number 15. The room was very pleasant, cool and comfortable. The hotel is located in a grove of palms and tropical plants. The front porch was elevated and provided a pleasant view over a quiet square—we never took the time to enjoy it.

Lunch consisted of dried milk and oatmeal. Emma mixed the dried milk with water—it is easier to eat it that way! In addition there was bread, oleo, and jelly. Not too bad. When we left the hotel for the afternoon we told the clerk that we would not be having dinner that evening. He was not told the reason—Emma's delicious cooking!

From the hotel we rode through several tropical villages. There was one named El May, followed by McDoun, then El Kantara. Along the sandy, narrow tracks were tiny little houses set back in the palm groves, many protected by fences of cacti. There are many little Mosques (I have to find another descriptive word for picturesque.) It is not possible to know what a place is really like unless you live there for some period of time. However, Djerba has made such a favorable impression upon us that, I think we might take that chance—we are surprised that many others have not done so.

Cathedrals, synagogue, churches, etc. fail to make much of an impression on me—except that I feel that the time, money, resources, and labor could have been better invested. The mosques scattered all over the island of Djerba did not make that impression on me. They seem to belong there, they "fit in". The low, white-washed, buildings with many white domes are impressive due to their simplicity. The graceful, thin, pencil-like minarets from which the muzzine gives the call to prayer, point to the clear blue sky and seem to have a purpose. Some minarets have a narrow circular balcony from which the calls are made. As he calls, the muzzine walks around the balcony and calls in every direction. The introduction of the Moslem religion was from the south when the camp of Sidi Oqba was set up in Kairouan in 670 AD. The Jewish population that has existed on the island of Djerba for more than one thousand years claim that they have been waiting until they are able to return to Jerusalem. Some claim that their ancestors were expelled from the Holy Land in 600 BC!

At one of the several synagogues we were told that many Jews have left the island and that those who remain are waiting to leave for Isreal as soon as possible. Our informant was a young Jew who had lived in the US, was doing some kind of social work on Djerba and expected to return to the States in the near future. He is of the opinion that a great number of Jews, now located in various cities across North Africa, will head for Isreal. Their departure will have an effect upon the areas that they vacate. There are two Jewish villages on Djerba. They are referred to as ghettos. Our Jewish informant told us that the synagogue El Ghriba is the oldest and one of the most famous in the world.

Djerba has had its bouts with pirates and with many foreign in vaders throughout its long history. It is very easy to understand that invaders would find it most pleasant. The pirate Dragut must have enjoyed his stay. It is recorded that, when he invaded the island he beheaded the entire garison of defenders and made a pyramid of their skulls. The pile of skulls existed until the French Protectorate. It was a mistake to dispose of them; they must have created a certain atmosphere. The Europeans have that characteristic; they think that they know best, that their way is the only way. It never seems to occur to them that the people who have lived in an area for hundreds or thousands of years just might have adapted to the environment in the most desirable fashion.

On our tour we reached the village of El Kantara. From El Kantara the only land—link runs to the mainland. The causeway was built by the Romans—with slave labor of course. (I like to mention that.)

Over the centuries it sank beneath the waves and was probably forgotten. There is the report that pirates cut through the causeway in order to create a back entrance into the bay—maybe they wanted an escape route.

About the year 1900 Djerba had a population between 30 and 40,000. At that time there were several hundred Maltese

Catholics on the island—they were sponge—fishermen. The village of Girba remains a Roman Catholic see in the ecclastical province of African Tripoli.

In legend Djerba is the land of the Lotus-Eaters. It is the island upon which the Greek sailor Ulysses stranded after more than a week of several storms at sea. After reaching shore Ulysses sent three of his men inland to find out what kind of people might inhabit the area. One of the men was supposed to act as the messenger. Herodotus wrote that it was the land of the Lotus-Eaters. No one seems to know what the Lotus is. It is small in size and as sweet as a date. Some think that it was a type of small apple. It is reported that wine was made from the Lotus fruit. Anthony, in his book on Tunisia reports that some scholars claim to have tasted the Lotus and that it is the fruit of a bush. I would like to offer an explanation of exactly what the Lotus is and what it tastes like. No one on the island with whom we were able to communicate knew anything about it. If I am to be honest—I have joined them.

The rest of the legend is that the three men sent out by Ulysses did not return nor did they send back the messenger. Upon imvestigation Ulysses learned that the natives gave his men Lotus fruit to eat. That made them lose the desire to return to the sea or to even think about their wives and children. They had to be forced to return to the ships and chained until well out to sea. Ulysses is fortunate indeed that more of his men did not have an opportunity to eat Lotus plants.

Numerous explanations have been offered to explain the behavior of the men. The one offered by Anthony makes the most sense to me. He thinks that the men had several days of severe storms at sea. They were certain that they would not live to see land again. When they were fortunate enough to reach the tropical island of Djerba and experience its safety, peace and quiet, it was a natural reaction not to want to return to the dangerous life of a sailor.

Ulysses was a dedicated man, blind to all possible temptations. He was unable to understand any point of view that differed from his preconceptions. He was not able to comprehend that other men's opinions might differ from his so, he blamed their odd behavior (to him) on some thing that they might have eaten. Are you able to find any evidence that so-called "human" nature has changed for the better over the past thousands of years?

Upon our return to the hostel we enjoyed another delicious evening meal prepared under the expert guidance and extensive experience of, Emma—oatmeal and dried milk!

The following morning we were off through the oasis to the village of Guellala where there are many pottery shops. The best description of the area might be "rural" or "basic". It appears that the potters moved in and set up their shops and outdoor ovens in a haphazard fashion. The sandy tracks run through the area in a disorganized fashion. As in the natural world, there are no sharp corners. Europeans might call it disorganized. We thought it just "natural". A pottery shop and required outdoor mound of rock and sand may be seen around any bend in the track.

The oven-mounds appear to have been "thrown together". Not so! They are very functional and from their interior the potter removes the beautiful and/or functional result of

225

his labors. The ovens we saw were quite large—and filling the air with smoke constantly. It was not possible for us to examine the interior of an oven so I can not describe exactly how they are constructed or how they function. All we know is that they heat, bake, and harden the potter's creations.

The potters have been creating every type of container for thousands of years. The art is passed from one generation to the next in an unbroken chain. That ability to create the unique designs is inherited along with the necessary drive, the desire, to do the work. There are two types of pottery: one turned by men, the other "modeled" by women. We were only able to see the men at work. The women's pottery is confined to "rural areas" and is "utilitarian" in design and nature. It seemed to us that we were in what we would call a "rural area". Anyway, the making of pottery in the area now called Tunisia dates back to the Neolithic Period.

Every piece of pottery is said to bear forms and decorations adapted to its function. Every form has a cultural value and is designed to fill a need. Working with clay is said to have appeared with the origin of man. (Women must have originated at about the same time!) Pottery, textiles', and leather work are rooted in the Tunisian culture. The Gafsa civilization was in close contact with that of Egypt, Greece, and Persia. (It would improve the attitude of such self-delusional countries as those of Europe and the United States if they were able to get into their brains, a better perspective of so-called "ancient" history.)

The renewal of ceramics, and an improvement in the creation and production of pottery happened in Tunisia when the Phoenicians introduced the potters lathe. Tunisian potters were inspired by the introduction of pottery from other Mediterranean countries by the Phoenicians. Punic artisans created new forms—for example the Amphora. (The earthen pottery vessel with the" pointed "bottom making it easier to stand, or pile them in the sand.) The Amphora was also easier to transport by sea. The Punis artisans created red and black varnished bowls and plates. The Romans introduced the African sigillate. It had bright red color and relief or stamped decorations with floral, animal, and/or mythological motives. Baked earth (terra-cotta) was introduced as a decorative element. It was used to some extent in the production of Christian tiles. The Christian tiles were relief decorated and four-angled so that they could be used on wall and ceiling decorating. They are called "Christian" because they were created to be used in Byzantine basilicas. The designs included animal, floral, and geometric themes. The inspiration seems to have originated from the Old and New Bible Testaments.

With the arrival of Islam Tunisian pottery and ceramics boomed. Numerous new forms, fancy decorations, and enameling and glazing were introduced. We had never thought of the importance of pottery in the history of man. The Moslem sect, the Aghlabites, inspired the production of more floral, animal, and geometric designs. They were produced in Nabel and Djerba. Another Moslem sect, the Fatimites, mixed human and animal figures with great harmony. With the domination of another sect, the decorations became more abstract and limited to geometric and floral motives.

Then another theme was introduced—The Andalus. The technique involved the coating of tiles with poly-chromatic galaze. The design included polygonal geometric figures. The technique was influenced by the saint Abu El Racem El Jazili and can be seen on and in his mausolium in Tunis. The fact that the history of Tunis is recorded in its production of pottery was impressive to us.

We learned that during the Turkish domination, their influence was recorded in pottery designs. The present-day potters of Djerba still are influenced and produce, Turkish designs. Their creations are said to reflect the design of the Ottoman Turks. Each region of Tunisia produces its own characteristic pottery designs. An expert is able to read the history of the region by an examination of its pottery. Each Tunisian region has gotten characterized over time through specific types of pottery influenced by past civilizations:

Djerba pottery reflects the influence of the Berbers, Greeks, and Romans—
The Sahel pottery reflects Berber, Byzantine, and Arab domination—
Nabuel—Punic, Roman, and Andulus influence
Tunis—Punic, Arab, and Andalus influence

There are many potters' shops as I have mentioned but, most of them were not in the right place for us—that is the sun did not shine through the door and onto the potter as he worked. In order to get the movie shots that we wanted we had to find a potter in such a location. As we looked for that type situation an oven was located in "just the right place". The bike was parked and I set up the tripod and got all set to shoot scenes of the smoking oven.

As I started to shoot the first scene the owner appeared. He appeared to be very upset, shouting in Tunisian Arabic and waving his arms like the vanes of a windmill. I stopped shooting, wondering how I should react. A young man appeared. He was shouting and waving his arms about. After a few minutes of that the two men were pushing each other back and forth in the middle of the sandy track. A small crowd heard the ruckus and started to gather—they were all talking to each other and to the two "combatants".

Suddenly they stopped pushing each other around and the young man was apparently giving the owner a stern lecture. In a moment the owner turned his back and, still talking and waving his arms, he stalked away. By that time we had packed all the equipment away and were ready to leave. The younger fellow came up to us with a smile and indicated, sign language, that we should take our pictures; the shots were taken and we thought it best to move out of that area.

A little further investigating resulted in our locating a potter working in direct sunlight! As we set up to photograph him at his wheel Emma made a comment about the recent incident—"Too bad that you did not get a shot of them having that "pushing match '!" She was right, I was not thinking. The incident did show, I thought, the difference between the older and younger generations. The younger people, to some extent, are more flexible, more reasonable, than the older people. Every time that we have had difficulty trying to take pictures, it has been with older men. They have been taught, and follow, the strict Moslem rule of "no graven images of men or animals." (Women included.)

229

The potter is a skilled artisan. It was difficult to get the shots that I wanted because I could not talk to him, I had to shoot whatever he was doing. We appreciated the fact that it was possible to get the shots that we did. He created one form after another, it looked so easy! As he worked he turned his potter's wheel by foot-power. A pedal on the floor supplied the energy that kept the wheel spinning. It is most impressive to see him create one unique form after another from a wet lump of clay.

His shop was what we might call "primitive". He was working as they have probably worked for the past thousand years. We felt very fortunate to have the opportunity to photograph him at his wheel. The shop was half-buried in the sand, with brush and what appeared to be a collection of debris covering the roof. I could not determine what the roof proper was made of.

There were no lights inside the building. The bright sun did light up the interior enough so that we could see his display. Emma selected much more than we would ever be able to carry on the bike—unless she would decide to stay on the island! An old box had to be found, everything packed into it with plenty of newspaper and left at the post-office. As I write we hope that the box is on its way to the United States. The mail does get out. Rolls of Kodachrome, 16mm, have reached the US, been processed and are now in the hands of one of our former professors in Ann Arbor, Michigan.

After leaving the potters shop we decided to take another tour of the island. We never seem to tire of riding along the sandy tracts under the tall palms, along the narrow, sandy roads lined by dead palm frond and cactus fences. It is such a peaceful, quiet, restful atmosphere—it is no wonder to us that Ulysses men did not want to leave! The women, wearing their long grey blankets draped over their heads topped off with the wide-brimmed, straw, oriental-style hats, seem to be ancient shadows from the past. Of course, certain customs have been imported from the mainland—the women do all the hard labor. They have and care for the numerous children, keep the hut clean and orderly, gather local food and fuel, and carry the water in those heavy, earthen, amphora's. The men here, like those on the mainland, are very busy discussing local and international affairs, drinking strong coffee or sweet, hot tea, and smoking their Turkish water-pipes.

About dusk we were back in the port of D"Adjorin. We walked along the shore looking at the docks, the sponge-fishing boats, and the drying nets and other fishing gear. Like the tracks through the island, we never tired of just visiting and walking along the port areas. Photographs are almost always taken, many several times over-then it was back to the hostel for another cooked meal—of oatmeal and dried milk??!!

One morning we were checking out the port area at D"Adjorin and saw the loading of three camels onto a sailing vessel. The camels were nervous and objected very much to boarding the ship—nothing unusual about their attitude and lack of cooperation. Emma thought that the men were very tolerant and patient. They pulled and pushed the poor animals but there was no beating—we liked their attitude. We have been impressed with the behavior of the camels. They have such a condescending air—they always seem to be just tolerating us so-called "superior" humans. The camel looks down upon man—physically and mentally.

After the camels were finally loaded the sails were unferrelled and away they went—very slowly. The camels had kneeled down and were looking over the gunwales of the boat in their characteristic superior manner. The little sail boat was loaded heavily with pottery and made a beautiful picture as it slowly and silently glided out over the blue waters of the Mediterranean. Emma ask the question that both of us had on our minds—For how many hundreds of years has this same scene been enacted?

We sat on an old pile of rope for a long time and talked as that little sail boat left the harbor and headed up the coast. There were several men aboard along with the camels and the colorful load of pottery. Where were they headed? What would happen to the men, the camels, and the pottery? We would never know.

The scene was so peaceful and quiet at the port that I hated to kick over the bike-It seemed so out of place! As we rode away I thought, it will not be very long before that scene will disappear into the mists of history. "Progress," American style, is on a relentless, and destructive march "forward" and around the world. The peace and quiet will be shattered by many such rackets as our bike makes. That old sailboat and those men will be forced by "progress" into the "Modern Age" of speed, high-pressure, and all the "advancement" of the American way of living. Will they be happier, more content and satisfied than they are now? Who is better adjusted to life and living—the average Tunisian or the average American?

Once again we wandered the sandy tracks. The palm leaf huts are always worth one more picture—maybe two or three. A woman weaving floor mats caught our attention. She was sitting outside against the wall of her thatched-roofed, palm leaf hut. No men were in sight and she was pleased to be photographed. She probably enjoyed the special attention.

The sandy track led us to a small cluster of huts and we shot pictures in that tiny village. Along one rather extensive length of the track a formidable prickly pear cactus fence had been cultivated. It must have required many years of attention. There was no danger of anyone penetrating that barrier! A man came down the track riding his camel—that made a great shot. He paid no attention to us—neither did the camel.

You may think that I am exaggerating when I say that it takes a lot of energy to get the pictures. I never will adjust to the noise that our bike makes—it disturbs the peace and quiet of the island. We would never buy another one like it. Very few shots can be taken from the bike. Each time it has to be shut off and parked—not usually easy to do in the sand. Next the tripod must be untied and opened and the camera attached and focused. By that time it is often too late—the scene has changed or the subject has "escaped".

Still, with persistence, we do get some good shots and, what we get is better than nothing. For us, it is great fun, we enjoy being here and seeing what life is like on the island. When I get frustrated Emma tries to remind me that we are very fortunate to be able to get here and see, and do, what we are doing—and, for the moment I get more frustrated! (But, when I calm down, I realize that I am very fortunate to have her—still, like the Arabs, a man must be careful not to "spoil" his wife, or wives!

Last evening a young man from Holland showed up at the hostel. He was able to speak English and very willing to do so. He was willing, and able, to express his ideas of what is right and wrong with the societies of Europe, North Africa, and the world. I thought, it must take a prodigious brain to process all that information.

He likes the French, hates the Germans (that seems to be popular at the moment.) He resents the fact that America helped Holland recover after the war. He thinks that the French also resent the assistance that they had to accept from America after the war. He is certain that most Americans are politically ignorant, they are far too materialistic, too ambitious, too germ conscious, and too militant. (In short, we Americans really do not amount to much that is worthwhile.)

If you do not allow people to talk how are you going to find out what they are thinking? Sometimes that is not easy to keep in mind. Some people would call him "pink", some would classify him as a "red". We wanted to listen and he wanted to talk—that combination usually works. We were not having a discussion, there was only one valid opinion worth considering—his.

He did not like the Americans and he did not like the Tunisians. The French were very fortunate that he liked them! After he praised the French for some time and mentioned their empire, I ventured to inquire as to how the French were helping the Tunisians. Holland, like the French and the English are living through the end-days of imperialism. The empires set up, mostly on paper, by the European nations are crumbling as we speak. One self-important, "superior" culture invading and attempting to dominate others is not in fashion at the moment. It may be revived by the US but, in the end, it will not work. I did not say that to our friend from Holland. He had enough information, knew what was right and wrong. Emma and I do not feel that our way is the only way, in fact, as I have frequently mentioned, we do not think that we are right when we interfere in the ways of foreign cultures. It is good to have opinions but, it is not good to be opinionated.

Yesterday we had some good luck. We were out in the desert looking around—I can not tell you what we might have been looking for. Five Berber women happened to pass by in typical blue robes, their heads covered and wearing the wide-brimmed, pointed, straw hats. No men in sight! A little dog ran along with them, a miniature of the adults. We were able to film them as they approached and as they walked down the desert track. They may be almost completely covered but they are very aware of everything happening around them. As the last lady passed she waved her hand, a simple gesture that seemed to say so much—

An elderly man came along riding the most loveable little donkey—that made a great combination and I had to get his picture. We were very pleased and Emma prompted me—"Give him some francs she said". I happened to have about 150 in my pocket and I handed them to him. I wish I could have gotten a picture of his gestures and his smile of appreciation. Those shots are about impossible for us to get.

When we returned to the hostel our Holland friend was there. We were so pleased with the shots that we were able to get that we told him about the old man and the donkey.

His response? "That is another thing that I do not like about Americans. They have spoiled the people in Europe by throwing money around and now they are at it in Africa." I looked at Emma, I did not know what to say—I suppose I should have said something, but I did not. We just walked away.

Djerba, to us, is the end of the line. We have been on the road for more than six months. Ghadames, down in the Sahara looks very tempting on the map—war and bad roads, no matter. In spite of the hardships, the trip has been a wonderful experience; I guess we had better take the advice of the officials. We were fortunate to get here—and, we do have to return. There are a great many places on this planet in which one might live comfortable and happily—travel should do a lot to eradicate provincialism. If we were to consider moving, leaving the States, Djerba would rank high on the list of potential new locations.

From London the road has taken us through many countries and over very beautiful areas. It has been just over seven thousand miles—and, of course, it will be just as far back. It would be great to do it all over again—but, with some minor changes. More power in the bike, and a side-car with an effective windscreen for Emma—or, even better, a French 2CV vehicle that would keep us out of the rain and the wind! The motorcycle enthusiasts would not like to hear that.

Djerba Tunisia North Africa
February 16 1955

Northeastern Pennsylvania has had a severe snowstorm recently! It does not look like snow here! The worst weather that might be expected would include high winds, short, heavy, dangerous rainstorms, and, cold nights. The sun shines almost every day and, the afternoons are very comfortable. I have to say that when our friends write us and describe how they have to shovel snow, and how low the temperature has gotten—well, we have to feel so very sorry for them!! It would be nice if it were possible to invite them to visit us here on the island for a few weeks! They would enjoy eating lots of Lotus!

Up about seven this AM. Emma made another exceptional breakfast of oatmeal, dried milk, bread and oleo, and tea. You could not get another breakfast like that anywhere in Tunisia! It makes a great change from beans and sardines or stew! On the bike and on the sandy tracks of Djerba by about eight. I know, it has been said over and over, how great it is to ride through this idyllic island at any time—but especially early in the morning when it is still shrouded by streamers of mist. It gives the impression of a fairy-land.

(I do not know what a fairy-land should look like.) Everything gives the impression of floating in the cool, misty air. The black robed figures also appear to float, weightless, as they silently move around.

At the port of Homt-Souk a sea-worn sailing ship was being unloaded. The internal combustion engine has not yet arrived on the island. Everything is done either by human labor or, with the assistance of camels or donkeys. That is why it is so peaceful, so tranquil here. But, it is going to change—and in the near-future, "progress", speed, and efficiency will soon come roaring down upon this isolated island and, the lives of many of these people will change forever. The "enlightenment" and "freedom" will be preached and they will be given the opportunity to live and be as happy as the average European or American. They will be able to buy homes and material things that they do not need and will not be able to pay for. They will be "free"!

The bike needed fuel so that was taken care of in Houmt-Souk. Emma had to do some shopping—maybe for oatmeal and dried milk! The camera had to be re-loaded. The Pathe 16mm movie camera is very rugged and dependable but, it holds only one, 100 foot roll of film and that runs for only three minutes. A number of ten or fifteen second scenes can be shot but, in an area like Djerba where there are so many shots to be taken, the camera must be re-loaded frequently. Longer running film cartridges are available but, where would we carry additional equipment?

From Houmt-Souk it was back over through the "pottery area". The sun was not quite right or we would have tried for additional scenes. Anyway, it is always interesting to just watch those potters create beautiful objects from those wet lumps of clay. Emma wanted to buy more pottery but had to resist the temptation—she also would like several carpets. So would I, too bad that our supply of cash is so limited. It is necessary that we keep enough money in reserve in case of an emergency. We are very fortunate just to be able to get here and see the people and their country.

Getting shots of the average person can be a real problem. Many of the women are afraid to pose for the camera. Some feel that it is too strange, some, most, are afraid that the men will not approve. Most of the men do not want pictures taken of the women and they will stop me if they happen to see what I am trying to do. I try to set up with Emma in the foreground and the scene that we really want behind her. Still, we have trouble.

Along the track to Port D Adjorn we passed two women walking, leading a donkey with woven grass baskets, one on each side. In addition, two children had been placed in two additional baskets, along with two earthen water jugs, carefully balanced, one on each side! Cute? Picturesque? Yes! But what about the poor, long-suffering, over-loaded donkey ?

Emma ran over to them and tried to ask if we might take their picture. I held up the slide camera. They failed to understand Emma but did recognize the camera, I think. I tried to get into position as quickly as possible because I was afraid that a man might come along. I was not fast enough! Just as I got the movie camera set up and was ready to start shooting a man came riding down the track on a bicycle. He realized what we were doing, said something to the women and one of them slapped the donkey on the rump—off they scurried down the track like frightened children. One woman almost lost a shoe. Two factors are at work—ignorance and religious indoctrination.

Not long after that incident, along another sandy tract, we were able to locate several young girls. They appeared to be gossiping. In that case we thought it best to just start shooting. By using the telephoto it was possible for us to shoot from a considerable distance. A young man noticed us, ran over to some men who were working nearby and told them what we were doing. When all of them headed in our direction we quickly decided that discretion was better than valor. (I know that I did!) Having had lots of practice, we quickly loaded our gear and headed in the opposite direction.

Our luck had not been favorable up to that point. I can not say that I was not very disgusted. Sometimes it is very difficult for me to see the situation from the other person's point of view.

From El Kantara we rode toward Homt-Souk again, photographing the grass huts, and a grave yard where the graves were marked simply by small stones. No elaborate markers used there. Everyone had been buried on the same level. In that instance the dictates of the Moslem religion were being followed but, that is not done in all cases.

During our wandering around in the south we have noticed that the prices are higher as you near the border with Libya and the area of Tripoli, located not far from the Tunisian border. The reason? The Americans stationed at the air base near Tripoli. The man from Holland does speak the truth when he says that the Americans spoil the natives when they throw their money around as they frequently do. The US has a large base near Tripoli. The military mind must be afraid that our country will be attacked by Libya, maybe

Tunisia, or Egypt? There are several such bases in Italy, no doubt serving as protection against a surprise attack from Sicily, or perhaps Albania!

Our experience with the potter is an example of US exaggerated generosity. We did have to pay two or three times the real price of the pottery because the Americans had been there. Reasonable generosity should be shown, but too many Americans do try to make an impression by spending money. It does make an impression-the people think that we are fools. Sometimes, the people are right.

Tomorrow morning we must leave. There are a couple more shots that we would like to get on the way out but, that situation would be the same if we had been here for a year. Just maybe, we are a little like those three men from Ulysses ship who had to be taken back to the ship and placed in irons. From our point of view, we hope that Djerba, and the people, never change but, we know that the situation will change and maybe not for the long-term betterment of the people. "Progress", in the form of tourism has already started and will turn into a flood as soon as Tunisia becomes independent. That will bring thousands of tourists and everything that they have to have. It will result in massive development, hotels, and lots of pollution. No one is able to predict the long-term effect upon the people of Tunisia and the country.

I must tell of one more incident here on the island of Djerba. An old man came riding along on his donkey and he made a lovely picture. We stopped him and tried to give him a few francs. He refused to take the money! There is a possibility that he is quite alone on the island. No—I am sure that there are many people like that old man on the island.

Our plan is to head north along the coast. That is our plan—at the moment, it might change even after we are on the bike. That freedom we enjoy and deeply appreciate. Life on the open road on the bike is not easy but, it is free! Not many people are fortunate enough to have experienced that for a period of one year.

Our plan-well, when we started to leave the island our world turned upside down. For the next several days we roamed the south of Tunisia. We almost got tossed into the sea in a storm, then had to ride through a sand storm and, just to top it off as, perhaps unusual, we had the fun of a locust plague! I will try to get it all on paper but, it might be a little jumbled—a lot of living in a short period of time—

Gabes Tunisia North Africa
February 17 1955

It is now 6:30, Emma is making supper and I am going to record the recent events. This might have been one of those times when you should have been there!

The morning that we left the Hotel Du Lotus we were up by six and making breakfast as usual. Emma was cooking cereal on the Swedish one-burner blow torch located in the closet so that the staff might not be able to hear it. Breakfast of oatmeal, dried milk, bread oleo, and coffee.

The dishes were being done silently when someone knocked on the door! We thought that we had been heard! One of the staff wanted the passport for the police—again. It was finally found and delivered. When I went down to retrieve it I met a policeman who was most pleasant. He turned out to be a friend of Habib's. The policeman has been trying to enter the US as a citizen for the past ten years. He must be very persistent. He invited us to his home—it was too bad that we did not accept his invitation. He knew the island very well and would have been an excellent guide. Why we did not accept that invitation I will never know.

Along the track to the port we were able to get a variety of shots—Djerban men drinking coffee, people in the port area, the market activity, mostly men buying and selling sheep camels, blankets, tin ware, and so on.

Before we reached the port Emma remarked that it seemed unusually sultry and hot. As usual, I did not pay much attention—I should have, as usual. The air was not clear, the wind was hot and dry and quite strong. None of those warnings were able to get into my brain.

At the port dock which consisted of a few planks arranged together, more or less, the little ferry boat was loading. It was the same over-sized row boat that had brought us over when we arrived, only this time it was bobbing around and they were having trouble getting it loaded.

There were several completely shrouded women huddled in the prow of the craft. Amidships on the extended platform partially hanging over the water was a vehicle that had definitely seen better days. One rear fender was completely missing, the rear window was smashed, the running boards were long-gone, and the headlights were arranged in a cross-eyed manner. The car was over-loaded with men and women. The men were constantly getting out, then back in. Alongside the car were two bicycles consisting of frames and wheels only and our motorcycle.

When we thought that there was no more room aboard for even another person, an old bus pulled alongside. It was full of people inside and cargo on top. Several men climbed to the top of the bus and started to throw things off in the most haphazard manner. Additional people boarded and the bus cargo was piled amidships. There were several bales of hay, mattresses, and boxes of all sizes, several sheep and a few chickens. Sacks of meal and potatoes were tossed on top of everything. On the backs of two of the three women in the prow babies were slung in the usual manner, and they

244

were shifted from back to front frequently for inspection. Only once during the entire crossing did one of the infants make any sounds.

The people appear to be very, very poor, but they seemed not to mind. They gave every indication that they were enjoying the voyage of five or six miles. That in spite of the fact that the wind was whipping up rather high waves which were pounding the extended platform of warped planks. As we cast off the waves pounded the craft and the spray soaked everything and everyone. I had to remove my glasses and the women in the prow were so huddled down that they were hardly visible. They did have more protection than we did. The air was filled with fine sand and saltwater.

The motor chugged and sputtered but it did not stop—fortunately for everyone and everything aboard. The tiny craft heaved and bobbed rather violently. The helmsman, if he was at all concerned, gave not outward indication. He was having trouble trying to determine where we were—visibility must have been close to zero. As the boat was tossed about I took pictures. Once, a rather large wave hit the vessel and almost swamped it, water rushed over the side and the women in the prow screamed. That made me nervous and I put the camera away. Emma just crouched down and gave no outward sign of how she really felt—she did not have to!

When the big wave hit the boat the car lurched toward the end of the plank platform. The front wheels reached the edge but the old rope lashing held and it did not go overboard. Had the front wheels gone over it would have tilted the boat and it would have been swamped. I looked at the helmsman, he did not react. He headed straight toward the high bank of sand that finally came into view. It offered some protection and the gyrations of the tiny craft lessened a bit. We traveled along the high sandy bank of sand and, finally, the landing site came into view.

Everyone appeared to be relieved as they stepped ashore, Emma was and I was very pleased to be able to join her. She said, "Had that thing been swamped and sank, who would have known about it or reported the inciden ?" I think that I know. By the time they unloaded our bike it was very obvious that we were in for a rough ride to Medenine—that was the closest village and the first available fuel station. We had checked the fuel in Houmt—Souk and the tank was half full. That would have been more than enough to reach Medenine—in normal weather. At that time we had no idea that we would have to buck a very strong headwind and sand storm. As we topped the high sandy bank that protected the dock area the full fury of the storm hit us. No hotel was there and it would be foolish to attempt to set up our tent in that gale and blowing sand. We had to get to Medenine.

The bike was not able to buck the force of the wind in high gear—not even on down grades. The thought of running out of fuel in that sand storm hit me right in the stomach. It was going to be a long, hard run in second gear. The blowing sand was stinging our faces and our hands and it was not easy to breath. The wind was hot but I put on my gloves. Emma tried to wrap a scarf around her head but finally just had to huddle down as much as possible behind me. I tried to pull my cap down to protect my eyes and huddle down behind our small wind screen, it deflected some of the sand.

I kept trying for high gear in an attempt to save fuel—no luck. The road side kilometer markers seemed to be miles apart.

The strong wind and blowing sand never slackened. The sand penetrated everything—into our eyes, ears, and our noses and mouths! The thought of getting either camera out and exposing it to the sand-driven wind was out of the question. The 35mm had gotten some salt water on the lens during the crossing of the channel. The sand penetrated our clothes and sifted down our necks. I could feel the sand trickling down over my chest. We wanted to turn back but—to what? Our only choice was to keep going.

Along the sand-covered track we saw camels grazing on the stunted vegetation. I thought that they might have the advantage of height. Most of the blowing sand seemed to be near the surface of the ground. Had we been riding camels it might not have been quite so bad. Anyway, the camels acted as if it were a pleasant, sunny, calm day. We thought that we were in the Sahara Desert—and we were! Shepherds were staying with their sheep—where would they go? Most of them were crouched down with the heavy hoods of their bournouse robes pulled up over their heads—some were lying down. One man came riding out of the storm on a camel—I still think that he was out of the full fury of the storm by being at that height.

Our fuel supply reached the bottom of the tank. Emma made an important suggestion—as she often does during an emergency. "Empty the fuel from the Swedish blow-torch cook stove into the tank." I am so pleased to have thought of that! We both hoped that it would take us on into

Medenine. I did get the slide camera out and take some pictures of the sand blowing over the track and some palm huts. There were sand drifts forming across the track and I had to be very careful when we hit one—they tended to deflect the bike. Then I ran out of film ! No way would I open a camera to re-load film in that wind-blown sand—we kept heading for Medenine. I worried that the sand might block the air-filter and stall the motor—it did not happen. Luck was with us!

The wind blew and the sand flew—every foot of the way into Medenine. The only variation was in intensity—at certain times there was less sand in the air. Our noses became blocked with sand, our throats were dry, and our lips were burning—our little bottle of very warm water did help. (A cold beer would have been nice!) As we headed toward Medenine the force of the wind lessened and of course there was less sand in the air.

I was able to use high gear. It was with great relief that we pulled into the station and filled the tank!

While we were getting the fuel an old fellow came along. He had some bracelets and other odd pieces of jewelry that he wanted to sell. He wanted one hundred francs for each bracelet in an attempt to get ride of him I offered him one hundred francs for two bracelets—he accepted and I had to pay!

The road from Djerba to Medenine was a sandy track but from Medenine to Gabes it was paved and we were able to make much better time. There was still a strong wind and some blowing sand but, compared to what we had just traveled through, it was not too bad. With less wind and sand we were able to ride into Gabes in relative comfort. I use the word "relative" because Emma still had to straddle that back saddle and prop her legs up on two iron rods that serve as foot-rests. We were both quite sore after the tense ride through the storm. It was still very hot and the wind, the air oppressive. The sand was still blowing over the road and, in several places; men were out trying to clear the sand away. Here, at this moment, they are clearing the road of sand-drifts—in Pennsylvania, it is snow!

The drifting sand covering the road was a constant danger—if we hit one going too fast we would end up flying! About 4:30 we pulled into Gabes. It was great to see the village—that is, what we were able to see of it. There was still a lot of sand being moved around. If the village were to become uninhabited for any length of time, it would be swallowed up by the desert sands.

We were very tired—I doubt that we were ever more tired! The sand had to be cleaned out of everything—eyes, ears, noses, mouths—we could feel the sand grinding between our teeth. The sand penetrated the plastic bags in which we carried the cameras—and, it got into the mechanism of the Pathe movie camera! Emma still had to shop for supper, and then we made our way to the hostel, signed in, washed and bathed, ate an orange, blew up the air-mattresses, and went to bed. We were glad that we lived through it, glad, that it was over—but, pleased that we did it.

Gabes, Southern Tunisia North Africa
February 19 1955

During the night the wind subsided and the weather cleared. It was a real pleasure to get out into the air, free of blowing sand. After breakfast we got on the bike and followed a track out into the desert. Every time that we do, we see something different. This time it was two black, pot-bellied children playing in front of a grass hut. The scene could have been in darkest Africa. I circled back to try for some pictures. As soon as the older child realized what we were doing he grabbed the other, smaller one by and hand and they disappeared into the hut. They, of course, knew that we were waiting outside and, while we waited, no one came out. It would have been wrong to push the situation any further—we left.

On down the track we photographed a similar hut but, no one came out. The setting was great but, it is the people who really make the scene. It is a completely different way of life when compared to ours. How might we ever be able to understand those people? How could we ever be able to accept them as they are, see the world as they do? There was a very small oasis out there in the desert with a small pool of water and a few palm trees. It was pleasant and quiet, no one was around. Maybe it was too small or perhaps a temporary pond. It was a great resting place for us—but we would not trust that water!

Then back to the hostel for lunch. Emma bought some meat. I wonder what it is. Sheep? Cow ? Goat ? Horse ? We ate it and it tasted good. The next desert track took us out toward Gafsa—about seventy miles North West of Gabes, Gafsa is an oasis in the mountains. It is just northwest of the extensive salt flats, Chottel Fedjadj.

Along the road to Gafsa small groups of people and individuals were moving in both directions. Some were riding camels, most were on donkeys or walking. When there was an option, the men rode, the women walked. Just beyond Gabes there were quite a few locusts. They looked, and acted, like the migratory phase. Still, they were not very numerous and I gave it little thought. The road into Gafsa was in very good shape. The Roman pools and the Mosque are, of course, "must see" attractions. They are worth much more than the time it takes to get there. There are beautiful views over the oasis to the mountains beyond.

Gafsa was a busy village but the people seemed friendly. They probably get a lot of visitors. Tourists pass through the village on their way to Tozeur, located to the south and west on the edge of the salt flat named Chott, El Djerid. Probably, we could have made it to Tozeur but, our time was running out and maybe the desert was starting to "get to us". I do not know—we decided to head back to Gabes. In Gafsa we did visit the kasba and the traditional quarters.

Gafsa, like many villages in Tunisia, has a very long history. It is said to date back to Numidian Times. The records indicate that it was destroyed by the Romans in one of their unending military campaigns into the south in 107 BC. As usual, the Romans rebuilt the village and it prospered. The thing about that is that people, nations, are still following the same path. They can not learn from history, maybe because they never read it or, maybe because they are not able to think. The Roman influence must have been all—pervasive—Latin was still the most common language up through the 12ᵗʰ century.

The history of Gabes is similar to that of Gafsa. After the Second Punis War in the second century, BC, it fell to the Romans. The Arabs moved in about the 7ᵗʰ century. In 1881 the people fell under the benevolent protection of the French—how fortunate could they be ? During the Second World War the city was bombed by the Allied Forces and the natives were once again "freed". They were most fortunate that time because we (the US) did the bombing! At this moment, Tunisia is about to become a free and independent nation—that is, if they are just left alone so that they can work out their problems. Only time will tell—

It was nearing dusk, late afternoon as we returned to the outer edge of Gabes. As we approached the oasis the locusts started to appear. First, just a few scattered here and there—then, suddenly we were bombarded from all directions! They splattered against the wind screen and hit us on the hands and in the face. It was a swarming. Crawling mass of insects! It was necessary to stop but useless to attempt to get them off our faces and clothing. They constantly crashed into our faces.

The swarming mass covered everything—the road, cactus fences, and most important, the trees and gardens. As the swarm began to settle, the individual locusts started collecting in dark masses in any depression that was available. You could watch as the vegetation disappeared. The leaves and even the bark of the trees were eaten. People were out in their gardens pounding on every pot and pan available—apparently they thought that the noise might make the locusts move. We saw no indication of success. At one point a man with an ancient blower came down the road along a garden fence. He was producing a cloud of some type of insecticide. Against the numbers involved in that invasion, the blower was useless. It might have made some people feel better-they were doing something.

As darkness fell the piles of locusts increased and so did the number of people standing around with bags, boxes, pottery and anything that might hold some locusts. A policeman arrived, apparently to maintain order. I thought that it would make a great shot if I drove the bike through one of the piles of swarming locusts. As I was about to take off the policemen held up his hand—they did not want the piles of locusts disturbed because they wanted to collect them! I should have realized that but, when it came to getting pictures, I was not able to think of anything else.

Dark clouds of locusts came out of the darkening sky. How did they navigate? Were they able to smell the water and/or the plant life? There must have been millions of them—how could anyone even guess at the numbers. People were climbing trees in an attempt to shake them out—we could not see that it helped. The poor people kept beating on their pots and pans and yelling—all to no avail as far as we could determine. It was a terrible scene for us to witness. The futility of those poor people trying to save their crops! We felt so useless, so frustrated. It was not possible for us to imagine how those people felt when they watched their crops being devoured by that senseless hoard of voracious insects. We would be able to move north and buy plenty of food—but, what about them?

They even tried to set old palm tree stumps on fire in order to create smoke, thinking that might keep the mass moving. Nothing seemed to help. Some insects did try to help—various species of beetles and ants quickly appeared to carry away the injured locusts that were unable to walk or fly. The whole scene was one of confusion and excitement, of apprehension and expectancy.

The people did not want the locust swarm to settle in the oasis—they wanted them to settle just outside, along the road. We think that their efforts did pay off—at least to some extent. As we watched the people gather and the locusts form ever-larger masses of squirming, restless life, the policeman walked over and, to our surprise, started talking to us in English about the locust plague. We were not only surprised that he is able to speak English, but, also his knowledge of the locusts, their life-cycle, and their capacity to destroy vegetation and the food supply of the people in the oasis.

The insect being discussed is the desert locust, Schistocerca gregaria. It lives in the deserts of Africa and Asia. The eggs are deposited in sandy soil, they develop into wingless "hoppers, they grow into adults with wings. The female will deposit into the sandy soil from 80 to 120 eggs. The weather conditions determine how many might live to form nymphs. A female might deposit three batches of eggs. One thousand egg pods have been counted in one square yard of damp desert sand. When the individual eggs hatch the young nymphs are called" hoppers'. If they are scattered, they are not a problem. It is when they build up into large masses that they change color and begin to act together. It is the present theory that as long as the locusts are scattered, not crowded together, they are not a problem. During a favorable season, when the sands are damp, the egg pods hatch, there are many locusts, they crowd each other and come into contact with each other—they then change color, their behavior changes and they change into the migratory phase.

Their masses can cover hundreds of square miles. Large swarms are able to consume enough food in a day to feed several thousand people. The large swarms have been recorded as plagues since ancient times. The masses are formed when there have been very heavy rains. That can happen in West Africa. Adults lay their eggs in the wet sand and the young develop rapidly, in a period of days or weeks. When a large swarm forms in West Africa it can then move across Morocco, Algeria, and Tunisia. From Tunisia, if the weather and the wind currents are favorable, the swarm might move on eastward toward Egypt. It is very difficult to predict the direction that the plague might take.

When the swarm descends upon a relatively small area, such as an oasis, the damage can create very serious food shortages. The insects destroy subsistence crops and, when they do, famine can be the result. It was no wonder that the citizens of Gabes were so disturbed. They had no idea as to how large the swarm might be. Cultivating the hard dry soil is difficult as is growing fruit trees and starting an olive orchard. Added to the problems of getting a living out of a harsh climate is that of dealing with the French authorities. Since the "Protectorate," the Tunisian farmers have had great difficulty holding onto their ancient tribal lands. There are obstacles, created by the French, to getting loans in order to start a farming operation.

The policeman told us that the Tunisians do not understand the land reforms put in place by the French. The Frenchman is able to borrow money easily and on fair terms—not so for the Tunisian. In a crisis such as this plague the farmers need to be able to borrow money in order to tide them over until next year. Loans like that are almost impossible for the local farmer to obtain with the French in control.

As darkness fell the locusts formed fairly large dark masses. Children and adults began to stuff them into their containers. The natives were turning the tables on the locusts—they were going to eat them! The policeman with whom we had been discussing the locust plague invited us to have coffee with him at the local social center down along the waterfront. Without any hesitation, we accepted.

At the coffee house, located outside along what we would call the sidewalk, we sat at a little table and watched the waiter pour the tea into the glasses. The boiling water was poured into the glasses from what seemed like two feet high! (Probably more like one foot.) The tea is very sweet but it tastes very good to me.

We soon learned that our new friend is not an ordinary policemen, he is the chief officer in the village. He hastened to tell us that he has almost no authority—that lies with the French officials and the military. What he does have is the respect of the native Tunisians, that we could tell from the manner in which he was welcomed at the coffee house. He did not want to talk about the locust plague, he had another plague on his mind, the French "Protectorate" plague!

He said that the period since 1950 has been the most critical in modern Tunisian history. The religious and cultural differences that existed in 1881 when the so-called Protectorate" was imposed by a force of some 30,000 French Foreign Legion troops marching in from Algeria, have been aggravated. The land policies enforced by the French have been most resented. Their constant efforts aimed at the redistribution of sacred Habous Lands have met with equally constant refusal on the part of the Tunisians. The Habous Lands are to be held in trust by the Tunisian government for the use of all the people. The French colonists have done everything possible to take the Habous Lands for their own use and profit. The French colonists are able to secure loans that are denied to the Tunisians, they have modern farming equipment unavailable to the locals. The Tunisians, if they want to live, wind up working for the few wealthy French farmers.

The control of everything is under the control of the French, farming, fishing, crafts, industry, shipping, the markets; it is a military, police-state. The French were not invited in, they were not welcome when they arrived, and they are even less welcome now ! The very deep-seated resentment led to the formation of the Dustor (constitution) party. That nationalist party is now called the Neo-Dustor Party and it has the support of almost all Tunisians. The leader of the Neo-Dustor Party has spent much time in various jails down in the Sahara and in various parts of France and Italy.

From time to time the French make minor concessions, too little and too late. When the people feel that they can take no more repression, they revolt and riots take place. The Foreign Legion then move is to restore order and it is done, at times, in a very savage manner. In one incident troops from Indo-China were flown in to quell a riot. They were unusually vicious, murders, rape, and looting followed.

Our friend was very disappointed by the fact that, when Tunisia tried to get the problem before the UN, the United States failed to offer any support. In fact, he told us they supported France in the UN and increased military supplies to the French military! "That", I thought, "from the land of the free and the home of the brave!" The policemen became quite excited, he is very involved in the struggle for freedom. He may be involved with the Tunisian guerilla units. The French refer to them as the "fellagas", "bandits", and "terrorists".

The Freedom fighters were formed as the result of the French attempts to place all the "trouble-makers" on the Cap bon peninsula in what can only be called prisoner-of-war camps. The escapees formed the present-day teams of freedom-fighters. The Tunisians strenuously objected to the arbitrary internments, repressions, "clean-ups", segregation, etc. The acts of terror and violence were natural consequences of a colonial policy that for almost a century had taken little note of the needs of the local population. The policeman said, "Our patience is at an end, if we do not get our freedom within the next year, there will be war. We will fight for our freedom with whatever we have".

From our point of view France just has no justification for being in North Africa at all. No country has the right to invade another sovereign country without due provocation. Tunisia was, at the time the French invaded, an independent nation. It was in debt due to bad judgment on the part of the Bey and his government but, that is not a valid reason for an invasion. Simply put, France, like England and many other European countries were greedy to take over other less advanced nations because they were greedy of profit, for natural resources and markets.

As of this moment France has created the serious problems it faces in various parts of the world. French veterans and colonists, and business profiteers were encouraged to settle in Tunisia. Now, or very soon, the Tunisians will get their freedom and be able to run their own country. What to do about the colonists? Some will be needed to operate the government until more Tunisians become qualified. That will require years of effort and education. The French have done everything that they can to hold the Tunisians back, to prevent them from learning how to make decisions on their own.

We know that the French settlers have never associated with the Tunisians. The French have a definite superior attitude, not only with the Tunisians, with any other peoples. The French have invaded the country of Tunisia and made the original owners of the country feel that they are second-class citizens. It should be obvious, even to the French that such an approach will not work.

Our experience in Tunisia has verified almost everything that the policeman has said. Suddenly we realized that it was quite late and that almost everyone had left the coffee shop. Also, it was chilly and we did not know if the hostel would be open. We wanted to hear more but it was time to get back to the hostel and then head up the coast to Bir El Bey. There we plan to meet Habib and try to get more movie shots. It is necessary to just take each day and deal with what happens, our plans have to be very flexible, fortunately, the way we are traveling, they can be.

When we said goodnight and goodbye to our friend, the policeman, we had much to think about. The French and the Tunisians have very serious problems and the resolution will be very difficult. A continued attitude of superiority and lack of flexibility will result in outright war or guerilla resistance. We are surprised and amazed that the United States is helping the French we are talking out of both sides of our mouths. Why are we helping the French deprive all the people of North Africa of their freedom?

Our personal problem is our safety. After what we just heard it would be very unpleasant to be mistaken for a French couple. That is why the girl at the hostel office said, and emphasized, "If you are stopped for any reason start to speak English at once." She knows that the freedom-fighters recognize the English language. Emma is nervous enough, it is not necessary to discuss our safety any further. We have to travel up the coast to Bir El Bey; then we will be returning south but, with Habib and his wife. That should not be a problem.

The morning after the locust plague we went back out to the edge of the oasis where the locusts were gathering and where the people were collecting them. Nothing was left! A few stragglers were clinging to the bare trees; the bark had been eaten off the trees. What the people did not collect, the beetles and ants did. However, there were several small, ragged children roaming around the area. One little boy was very generous. He approached me very slowly, cautiously, and then reached into a greasy, soiled pocket and removed several locusts that had been cooked. He deftly removed the tough, spiney legs and wings and popped the remainder into his mouth. Was he telling me what to do? I noticed that Emma kept her distance. The boy looked at me and waited, he did not have to say anything, I knew what I had to do, and I popped one into my mouth just as he had done. I expected it to be crisp, maybe like a potato chip. It was not! It was oily, soggy, and mushy! He must have been impressed, he gave me another! I got the second one down, it was as tasty as the first, I thanked him and we left the area!

How do you like your locusts? You should remove the wings and hind legs, boil in a little water until soft, add salt and a little fat and fry until brown. Serve with cooked, dried corn. You can prepare embers and roast the entire locust on the embers. Remove the head, legs, and wings. Eat only the "breast", the thorax and abdomen. Do you want to take locust food with you when you travel? Then you roast them, grind on grinding stones until a fine powder is produced. The powder will keep for many weeks and can be used as emergency food. You might open the abdomen, place a few peanuts inside and then roast, grill, or fry the animal. Add oil and salt to taste. If you prefer place as many locusts as you think you might want to eat on a skewer, place skewer over hot coals and keep turning until golden brown, again you might want to add oil and salt, if available. Locusts can be fried with chopped onion and seasoned with curry powder. It is our opinion that locusts can be prepared in any manner that you might think desirable—use your own imagination and serve with a beverage of your choice, or, if you prefer, drink plenty of the beverage first !

February 21 1955

Last evening we were wandering around an area not far from the hostel called Chennine. A well-dressed man approached us and started to speak English. He said later that he thought that we were English because of the bike and the fact that we had bought most of our clothes in London. He had traveled throughout Europe and always stayed in hostels if at all possible because, he said, "That is where you are able to meet the greatest variety of people. We agreed with that. We learned that he is German and his home is in Kaiserslauten, a town not very far from where Emma's relatives live. They are the people we lived with for about three week when we first started on our travels. We spent a long time talking with him over a rough wooden picnic table at the hostel.

After some time he said that he knew of a little coffee shop not far from the hostel, would we like to walk down there? Of course we wanted to do that, he is an interesting man and seems quite intelligent. From the outside the place was just mud and cement with typical Arab arches copied from the Romans. Maybe they are actual Roman ruins; a lot of ruins found all over Tunisia are being recycled. There were no windows; the Tunisians seem not to like windows. Maybe they are like a man I knew many years ago in the Poconos. When his wife complained about a not having a window, he told her that she could go outside if she wanted to see what was out there." Inside the shop were a few dim electric lights, along one side of the room was a long wooden counter. On the counter a variety of utensils are placed, pots, pans, etc. I doubt that the counter had ever been cleaned; when a certain critical amount of debris collected it fell to the floor where it is still visible. Scattered over about one-half of the floor were small tables and some uncomfortable chairs. The other half of the floor is covered with grass or straw mats. On the mats there are low tables around which many Tunisians were gathered, talking, smoking Turkish-style pipes, or playing some sort of game. They sat Indian-style, some leaning against the wall quite relaxed. It made me wonder what might be in those pipes.

One young man sat in the middle of the floor. In front of him was an earthen pot full of glowing charcoal embers. The pot was about four inches high, had a solid bottom and holes around the sides about half way up. On the coals sat a little tea pot. With a straw fan the man fanned the glowing coals and the pot began to boil. The boiling brew was poured into small glasses about the size of whiskey glasses and passed around to nearby men sitting on the straw mats. We were there for more than an hour and he was still brewing tea when we left.

The men, their dress and customs created the atmosphere of the East. Their way of life and their thinking is so different than ours. We wonder, could we ever learn enough to even begin to understand them? How will they ever be able to understand us ? The land, the environment, the customs, the history, their religion, their dress, the gulf is far greater than the Mediterranean Sea or the Atlantic Ocean. We have learned a great deal about their culture since we have been here, but have so much more that we need to know.

Our German host was a prisoner-of-war in the United States for three years during World War II. He said that he liked the States and wanted to stay but it was not possible. He is a mechanic in Germany; he repairs small motors and mechanical devices. He, like the policeman in Djerba, would like to get into the States. We have met many people with the same idea, if they were all allowed into the US it would soon be as over-populated as India and China!

The German, the Dutchman, the policemen, they all have a very good understanding of the Tunisian Problem. They do not understand why America is helping the French subjugate the entire population of North Africa and also West Africa. We all wonder, "What is going on, what is wrong with our foreign policy and/or our so-called diplomats?".

Gabes Tunisia North Africa
February 21 1955

This morning we went out and tried to get some shots around the pool of water in the oasis. There are usually many people around. They seem to rise out of the sand. We start to shoot a scene and it appears that no one is in sight, before you finish there is a crowd watching every move that you make. They never interfere; they are very well behaved, just curious. Girls are seldom seen, the boys of all types, sizes, and ages seem to roam at will.

Some women arrived to fill their earthen water jugs. Those jugs are heavy, I have tried lifting one, not one full of water! They spotted me with the camera at once and would not approach the water until I put the camera away. I try my best to understand their point of view and their right to privacy but, I have to say, I really get frustrated when it is not possible to get many excellent shots.

From the center of the oasis we rode over to Chennini where we shot several young boys eating grasshoppers. As we talked to a man there they quietly occupied themselves stripping off the wings and legs of their "hoppers and popping them into their mouths. Each of the boys had their pockets stuffed with "hoppers, this time we were not offered any. Emma did not seem to mind. I got the impression that they found the "hoppers very tasty, probably one just might have to acquire a taste for them. And then, a lot might depend upon how hungry you are!

As usual, we had considerable difficulty trying to explain to the man that we wanted to photograph a few of the boys eating their "hoppers. He finally got the idea and collected several youngsters and arranged them in front of an old building. They did not seem to mind, they were "naturals" and just kept stuffing the "hoppers into their mouths. The shots looked great in the camera but you never know until the finished photograph appears.

The locust plague is difficult to figure out. When we returned to the original collecting site there were practically no locusts in that area. Today there were quite a few still wandering around, we got the impression that they were "lost", had separated from the main swarm. The poor farmers are still trying to get the remaining locusts out of their gardens. We feel so sorry for them!

By late this afternoon it seemed to us that the main swarm was moving off toward the west—but it is impossible to determine which way they might be headed. These people just want them to leave. As I mentioned, it is hard to believe that they will actually eat the bark off the trees! It is very obvious that the crops have been seriously damaged, the trees stripped of nay foliage. Along the track there were clusters of locusts, they gave me the impression that they were eating each other !

Today is Sunday. The ever-changing plan is to stay here until Tuesday, maybe Wednesday, then head for Mahdia, spend some time there, and then continue up along the east coast toward Bir El Bey. When we talk about returning to Bir El Bey it seems that we are talking about returning "home". That is our home-base here in Tunisia. It really is a beautiful location on a small inlet with a white sandy beach and huge blooming Eucalyptus trees. It would be a wonderful place in which to retire. By the way, there are many people living here in Tunisia who are retired. They form their own societies, like the French, they socialize with each other and, so far as we are able to determine, enjoy the climate, but not the people !

Today, along a deserted sandy tract we photographed a beautiful almond tree in bloom. As usual, I hope that I got the exposure right. The tree had survived by growing out of a cactus "fence" along the tract. It exemplified how determined the will to survive can be. A good photographer would be able to record that scene and it would be a classic! What a shame that many more people will never even get to see it. The twisted form of the tree, the white flowers standing out against the crystal blue of the Tunisian sky! (Again I felt, how lucky we were to be there.)

Mahdia Tunisia North Africa
February 22 1955

Now we are finally on our way from the south to Bir El Bey. The southern half of Tunisia is desert, the Sahara Desert. We found that it can be as life-threatening as it can be beautiful. The desert, to us, is like the ocean and each oasis is a welcome port-of-call. We were able to leave one port on our bike and "set-sail" toward the next one—it was great! You get used to the great open expanses of sand and rock and the over-arching beautiful blue sky. Of course it is nice to know that you will have a fairly pleasant place in which to sleep and something to eat. I do not think that I would enjoy going to bed and trying to sleep every might with my stomach empty. Far too many people around the desert have to do that.

We will always remember the pleasant days that we spent in and around the port city of Gabes, the oasis by the ocean. What a fascinating area of the planet! The troglodytes out in the desert, the sand storm, the rough crossing from Djerba to the mainland, the locust plague—no tourist office could arrange such a schedule, such a safari! We would like to stay in Djerba, or maybe Gabes, or maybe out in the desert in Medenine, or all of them—but that is not possible, we are not really free to do as we please. It will be necessary to think about returning to the States; locating a new position, saving more money, and getting ready to make our next journey. Well, at least we have that in mind; it is a plan and something to look forward to—

Here in Mahdia we met a woman whose husband is stationed south of Gabes in the mountains. She has spent some time in the States, worked in New York City. She told the story of being picked up by a "shark" the second day that she was in the city. She said that she had a rough time with him but hesitated to give us the details of what happened. At any rate, she got away from him and returned to Tunisia. She took us on a tour of the museum where we were able to see displays of pottery, mosaics, and large amounts of art work collected from the area around Mahdia. We could not buy anything for two reasons—no money and no place to carry it. I managed to get some pictures until the attendant saw me.

You know, I wonder about some of these men and their attitude toward pictures, especially where women are involved. Is it all religious belief or is it also jealousy? I just suspect that it might be the latter to a considerable degree. The men will usually cooperate if their picture is being taken, when women are given the attention the attitude usually changes. I think that it will take a long time for women in the States to gain their freedom and equality—how long will it take here?

In one room about eight women and children were weaving rugs. We could not find out how many hours they worked each day. I think the man understood quite clearly what my question was. It looks like a lot of work for a little pay. The women and children do the labor and the traders make the money—a great arrangement for them. Telling me, "That is the custom", doesn't make me feel any better. That is not a satisfactory answer. How is it going to be changed? When? The men ride, the women walk, the men play games, the women do the work, the women carry the wood and water on their backs and heads—but it is the men who are really using their heads!

This state of affairs has been mentioned throughout this entire record of our journey—and, I feel, it can not be stressed too much. We are tourists and tourists should be careful about jumping to conclusions. The tourist sees only what is on the surface. I am trying not to be too critical but, it is very difficult. The entire burden rests on the women and children—and there are far too many children. The children are also the responsibility of the women! I do have a final question—how in the hell did this custom ever originate?

Again, I have to say that we were very reluctant about leaving Gabes, so many exciting things happened to us while we were there—those events kept our visit alive and exciting. It is pleasant to think that some day we might be able to return-but, that is not very likely. There are so many places to go, so much to do and see—and only one life-time! Time runs only one way—a day lost is a day gone forever.

Some people say that this country will never change. Emma and I do not agree with that. The land now called Tunisia has changed frequently just during the two thousand years of recorder history. The original Berber population has been altered by one invasion after another. With each invasion a new and different culture was introduced. Why would that process not continue? Tunisia will get its freedom, one way or another, and with freedom will come drastic changes. Travelers like us have already discovered the country.

Bir El Bey Tunisia North Africa
February 28 1955

We arrived here on February 23rd. Habib was on hand to greet us. He seemed to be interested in our trip south, what we did and what we were able to see. We enjoyed telling him about the storm during the crossing from Djerba, the sand storm, and the locust plague.

At the hostel we found two girls, school teachers, from England. They had no means of transportation, they were hitch-hiking! The first evening was spent exchanging stories and travel information with them. They are on their way to Yugoslavia and points east, whatever that might mean. Every country produces a certain number of strange individuals; England seems to have an ample supply. I think it is OK for me to make that statement, I am half English. Is that why we are here?

The girls have taken no meals at the hostel, did not rent sleeping bags. To the warden they are, apparently of no interest or value. The warden quickly found fault with the girls and was yelling at them about something, we do not know what it might have been. (Except, of course, they were not spending any francs!) The warden's wife told them that they would have to leave.

We buy our evening meal here every day because it is about as reasonable as Emma would be able to make it. However, if any hosteller fails to rent a sac and buy at least one meal per day, he is not welcome at this hostel. In Europe there is a small fee and that is it—you are free to do as you please. This is not Europe, maybe the rules are different.

The girls were ejected about dusk with no place to go and no way to get there. They could not afford a cab and a hotel that is obvious even to a Frenchman. We talked to Habib and he found room for them at his home. The next morning they were on the road to Gabes. Emma and I tried to talk to them about attempting to hitch-hike in an Arab country. Men have some strange ideas about women and girls, especially two young women traveling alone! They seemed not to be listening. We wonder what will happen to them. They said that they plan to return on Tuesday and leave Tunisia for Sicily on Wednesday.

Could they possibly plan to stay in this hostel? Maybe with Habib?

Since the incident with the girls it has been quiet here at the hostel. Yesterday several girls and boys arrived, some of them with small children. Our concept is that hostels are for people who want to travel at the most reasonable cost. This hostel seems to serve the French office staff in Tunis. The warden is very happy to greet them. All are welcome, men, their wives and children, and their co-workers. Here they hold their outings and Sunday picnics. A private setting like this would be very expensive but, they, and the warden and his wife are all French. A group of Tunisians would never be able to get into this hostel!

Today we worked on the bike. The whole thing had to be gone over and cleaned. The fuel and oil filters had to be cleaned in gasoline. We switched the tires and shortened the chain. Several links have been taken out of the chain, we hope that it continues to hold together, cleaning and greasing it should help. A few bolts had fallen out, we replaced them. We think that we got all the parts back together—it runs!

Yesterday we headed for a village up in the mountains called Dougga. It was our third attempt. The first time the weather suddenly turned wet and cold and we had to return. The second time the chain broke and we had to put in some new links. On this last try we were able to make it. The climb is well-worth the effort. The Roman ruin is very well preserved considering the treatment, or mistreatment that it has suffered. Many of the beautiful columns still stand and many more would, had the area, like many others, not been used as a quarry over the many centuries. Someone wrote that Roman ruins might be able to withstand the weather and climatic changes but they can not withstand the destruction of the shepherd. The amphitheatre is very well preserved, the tiers of stone seats are in very good condition, that is, if you have your own pillow!

We were told that Dougga was originally a fortified Berber village. During the frequent invasions of the lowland area the people were forced to take refuge up in the mountains. It could not have been pleasant. The population of the plains must have been quite large, and they all had to live together during the times of siege or occupation. Food and sanitation must have been in short supply.

While we were there s small group of young French men and women arrived. They swarmed all over the place and made plenty of noise. We tried to talk to three different individuals but they were either not interested or could not speak English. That is not the first such experience for us. They probably feel insecure, threatened, here in Tunisia—they do not belong here. Many of them have been sent here by the French government or they have been encouraged to come by being offered desirable positions and/or more money than they could earn in France. Anyway, they tend to stay together in groups, like the Berbers who took refuge here in Dougga centuries ago when the country was invaded or threatened.

The original village was, of course, fortified. The first name was "Thugga", Thugga meant "pastures". It was founded about the first or second century B.C. The Romans appeared on the scene during the second century B.C. The theatre was built about 168 AD. Dougga declined as the power of the Roman Empire waned during the following centuries. The Berbers were able to reclaim their village. After the Romans, the Byzantines and the Vandals invaded. The Berber civilization, culture, was able to withstand all such trials and survive intact.

Beyond Dougga there are extensive cork forests. We were not able to reach that area but plan to attempt it next time. The time passes quickly when you are investigating an old ruin and trying to use your imagination and visualize what life must have been like for the original inhabitants. During the afternoon we sat on the stone seats in the theatre, ate two sandwiches that Emma had thoughtfully prepared, listened to the French chatter, and enjoyed the view in the warm sunshine. Not a bad way to spend a day!

During this past week we have produced very few good pictures. So, we put our hopes on next week. One shot of a snake looked Ok and a general view of Tunis along with additional views in the souks. The best farm land around Tunis is held by French absentee farmers. The nomads and Berbers work as day-laborers on those farms. From the road we have been able to get some shots of that situation. In Tunis we happened upon a large crowd of men waiting in front of an office building. Investigation revealed that they were Nomads and Berber laborers seeking any type work that might be offered. Those men are hungry, they have families, and they have to accept anything that the French offer them. How would you like to be in their shoes? (That is, if they have shoes.)

Next week the plan is to visit Habib's home in the south. There we hope to get more shots of the inside, the tile work, and the activities of the people who work for him. More shots like that are needed if the film is going to show the daily life of the people. More on the mud huts is also needed, if possible.

Yesterday, on one of our rides out through the country a convoy of French Foreign Legion trucks came down the road traveling at a rather fast speed. I saw the convoy and moved to the right as close to the edge of the road as possible. There was plenty of room for them to pass and no oncoming traffic. All went well until the last truck was passing—he cut sharply to the right and forced me off the road and into the sand. I had considerable difficulty keeping the bike from turning over in the soft sand. We were traveling at about forty-five MPH. The bike came to rest partly buried in the sand. We got it out and back onto the paved road. I was just plain mad as hell! I knew that it had been done deliberately.

We brushed most of the sand away and I kicked over the starter—it started. Emma got aboard and we headed down the road after that convoy of trucks. I got into the center of the road and twisted the throttle wide open. Our top speed was about 50-55 MPH. The trucks were moving right along so it required some time for us to get to the lead truck. I was very angry about the way we were forced off into the soft sand so I probably was not thinking rationally—well, I was not thinking at all!

We swerved in front of the truck and I slammed on the brakes. The entire convoy stopped and the officer who had been riding in the lead truck approached us with an expression that, translated, might have meant "You must be out of your mind". He was French and could not speak or understand English but he knew that I was very angry. He found a stick and handed it to me and smoothed out an area of sand. I tried to illustrate in the sand what had happened. He understood instantly.

The officer sent for the driver of that last truck and, when he appeared, he ordered him to get into the back of the lead vehicle. He then sent another driver back to the end of the line. He was very pleasant about the incident, he said in French, several times, "Pardon", we shook hands and parted company.

It would be very difficult for me to live in an occupied country under constant surveillance by the police, secret agents, and the military. My hope is that the US will never adopt such tactics for any reason. Certainly we hope that the US will never be occupied the way Tunisia has been for almost one hundred years! The US has been involved in many wars since 1776. No one has ever won a war. Every war bleeds the life-blood out of each country literally and figuratively. History is littered with records of constant warfare. The time, energy, resources, brain-power and wasted lives expended in wars would have elevated man to undreamed of heights. I have a few intelligent friends—they tell me that war is inevitable, even necessary, that it is genetic, inherited. I believe in evolution and genetics, in inheritance—but I really hate to believe that!

Bir El Bey Tunisia North Africa
March 4th 1955

For the past two days Emma and I have spent all our time working on the bike. Maybe I pushed it too hard when I raced to the front of that convoy. At any rate we checked it over as much as we could, oiled and greased everything and cleaned the filters. It now has over nine thousand miles on the odometer and they were very difficult miles over the Alps in Europe and through the sand storm and salty crossing from Djerba. All that and very much over-loaded! The wonder is not that we are starting to have trouble—the wonder is what keeps it going? Well, we got it operating OK and rode into Tunis as a test—run; everything went along quite well until I tried to cross some trolley tracks. Apparently I spilled some oil on the front tire and when that oil spot hit the tracks it sent the bike into a spiral spin. Emma was thrown off in one direction and I flew through the air and landed some distance away. We were very fortunate. We do not have helmets but did not strike our heads. We each slid along the pavement for some distance and that ripped our clothing and skin along one side. No bones were broken but the wind-screen and the leg-shields were shattered and twisted. The bike continued on down the street before falling onto one side, the motor still running.

After I got Emma back on her feet and found that she was OK physically but badly shaken up mentally and emotionally, I shut the motor off and put the bike back on its wheels. Emma landed hard on one side, she had many scratches

278

and bruises but insisted that she felt good and was ready to get back on the bike! I thought that was amazing! I had some protection from the leg-shields and the wind-screen as well the handle-bars. I did not slide as far as she did.

With the bike back on its wheels Emma held it upright and I did what I could with the leg-shields to bend them back out of the way. By the time all this happened a large crowd had gathered along the sidewalk. They all just stood, talked, and watched us, no one offered to help. Nothing could be done with the wind-screen, it was far beyond any possibility of repair and, we knew that it would be useless to attempt to replace it. Mr. Erne back in London, from whom we purchased the bike, insisted that the rack, the leg-shields, and the wind-screen be installed.

Back at the hostel we did what we could with our scratches and bruises. More work was required on the bike but the possibility of complete repair was out of the question. A local garage near-by operated by several Italians was tried but they were not able to help—no parts available and just about impossible to have them shipped in from England. As long as the bike would run, we decided to run it.

Late in the afternoon Habib showed up. He had made arrangement with a family living in one of the mud-hut village's near-by for us to get some shots. We jumped at the opportunity. The sun had come out and the light would be right. Habib would act as the interpreter and director. There was one requirement—if shots of them eating were to be taken; then we had to supply the food. That seemed very reasonable to us.

Habit raced off to buy the fresh vegetables and the cous-cous. While he was doing that we took some shots of the women sweeping up the compound, carrying water and working in the garden. Also, we were able to shoot the older children taking care of the younger ones—there were many of them and we hoped that Habib bought a good supply of vegetables and cous-cous.

There were three requirements to be met before shooting could start. Habib had to be the interpreter and director if the people were to understand what we wanted them to do. The husband had to be at home. It would not be possible to approach the place if he were not there. Finally, if they were going to demonstrate the manner in which they eat, we had to supply the food. Of course the shooting had to be done when everyone felt in a cooperative mood and the weather was clear. All requirements having been complied with—we were ready to shoot—

It is a typical mud-hut located out in an open field a few miles southeast of Tunis. There were other similar huts a short distance away; there were no fences except a cactus-brush engagement that would keep just about anything out of the garden patch. The people were very pleasant and cooperative. Habib knew what to say, how to direct them and they appeared to enjoy the whole procedure which must have been strange, and their first experience of being "in the movies". The hut had only one low, small door and no windows. Photography would have been impossible inside even on the brightest day, which this one was not. A mud, brush, cactus fence formed an enclosure around the front door. Emma and I think that the people are Bedouins trying to make a living, that is stay alive, by having a garden and finding any type of work that they can in and around Tunis.

All the children behaved, they followed Habib's instructions to the letter, they were very curious but they talked and laughed among themselves and they kept out of the way. There appeared to be only one wife and she too cooperated. She demonstrated how she worked in the garden and, that demonstration was very realistic. It is only possible to operate a heavy hoe in that manner unless you have had plenty of genuine practice. Next she slung a heavy earthen water jug with the tapered bottom over her shoulder in order to demonstrate how the water is carried. We do not know how far away the water is but it is out of sight across the open, wind and sand-swept field. (A full-scale tree planting program is badly needed!)

The oldest of the many children lifted one of the smaller ones onto her back in the ever-present cloth shawl or blanket. The tiny child accepted the treatment with no show of emotion; in fact it appeared to enjoy the attention. The children were so cooperative; they did everything that they could think of in an effort to help us. Emma felt so sorry for them! She set off a sad train of thought in my brain. What chance do they have? There is no school in the area for them. The man is not able to make enough to live on—how could he ever afford to buy decent clothes for them? And if, by some miracle, they were able to get to school and get an education, what would they be able to do with it? The French have the country in a vice—they have control of education, production, the markets, trade, everything!

Near the gate there was a huge pile of brush that the woman, probably with the help of all the children, had collected in the surrounding fields—which looked barren to us as far as we could see. She swung that load of brush over her back like the expert that she is to show that it had been collected and carried to the hut in order to supply heat and fire for cooking.

The women and children were getting our full attention. I had completely forgotten about the man. He said something to Habib and Habib said that we must take some pictures of him doing something. The man picked up the hoe and made believe that he too worked in the garden. (During all the time and travel that we have done in Tunisia, we have never seen a man working in the garden.) Next he wanted to be photographed tending his bee-hives, and that was of interest. The hives appeared to have been man-made of grass and mud. He walked up and moved the hives slightly so that many of the bees swarmed out. He paid no attention to them and they just investigated the disturbance and returned to their work. Emma and I photographed that event from a respectable distance.

While we were photographing the man, his wife and children had built a charcoal fire and started cooking the cous-cous. They required very little instruction with respect to that operation. While the cous-cous was being tended we sat around the fire and visited as best we could. Habib did his best to interpret. Everyone was so pleasant, the atmosphere around the fire so warm and comfortable—it was very relaxing. It was also very frustrating! How could these people really be helped? Just giving them one good meal of cous-cous, vegetables and meat was far from any real assistance. The man wanted to work, he needed the environment in which he could do so—and create a decent life for his family. And, he and his wife needed to be educated in such a way that they would not have so many children that they are obviously not able to give even the bare essentials. It will never happen while the French "protectorate" exists!

The cous-cous was removed from the charcoal fire and put into a large bowl in the center of a colorful blanket. The whole family gathered around the bowl of steaming stew—it smelled very good! Even the cat tried to join in. But not the wife, she did the cooking and serving. And not the older girls—the younger ones joined us. There must be a cut-off age at which the sexes are separated.

While in Tunisia we have eaten a lot of cous-cous and it is always delicious, but, I have to say honestly that the cous-cous we ate with that Bedouin family, out in the yard, gathered around the charcoal fire tasted the best! Emma and I will never forget that family.

The bike is just not running like it did. We had it back to the garage but it did not help much, if at all. It makes us nervous; the bike is our only means of transport and the most economical. It has to get us back through Europe. It would be best if we could sail home from Germany or Holland. Emma is ready to leave I know but I want to get some shots down at Habib's home near Gabes. Gabes and Djerba! They are just plain fascinating places!

Last evening we walked along the beach to Hammon Lif. Emma wanted to shop for bread and eggs. Not another person was on the beach, it was a beautiful evening, and the only sound was the gentle action of the water along the white sand. Some distance back from the edge of the bay we saw a rather large village of mud huts. It seemed a little strange, all those huts and no people, no sound. All those people living on the edge—on the edge of the sea and on the edge of starvation. We walked up to one hut very cautiously, the man came out and was friendly but, of course, we were not able to talk with him. He seemed to know us—we are in the hostel a very short distance away and when we do go out we are very visible—and noisy!

There was a glowing charcoal fire burning just inside the door. It seemed friendly and even comfortable—that is if they had any comfortable furniture. Everyone sits on a carpet on the ground. No other heat, no light, no furniture, no sanitation. Still, they get by, they seem to be able to make the best of what is available. (Too many of us Americans complain that we do not have enough and, in fact, too many of us have too much, and too many do not have enough!)

Hamman—Lif is a quiet, laid-back, market village. It is about 12 miles southeast of Tunis and has been famous for its thermal springs that originate in a near-by mountain Mount ou Kornine. The ruins of an ancient synagogue were found in Hammon—Lif after the French "protectorate" was put into effect in 1881. The synagogue is thought to date from the 3rd-5th centuries. Hammon—Lif was, at one time, the home of Italian, Greek, and Jewish residents.

Hammon—Lif today is most famous because it was the residence of Ali II Bey, the fourth Bey of Tunisia. We believe that the hostel in which we are staying was part of that residence. If it was, it is very easy for us to understand why such a location would have been selected.

Another village that we like is right on the Bay of Hammamet. It is right on the edge of the sea with a very attractive beach. The massive walls surrounding the village front right along the edge of the water. The village is close to Cap Bon, a popular area with many French visitors. One man in Hammamet was quite proud of the fact that some Italian millionaire had built a home there. A Romanian millionaire also had a villa in Hammamet. While we are mentioning people who are supposed to have been famous we might mention Erwin Rommel, the "Desert Fox" of World War II and Winston Churchill. Winston was an English genius and he found the best locations in the world in which to spend his frequent vacations. (Like us??)

Bir El Bey Tunisia North Africa
March 7th 1955

Once again the old cycle seems to be back in shape. We have had a lot of trouble with it. The bike just was not built or intended to do what we have done. Now we know that a more powerful bike with a side-car would have been a much better choice. However, we did not know exactly how far we would travel and so we were not able to give Mr. Ernie at Marble Arch Motors on Piccadilly Circus in London that information. He probably thought that we intended to tour around the British Isles and then return to the States. It has not turned out that way!

Emma now knows that I am not a mechanic. I thought that I had her believing that but, now she knows. When a man works on a bike for two days and then has to take it to the garage with several extra bolts—well, it just makes a bad impression. With that in mind Emma is more certain that we should finish up our shooting here and head back to Marseille and across France. I still want to get those shots down at Habib's home in Motmir near Gabes. Emma has given me an ultimatum—Finish up here in one month and get across France within two months!

Two nights ago Habib and his wife invited us to attend an Arab Musical with them. It was to be modern music and dancing. The show lasted from 9:30 until 1:30! It seemed like a long time to us. We made it through the first two hours OK, the last two hours made us rather tired. I do enjoy Tunisian and Arab music. However, when the dancing girls appeared I got into trouble. The featured belly-dancer made my glasses steam up. When I removed my glasses to clear them I missed part of the show.

During certain parts of the belly-dancing it was probably best that Emma was there to keep me in my seat. Her belly certainly did dance, in fact every part of her anatomy seemed to be in constant motion, and it was difficult to know where to look. Then there was the problem that I thought she was having keeping the meager clothes on that more or less covered a minimum of her vital parts. I am not able to report on the reaction of the other men who might have been present—I had no time to observe them. Perhaps an engineer with an advanced degree would be able to explain how she was able to control all that vibration and simply not fly apart!

The following day we spent in and around the hostel. I needed the rest. In the afternoon a man appeared who was trying to sell Halfa Grass mats and baskets. It is amazing what a craftsman is able to do with a needle and some stems of that grass. The grass grows wild along the East coast of Tunisia. They say that it can not be transplanted or cultivated. It just has to be gathered by the families living in that area. Many people are involved and it is hard work. The harvested grass has to be marketed through French merchants who have control of the prices. Much of it has been shipped to England where a fine grade of paper is manufactured. My point here is that, once again, the Bedouin or Nomad family that does the labor is not adequately compensated. There is only one way that I can see to fix that situation.

Emma bought two baskets and several mats. The baskets work quite well on the bike. One is used to store food and Emma uses the other one when she goes shopping. They seem to be very tough and durable. They should be, they are used during the process of pressing olives. We tried to get pictures.

Bir El Bey Tunisia North Africa
March 9th 1955

Events sometimes take place so fast that, after a short time, it is difficult to recall exactly what happened. Life here in Bir El Bey had been hectic these past few days. A couple from Denmark arrived at the hostel. They have been on the road for the past nine months. Hitch-hiking has taken them through Europe, Turkey, Iran, Egypt, Libya, and now they are in Tunisia. Their hostel cards have expired as of March 1st. The warden has refused to admit them into the hostel and so they were forced to camp near the beach. In the morning the warden discovered their tent and attempted to tear it down. The young man had to restrain him because his wife was inside!

At that point they decided to leave. We happened to meet them walking out the road past the little white Kouba. They were headed for Tunis. When we heard their story we invited them to return with us to our building, we have a key. Emma made breakfast and they related parts of their story. They left their back-packs with us and went into Tunis. The plan is to locate a fishing boat going to Sicily.

When we returned about 7:30 in the evening we found them waiting, we were with Habib. He received his new 2CV yesterday and we all went for a ride. He had to buy a French 2CV because the tax on any other type vehicle is so high that he can not afford it. We had told Habib about them and he offered to provide supper and a place to sleep. He took them to the village of Soliman this morning. North of Soliman they will try again to find a fishing boat. They have not returned so we think that they were successful.

A new man arrived at the hostel; fortunately his hostel card has not expired. He has been talking a lot but has not said anything that I would care to remember. He does not say who he is, where he comes from, what type work he does, nothing. However, he is very curious about us. His questions include such things as: where we came from, where we have been, where we plan to go, how long have we been traveling? Maybe he will want to check our birth certificates. Since we are not secret agents we see no harm in his questions.

Today we were photographing a family that is living in a cave along the main road into Tunis. We think that they might be Bedouins; they do not appear to have any equipment or pack animals. They are really pathetic, but, they have several surviving children. Every one of them is dressed in the most ragged clothing that we have ever seen. Everything is relative—compared to them, the people we have seen in the mud-huts are quite well off!

Using sign language we asked if we could take their picture. One younger man shook his head "yes". I had just set up and was shooting when an American Jeep arrived with four French Foreign Legion troops aboard. One man covered the lens of the camera and indicated that we should follow them. I packed up the camera and complied with that order. They led us to a military compound located along the road leading into Tunis, actually not far from where we were shooting.

After a brief wait we were taken before the commandant, a veteran with a chest covered with multi-colored ribbons such as you might find in a Cracker Jack box. He very carefully checked our pass ports, noting each stamp of which there were several. Following the pass port exam he just as carefully looked us over. We probably did not make mu.ch of a favorable impression—we have been on the bike, camping and staying in hostels since September. Finally not having found anything with which we might be charged, he stood up and pushed the pass ports across the desk. I considered that a provocation but, under the circumstances thought it best not to challenge his authority. He said, "Savau", "OK" in English and we headed back to the hostel. It was decided to make-do with the pictures that we did get. Fortunately, Emma handed the man about 100 francs as we left, more money than he has seen in quite sometime.

When we were "arrester" by the Foreign Legion troops it gave us the experience of what it must be like when one is living in an occupied country. It is not possible to have that feeling unless it happens to you. We Americans have never been occupied by a foreign power—not since the country became free more than two hundred years ago. It could happen if we are not very careful. The danger might originate outside our country or it could happen as the result of mistakes by our elected leaders. An individual seems not to be aware of what he has until he loses it.

The French have worked out a system by means of which they deal with the Tunisians who place too much emphasis upon freedom—they ship them down into the Sahara Desert. In one instance there were so many Tunisians involved that the French set up prisoner camps up in Cap Bon—it all depends upon the nature of your case. By the way, violators of French "protection" are not arrested, they are "detained".

Bir El Bey Tunisia North Africa
March 10th 1955

This has been a very good day! This morning after breakfast of sausage, eggs, tea, bread, butter and jelly we went over to see Habib. We ask him if it might be possible for us to get some additional shots in and around the mud hut village. He is going to try to make some time for us but said that he will have to check with the husband to make certain that it will be OK for us to visit again. He talked with the man for a long time. Finally, the answer was "Yes". It seems to be one of the customs here in Tunisia; almost any decision requires lengthy discussion.

Habib checked the paper and found that the weather report indicated a cloudy afternoon. The man told Habib that it would take his wife until about 2 PM to make the cous-cous. Maybe every activity centers around a meal of cous-cous. The situation for filming looked dismal. We talked, Habib talked, we held a longer discussion than Habib did with the man from the mud hut. The decision was made to shoot. It turned out to be the right decision.

We slowly walked toward the village with Habib's workman. The custom is to give ample notice that you are about to pay a visit. Habib had to take his wife to Hammam Lif. She took the local train into Tunis. He returned with all the required materials for the coos-coos.

Once again, while the cous-cous was being prepared by his wife, we shot various scenes in and around the hut.

We were surprised by the fact that we were given almost complete freedom. There must have been discussion among the villagers relating to our filming attempts. A rather large crowd of men, women, and children gathered. As usual, they were very curious but, they were very careful about staying out of the way. The longer we work with these people the more we respect them. They really are victims—victims of the French "protectorate", victims of a harsh, depleted environment, and victims of ignorance leading to over-population.

Maybe looking at the situation through the lens of the camera focuses my brain upon the situation in front of us. Maybe focusing the lens focuses my attention, I do not know. When those huts, the barren environment, the sparse furnishings, the ragged clothes, the children suffering from various diseases, uppermost, malnutrition, when it all comes into focus in your brain, well, it is almost too much to comprehend. How, and where should the complex problems of Tunisia be attacked When the French finally leave or are ejected by force, how will the situation be improved for the common people? Will the new leaders be better than the old? The new leaders better have long-range plans for Tunisia and the people.

The future of Tunisia depends upon its resources. The new government will have to really start at the bottom—with the soil. Tunisia has serious erosion problems. The Sahara Desert is moving north and the habits of the Nomads and Bedouins are helping the process. Improving the infra-structure, roads, schools, hospitals, will improve the health of the people and result in many additional individuals—then, what will they do? Where will the jobs come from? How, and who, will protect the fundamental basis of real progress; the resources of the country!

When we have talked with some of the people who are trying to plan the future of Tunisia they seem to be thinking of immediate, short-term solutions. Of course that must be done. However, only long-term plans will avoid a future crisis. The population must be adjusted to the available resources. That is a fundamental law of nature and it can only be violated at the risk of ultimate disaster.

Some of the planners talk about tourism as the answer to all their problems. From what we have seen, we do not believe that tourism will solve the long-range problems of Tunisia. In the long-term it will create more problems. In the short-term it will bring in more people and lots of money. That will create the potential for "progress" and a larger population. But tourism is not a long-range solution to the population problem in Tunisia, in the long-term it will make the problems much more serious. Simply stated—what will all the additional people do when, eventually, the tourist trade ends?

In Djerba there are great plans to build hotels. People from all over the world will fly in and spend their money. There will be many jobs and lots of money to be made by a few people. The population will explode and the entire area will be destroyed by pollution. Then, eventually, the tourist trade will end one way or another. When that happens what will all the people in Tunisia do?

Maybe we should not have brought the cameras along. Maybe we should have just visited the way most tourists visit. You stay in a plush hotel, ride through the country and marvel at how "quaint" the people are and remark to each other "Why, it is just like going back a thousand years! "Then, when you get thirsty and hungry you return to the hotel, eat, drink until you are even more senseless than you are normally, and go to bed and sleep soundly. After all, you have had a very strenuous, tiring day and are quite exhausted.

Did you know that all that might happen when you look through the lens of a camera? I did not know it when we decided to buy the camera in Monaco. Actually, we were not at all certain of just what we were going to do with it. Of course we did have a rather vague plan that included getting to North Africa but, we were not at all sure that we would be able to do it. It is not required that you be mentally unstable if you have such plans—but, it does help!

We are still taking pictures in and around the mud huts, remember? It is not possible to get too many shots of these people and their customs. We can get the pictures on film but, can we really understand what we have photographed? Once again the husband did not want to be ignored, he really wanted his picture taken and we did our best to include him. After they all sat around and ate the cous-cous, he decided to make tea. The pot boiled on the charcoal fire and he stuffed the dried tea into the pot with plenty of sugar. That tea is really hot and swee ! They make me nervous every time they pour the tea. The water is boiling hot and it is poured into a rather small glass at considerable height! I know I have mentioned that before but, it always gets by full attention—they have never missed the glass!

After we said good-bye to our friends at the mud huts we headed back towards the hostel. Habib had to get into Tunis and pick up his wife. We were thinking about the people in the huts and talking about them when, down the road, came a very large, and long caravan. They were headed north, maybe toward better pastures in the northwest up toward the mountains. They were nomads on the move. I used to think of nomads as people who just wandered about foot-loose and fancy-free. Nothing could be more wrong. They know very accurately where they were, where they are, and where they are going. They follow a definite route dictated by the weather and the season. I think that they are nomads only in the sense that they are constantly moving from one area to another.

It was necessary to get ahead of the caravan in order to get the shots that we wanted. After speeding some distance ahead we stopped and set up the comers. Some of the loads on those camels appeared impossible for them to carry! On average they say that a camel is able to carry about five hundred pounds. I think that, in the heat of the desert, and trying to walk in the sand, even with their split, wide feet, that is asking a lot of the animal. The entire camp has to be carried by those poor animals. The huge goat-skin, black tents, tent poles, pots and pans, chickens, and small children are all lashed together. The caravan had camels, horses, sheep, goats and several loaded donkeys. There were several large, earthen, water jugs.

The situation was normal, the men were riding the donkeys and the women and older children were walking. Would it not be great to be able to get movie shots of that caravan being unloaded and set up! Not even Habib was able to arrange that. There the Nomads drew the line. We would not go near one of their camps with those vicious, white dogs on guard. We have not seen one caravan that has not had one or more of those dogs tied under one of the ever-present two-wheel carts.

The last of our film was used on the caravan—that is, all the film that we had with us. It was necessary that we return to the hostel. Anyway, the light was fading. Again we were invited to have dinner with Habib and his wife. I wonder if she is tired of making dinners for us. If she is it does not show up in her cooking. There was plenty of meat, some wine, bread, coffee, etc. After dinner there was the usual talk about the French "protectorate", and the plans some people have for the future of Tunisia. Everyone is looking forward to Habib Bourguiba being the President and leading the government of a new Tunisia.

The people of Tunisia are like the Americans just before an election—they are full of hope for the future. The people think that getting rid of the French will solve all their problems. It would be great if their problems could be solved that easily. Ending the dam "protectorate" will help, but the problems of over-population, lack of good land, soil erosion, education, poverty, etc., will not go away with the French.

It must be admitted that the French have tried, in limited fashion, to help the Tunisians. That is to the extent that they have had constructed some schools, clinics and hospitals, they have had built, with Tunisian labor railroads and highways and improved the infrastructure to a considerable degree. Safety has been improved. What has been their real reason? Some people here think that the main purpose has been in order to carry out a more efficient job of raping the country of its resources. Does anyone really believe that the French took over this country in order to protect it?

The past several days have been rainy and windy, terrible weather for picture-taking of any nature. We were walking along the beach in the rain and Emma was worrying about the people we had seen and photographed in the mud huts. She asks, "What do they do ? How do they occupy their time?" The truth is that I just have no idea. Whatever they do, they have been doing it all their lives. I am not trying to be humorous; I see nothing funny about how they have to try to stay alive. I do know that, at times, when the rains have been heavy and prolonged, many people have been washed out and drowned by the resulting floods. There is nothing here, no vegetation, to break or slow down the run-off. That is why the erosion problem is so life-threatening. Many of the hut-clusters are on open, unprotected ground, and down in depressions in order to escape the full blast of the wind. There are many vital reasons for pushing a vigorous reforestation program in this country. (And for doing the same in our own country!)

When we are not able to get out and ride around the country, observe the people and how they are living, and try to take pictures, I get very irritable. When we are able to roam around we see new things and think of different scenes that we might be able to photograph. An uncle of mine said that when he traveled around the world he never took pictures. He said that he traveled for his own personal pleasure and did not want to be encumbered by camera equipment. To a considerable degree he was right. Cameras do slow you down and they can be a bother. However, Emma and I feel that taking pictures helps focus your attention on the subject and, the pictures create a record of your journey. Every situation, every decision in life, no matter how trivial it might seem; is a compromise.

Two days ago the Danes returned. That was a surprise! They are living in the woods in their little tent in all this rain. We have to be careful about having them in for sandwiches and coffee—the warden is so temperamental that we might all be camped out in the rain! Many people just do not have any empathy for the predicament of others.

Of course we do have them visit us frequently—they seem to be traveling on even less than we are. I did not think that possible. For one main thing, we have our own means of transport—that is very important in a country like Tunisia where public facilities are very limited. This is not at all like Denmark. The Danes have traveled through several Arab or Moslem countries. They tell us that Tunisia is about average or maybe just a little above average if one is considering an over-all view. We were pleased to hear that because all our pictures and experience has been right here in Tunisia.

They have been relating their exploits with the Arabs, the Bedouins, and the Nomads. When you are on the road hitch-hiking you have to contact the people even more than we do. They have, at times, lived with the Nomads—but, I thought, they have no camera equipment! Well, the most important thing is to get there and experience life with the people. The Danes tell us that there are many more Nomads and Bedouins to the east of Tunisia. They say that the living conditions are even more basic, lower than they are here.

That is something to think about. Our goal is not to see and experience the worst that humanity has to offer. We are not after just the primitive, the lack of food and sanitation. We just want to see and record the lives of the Tunisians at the present time.

This afternoon we talked with a group of Tunisian girls who were visiting the hostel on some type of outing. They appeared to be well-dressed, well-fed, happy and contented. It was obvious that they were from so-called "upper-class" neighborhoods. Their ideas were of great interest to us. They are at what we would call high school level. With respect to world affairs they are very poorly informed. They seem to have an uninformed concept of what freedom really is. Most of them think that boys are more intelligent and that the male should be dominant in the family. (I think that Habib also believes that in spite of his education in Paris.)

The girls are not at all agreed that the veil should be dropped or outlawed. That was an idea that they did not seem to like—but none of them had a veil on. Some thought that the veil would just die out after the French leave. They did all agree that the French should leave and, the sooner, the better. Some of them believe that if a girl works in an office she is required to go out with the boss at night if he wishes her to do so. We have the impression that, in Tunisia, the women definitely feel inferior to the men. They accept that custom as being right and seem not to question it. I doubt that the men, in general, are doing much to change that situation.

All the girls agreed that the problems in Tunisia are the fault of the French. Of course we do not believe that and said so. That possibility was not accepted—when the French leave, they will take all the problems with them. The Tunisians are going to learn one thing—all the problems are not the fault of the French. We all like to do that—even I blame Emma when anything goes wrong!

With respect to family affairs the girls firmly believe that the man, the husband, should decide upon the size of the family. (I thought, from what we have been able to observe, a lot of very unwise decisions have been made.) Most of them think that one wife is enough. (So do I!) They feel that if the first wife fails to produce sons, male heirs, then the man should take another wife. Emma tried to find out why all the blame should be placed upon the wife—she failed.

Some of these ideas will require a lot of time and education—if they can ever be changed. The truth is that, in the States we have a long way to go with respect to many of these ideas. With enough time, good teachers, more schools, the situation will improve. Societies evolve slowly and they probably should change slowly so that the people are able to adjust in a sane and sensible fashion. Too much change, too fast might result in confusion and disintegration of the basic fabric of the culture. There is the opinion that since it is a proven fact that man evolved very slowly over the past several million years, he should be given enough time to adjust to new and different ways of living. Maybe patience would be the operative term.

Tomorrow at two o'clock we leave for Motmir, Habib's home in the south near Gabes. His home in the south of Tunisia is about six miles southwest of Gabes, the oasis along the coast. It is an interesting location on the edge of the Sahara. There, in Motmir, we are to attend a circumcision ceremony and, of course, get more pictures. We hope for a safe journey and good weather. If all goes well in Motmir we might visit Dougga, try for more Nomad shots, and then head for the US.

Bir El Bey Tunisia North Africa
March 18 1955

We left for Motmir in the south with Habib—but had we known what he had in mind we never would have done it. We did have several warnings that he was interested in Emma but I did not give the situation any serious consideration. She did tell me that he made several remarks when I was busy with the cameras. She said that he had made "eyes" at her. Emma is very attractive and, I thought, such things are to be expected. The fact is that I did not give it any thought at all. It never entered my brain that he would try anything. I was always present so I did not think that any problem existed. I did sense that Emma was nervous but, under the circumstances, I thought that she was holding up very well.

Our reason for going down to Motmir was to secure more pictures—pictures that we would never be able to get without the assistance of someone like Habib. My interest had so centered on the film that I was blind to everything else. As we walked over to Habib's car Emma told me that Habib had just mentioned that his wife would not be going down to Motmir with us. That did strike me as very odd and, coupled with her report that earlier in the day Habib had said to her, "You are lovely", I should have been alerted to the developing situation. I did say that, had arrangements not gone so far, I would have changed my mind and cancelled the trip. I put everything out of my mind—I wanted those picture!

Earlier in the day I happened to turn around and noticed that Habib was looking at me. It struck me as a strange look—I thought at the time that it was weird, then I forgot about it. Now, in the light of what happened, I feel very stupid.

On our way south we were able to get some Halfa Grass pictures. They were not special but they were interesting. I have mentioned the importance of Halfa Grass to the natives along the coast of Tunisia. It was nearly dusk when we arrived in Motmir. Habib talked with his mother for a moment then said, "We are in luck. The circumcision ceremony is taking place now in the Kouba up in the cemetery." Up we raced and saw a strange sight indeed! Many of the villagers were gathered in the little courtyard in front of the dome-shaped Kouba. They were a ragged but happy lot. Five musicians from the village were supplying the music. Three had drums, one a tambourine, and one a flute. Most of the people were bare-footed. All the adult men wore heavy robes and Arab head-dress.

The music was, to me, primitive, but rhythmic. The longer they played, the more enthusiastic they became until they reached the level of entering a trance-like stage. The by-standers, crowded into the court-yard clapped their hands and stamped their bare feet. The old men nodded their heads and sat cross-legged, crowded around the musicians. Many, many, ragged and bare-footed children milled and crowded around in the little, walled-in court-yard.

The entire scene fascinated us! It was strange, almost weird, so different, and so foreign. I was very impressed, Emma was not. She seemed uneasy. I wanted to record the entire procedure on film that was all that I had on my mind. Habib talked to the musicians and said that they agreed to play for us the next day. I was very pleased; it seemed like a great opportunity. Habib said that we were the first Europeans ever to enter the courtyard of the Kouba. Probably we were among the first to visit the village. The fact is that Motmir is not really a very important place. It probably would not have attracted the attention of invaders.

As the musicians and the people left the courtyard we gave the headman 500 francs. In his hands he had two old pieces of cloth—he swung them around his head and danced for us as he left. The dance was not graceful but, he made the effort, he was happy and the scene was interesting.

From the Kouba we all returned to the house and ate. After we finished eating Habib said that the wedding was being celebrated by the women. He said that Emma would be allowed to attend but, men were not allowed. That eliminated me.

Habib's mother and two of her assistants said that they would dress Emma in Arab clothes for the wedding. It was arranged for me to visit with a local group of men in the village. I would go with Habib's cousin who would act as interpreter. Emma was to attend the wedding with Habib's mother. Habib and I picked up his cousin and we all went to the village meeting where we drank tea and tried to talk. At that point I learned that Habib's cousin did not really understand or speak English. Habib said that he would return home and take his mother and Emma to the wedding. The whole thing turned out to be an elaborate plan, it was diabolical!

When Habib returned to his home he told Emma that his cousin's wife wanted to see her in Arab dress and, since his mother was not yet ready they should go down for a minute. She got into his car with him. I had advised her several times to remain with his mother. Habib has a very clever way of rushing people into things and I understand how Emma was taken in by this part of his elaborate scheme. Once in the car he drove out of the village, not into it and Emma knew that she was in trouble!

The conversation that ensued is difficult for Emma to recall in detail. She was in a state of shock. She realized that she was dealing with a sex maniac. Habib is a very intelligent man and he had used his brain, time, and energy in order to get her alone. Imagine trying to reason with a man who would elaborate such a complicated plan in order to gain his ends. That would require a man with no morals, no principles, and no respect for women and the customs of another culture. His plan required considerable thought, planning and expense.

Emma remembers that she tried to get out of the car—he stopped, ran around to her side and pulled her out she resisted and tried to talk to him. He tried to kiss her and she tried to push him away. (Not an easy thing to do because he is in excellent physical condition.) Next he attempted to force her down and again she resisted. At that point she told him that she was menstruating and that it would not be possible to do anything. She tried to explain that she needed time to think and that they would be able to meet the following Saturday night at about 1 AM. She recalls saying that I carried a gun, knew how to use it, and might kill him. She tells me that he appeared to calm down and that he started to talk.

Habib informed her that I am a cold man, that I do not really love her and that I have more interest in making the film than I have in her. He hates his wife; she does not love him, and refuses to have intercourse with him whenever possible. He feels that Emma is warm and a loving person. They would be able to spend the winters in Tunisia and the summers in Paris. He could easily get rid of his wife and of me. (He has said to me that it is easy in Tunisia to have people eliminated.)

It had to be a long and difficult conversation for Emma. Finally, it started to rain, Emma said she was cold and wanted to return to his mothers place. Why would a man, educated in Paris, supposedly a leader in his country, attempt such a thing? It is beyond reason, beyond what is normal; it is the action of a distorted personality. He agreed to take her back to his mother's home.

He then came and picked up his cousin and me, took him home, and we returned to his mothers place. Emma did not tell me what had happened but, I did sense that something was wrong. I knew that she wanted to leave Tunisia but I did not know why. Now I realize that it was because of Habib's antics. It is easy to look back and say that she should have warned me. Maybe that would have brought me to my senses.

We were dealing with an educated Tunisian, not the run-of-the-mill ignoramus who might have the excuse that he did not know any better. However, I do have to accept the blame. I should have been much more alert, I did have warning signals and I chose to ignore them. At a party in Rome an Egyptian diplomat made advances to Emmas in my presence and I dispatched him without any difficulty. When I was informed of the facts my first impulse was to get Habib alone and shoot him. In a foreign country such as Tunisia that would not have been a good idea. The most sensible thing to do is leave. That will not be possible until Tuesday at 9 AM, the first available passage to Marseille, France.

It is not possible for us to know what Habib might have in mind. We had no idea that he would attempt such a thing as this—what else is he capable of? When I think back about his behavior several strange events did take place. He encouraged me to go across into Libya and photograph the Partisans, Tunisian Guerilla resistance fighters. He remarked, "You would have to leave Emma by me." I was suspicious of that and said, "If I try that, the Freedom Fighters might shoot me. If they do not the French Foreign Legion surely will when I return." "Yes, he said, I did not think of that." On another occasion he tried to arrange for me to go out on a Tunisian fishing boat. Again I was suspicious. Why did I not catch on to this latest maneuver In spite of the warnings, I failed!

Emma and I feel that our best option is to stay close to each other, do not give him any additional opportunity to attempt any additional stupid maneuver and get out of here. We have three days to go. That will seem like a very long time! I have heard him say that he would not dirty his hands if he wanted anything done about a quarrel or disagreement, he would hire it done. Many of these poor Tunisians would do anything in order to make a few francs. The life of a Christian is still not worth much in the Moslem

World. Not knowing how far he is prepared to go is the problem. We just want to get out.

The difficult part of all this is that Habib is supposed to be an educated man. He has been educated in two different cultures, both of them outstanding. Is this typical Arab behavior? Is this the real Arab attitude toward Europeans? Is this the best that European women can expect in Arab countries? The warnings are in all the guidebooks for North Africa. We have heard some very weird stories of harrowing experiences by women in Arab countries. Much of this is my fault.

After a lifetime of studying people, Sir Arthur Clark ask, "Why do people do the things that they do?" To my knowledge, he never received a sensible answer. Habib must have a split personality, he personifies, Jekyll and Hyde behavior. To us he claimed to be a dedicated Tunisian Patriot, a man who would give his life for his country. In reality he is a very low-class person without any genuine morals or concept of what ethical behavior might be—

For the chance of a momentary thrill, he threw away the possibility of a lifetime friendship—

Now it is my turn to ask—Why do people do the things that they do?

Tunis North Africa
March 20 1955

This Sunday evening I am writing on an improvised table in a hotel room in Tunis. Events have unfolded very rapidly over the past two days.

On Saturday morning we said good-bye to the English and American girls, ordered our lunch at the hostel and rode into Hammam Lif to mail a package to Emmas father in Locust Ridge, Penna. We mailed the package and, knowing that we would have to pay our bill at the hostel, we tried to cash some Travelers Checks. The man at the post-office said that we would have to go to a bank in Tunis. We rode into Tunis.

The bank was closed but the guard at the door went inside and talked to someone who then came out and asked what we wanted. When he saw the Travelers Checks he let us in. We knew about what the hostel bill would be (12,000 francs), so we cashed forty dollars.

When we left the bank we were talking about getting out of Tunis, trying to avoid trouble, etc. After some discussion we decided that we should inform the U.S. Counsel as to what had happened. We should have done so at once but neither of us was thinking straight Emma was to meet Habib late Saturday evening. We both felt very frustrated. I felt that we might be in for a rough time. We copied down the name and phone number of a vice-counsel with whom we had discussed our film several days previously. As we walked down the steps and out into the street we were feeling very low and disappointed.

In front of the Counsel Building we saw a Chevrolet station wagon arrive with a small American flag on the front left fender. The man was on his way up to the office. We realized that he would only be there for a moment—we dashed back into the building and raced up the steps trying to keep up with the elevator. We reached the door to the office just as it closed. He heard us talking outside, opened the door and inquired as to what we wanted.

After hearing a brief summary of our story he got on the phone. The Head Counsel and his wife arrived within minutes. The Counsel took charge and directed the entire operation. He instructed his chauffer to take us back to the hostel, pick up our belongings, pay our bill, and explain what had happened to the warden. Before we left for the hostel the chauffer found us a safe hotel room near the Consulate Office. The Counsels wife invited us to have dinner with them on Monday evening. He asked me if I had enough money. They could not have done more for us.

At the hostel we gathered up our baggage quickly—possible only because Emma had packed up everything the previous evening. The warden, a true Frenchman, charged us for the lunch that we ordered and could not eat. Our sheets, blankets, and dishes were turned in.

On our way out we passed Habib on his way in with his wife. Tight behind them was an American Jeep with four armed French Foreign Legion soldiers. As we passed Habib stopped and got out, a question on his face, just as though he had no idea as to what had precipitated these events. We doubt that the Troopers were impressed, or cared. The chauffer said that, under more private circumstances, he would recommend the use of a tire-iron. My preference is a 38. I will never be able to understand what he tried to do or why.

What can I say about Habib? I simply do not have the background, education, experience, or ability to really describe or explain his behavior. He and I are from two very different cultures. Is he an exception? From what we hear he is not. The Danes told us that they were riding in an Arab taxi when an Arab man attempted to attack his wife while she was sitting alongside of him! The result was that they were left along the track out in the desert and reached the next village by riding on top of a passing, loaded, lorry.

At this point it would be possible to go into great detail and discuss the Moslem-Christian situation. Even in the light of this situation I have to admit that the Moslems have their reasons for hating the Christians. I doubt that any rational person would attempt to justify Habib's behavior on the basis of the Christian Crusades or the cheap American movies peddled around the world by American corporations driven by greed.

Emma and I work in the field of education. What is the true value of an education? Does an education really improve and change the individual? Habib has had a so-called "modern" education; he is, by any standard, highly educated. But what about his basic nature, his fundamental drives, has education improved or changed them?

The chauffer returned us to Tunis and helped us get located in our room. We are nervous and will be until get aboard the ship for Marseille. It is a shame that it has become necessary for us to leave Tunisia and the people that we have come to know and have great sympathy for in this with Habib, his wife and family, and with the Tunisian people that would last through our lifetime. Now, all that has been destroyed in just a few minutes by a man who has never learned to control his emotions.

Habib introduced us to several influential people in Tunisia. He, and they, expressed the desire to lead the country into a better, brighter future. Is Habib an example of those future leaders? Will conditions improve for the Tunisian people with men like Habib leading the country?

This incident has had an added impact upon Emma because of what a cracked fortune-teller told her several years ago while she was in nurses training in Philadelphia. That fake warned her to be careful during a long trip.(To North Africa ?) The black tassel is the sign of death, she said. Emma has combined that faulty "information" with the recent events with the result that she is a nervous wreck. I consider fortune-telling as nothing more that superstition.

Tunis North Africa
March 21 1955

This evening we had dinner with the counsel and his wife. The chauffeur took us to their home near Carthage. We were treated very well; they have done everything possible in an attempt to get Emma to relax. I think that they have had some success. They also invited the vice-counsel and his wife, Mr. and Mrs. Hill, to dinner. It was the first time that we ate in such style since leaving the States. The food was very good, the conversation was better. It did relieve the tension and we appreciate their time and effort.

About 2;30 in the afternoon, before we left for dinner, the Danes visited us at the hotel. They said the Legion Troopers apparently were holding Habib under "house arrest" and that when they talked with him he was very nervous. He had learned that we were under the protection of the American Consulate and that we are in a hotel somewhere in Tunis. He asked them to find out where we are and to let him know. Of course they plan to tell him nothing. When I called the Counsel and informed him that Habib was looking for us, a Tunisian policeman appeared in the hallway. A policeman was still on duty until we left the hotel to board the ship. We were followed by the counsel's chauffeur until we boarded the ship.

Boarding was not easy. The Tunisian porters created a real problem. They are dirt-poor, ragged, hungry, and out to get every franc possible. We were able to avoid all of them except two. Those two were unusually persistent and aggressive.

Emma, as usual, was taking care of the paperwork, I was sitting on the bike holding one woven basket and waiting for the signal to ride the bike into the hold of the ship. The one porter tried to grab the basket out of my hands. I let him get a firm grip on it and then swung him over the front of the bike. He landed safely, got up and, as he walked away said, in perfect English, everything that I had heard, years ago, in the US Air Force.

Emma returned with all the papers in order and she got aboard, I ran the bike up the ramp and into the hold and a crew member secured it. From the deck we saw the two porters with whom I had the trouble, pull a woman's large suitcase apart. The contents scattered around the dock area, they calmly walked away and she, nervous and frantic, tried to stuff everything back into the suitcase.

On board we soon discovered that we had secured what is called "deck-passage". That means that you are confined to the bow area of the ship—and that area only. Well, we thought, it only takes about 24 hours to cross and we will just make the best of it on the open deck. Not quite! At dusk everyone was herded below deck and into the hold. That was a shock. What we had was fourth-class passage. Below deck what we had was an international mixture of two naïve Americans along with Tunisians of many nationalities and French, Italian, Libyan, Algerian, and southern Europeans of various ethnic backgrounds. The people carried bags and boxes of every description, there were chickens, goats, and sheep! One man carried his bicycle with him as he wandered back and forth through the human melee.

The more experienced travelers were prepared. They carried chairs and folding cots and they formed defensive circles impossible to penetrate. Sanitation was almost non-existent and the smell of urine quickly spread throughout the confined area. The deck was quickly littered with garbage and some of it flew through the air. We tried to take cover along one wall but, when Emma was hit by a flying tin can I realized that some action had to be taken. I pounded on one of the steel bulkhead doors until an officer appeared. He understood our predicament instantly and escorted us to a most welcome stateroom. Neither of us asked or cared what it might cost. We were able to relax and eat the sandwiches that Emma had prepared for just such an emergency.

Just after dawn the ship docked in Marseille. It required the two of us to make our way through the docking formalities. Emma handled the paper work, I managed to locate the bike and our suitcases, load the bike and ride it down the narrow plank and onto French soil!

The ride across France in the spring lay ahead of us—The pleasant experience of Tunisia and the unpleasantness of Habib was behind us—Our thoughts and conversation centered upon returning to the States, saving enough money and getting ready for our next journey—to South Africa and The Great North Road!

THE END
BY
TED AND EMMA SELIG JONES
211 Roberts Road, Box 319
Pittston, PA 18640
Jonem5@yahoo.com

ABOUT THE AUTHORS

Emma and Ted grew up in the Pocono Mountains of Northeastern Pennsylvania. They met as seniors in high school, maintained a close relationship during the Second World War and were married June 1ˢᵗ, 1946. During the war Emma trained and graduated as a Registered Nurse. Ted served in the U.S. Air Force as an aircraft radio communications technician.

From 1946-50 Emma and Ted worked their way through East Stroudsburg University taking most of their classes together and qualifying as high school teachers of Biology. From 1950-51 they were graduate students at Pennsylvania State University where they earned their Masters Degrees.

From 1951-54 they worked in the Ann Arbor School System, Emma as School Nurse and Ted as a Biology Teacher. Graduate work was completed at the University of Michigan, Ann Arbor—1951-54. During 1954-55 a ten month camping tour through Europe and Tunisia, North Africa was done on a 150cc BSA motorcycle. Graduate work in various fields of Biological Science was concluded through the years at Hopkins Marine Station in California, Arizona State University in Tucson where Ted received his PhD in Zoology, and at the Pennsylvania State University, State College where his thesis dealing with the occurrence and distribution of aquatic insects was completed.

IN 1965 Ted resigned his position as Assistant Professor of Biology at Georgia Tech. in order to make a ten month camping trip from Cape Town, South Africa through Central Africa, to Mombasa, Kenya with Emma. VW Camping trips were also made to Morocco, The Sahara, Lapland, Norway, and Turkey.

It is the sincere hope of the authors that our six month camping trip through, and stories about, Tunisia will instill genuine curiosity and respect for the variety of peoples and cultures that have evolved throughout Tunisia over the past several thousand years.

Emma & Ted.